Francis X. Bushman

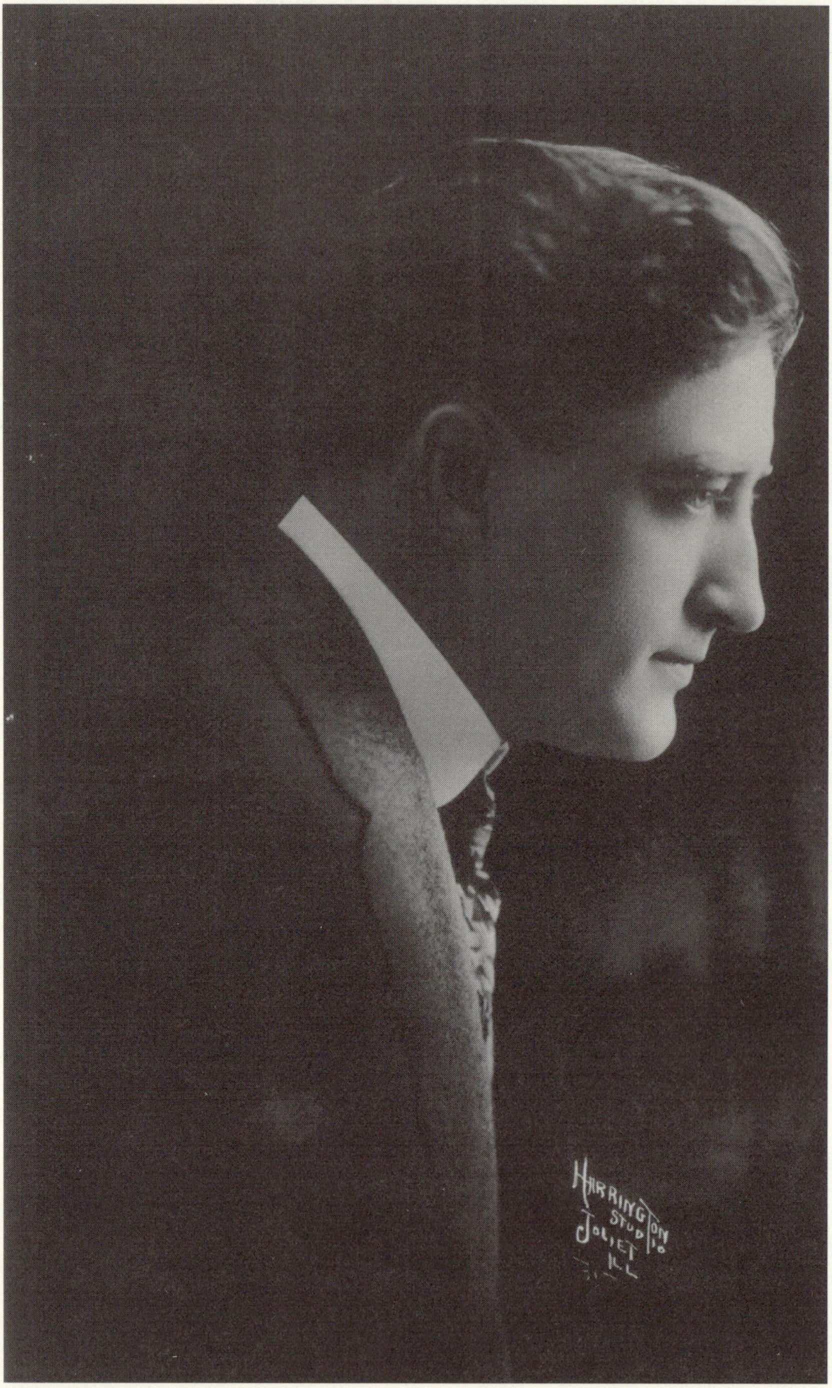
HARRINGTON
STUDIO
JOLIET
ILL

Francis X. Bushman
A Biography and Filmography

by
Richard J. Maturi *and*
Mary Buckingham Maturi

McFarland & Company, Inc., Publishers
Jefferson, North Carolina and London

Also by Richard J. Maturi and Mary B. Maturi

Cultural Gems: An Eclectic Look at
Unique United States Libraries
Wyoming: Off the Beaten Path
Nevada: Off the Beaten Path

Also By Richard J. Maturi

Wall Street Words
Stock Picking
Divining the Dow
Main Street Beats Wall Street
Money Making Investments
The 105 Best Investments for the 21st Century
The Hometown Investor
Investor's Guide for Making MegaBucks on Mergers

Frontispiece: Francis X. Bushman in ca. 1911–1915

British Library Cataloguing-in-Publication data are available

Library of Congress Cataloguing-in-Publication Data

Maturi, Richard J.
    Francis X. Bushman : a biography and filmography / by Richard J. Maturi and Mary Buckingham Maturi.
       p.   cm.
    Filmography: p.
    Includes bibliographical references and index.
    ISBN 0-7864-0485-X (library binding : 50# alkaline paper) ∞
    1. Bushman, Francis X., 1883–1966. 2. Motion picture actors and actresses—United States—Biography. I. Maturi, Mary Buckingham.
II. Title
PN2287.B885M38   1998
791.43'028'092—dc21
[b]   98-7400
                                             CIP

©1998 Richard J. Maturi and Mary Buckingham Maturi. All rights reserved

No part of this book may be reproduced or transmitted in any form or by any means, electronic or mechanical, including photocopying or recording, or by any information storage and retrieval system, without permission in writing from the publisher.

Manufactured in the United States of America

McFarland & Company, Inc., Publishers

First and foremost,
to Virginia Bushman Conway Stuart,
a special lady and daughter of Bushman.

And to the millions of fans
who loved and admired Francis X. Bushman
and have kept a vigil all these years.

Acknowledgments

Special thanks to the Bushman relatives who helped in our research and generously provided family photos and stories which give added insight into the man behind the movies. In addition to Virginia, we wish to thank Chris, June, Kathleen, Rita, Robert A. and Robert L. for their gracious help. Besides gaining a wealth of information on Francis X. Bushman, we also found some dear new friends. We also owe a debt of gratitude to Gene Gressley, founding director of the American Heritage Center, for research leads; and to Arthur Guy Kaplan, Judith Clemente, Roz Berson Stein and our sons, Craig and Matthew, for research assistance.

Our gratitude to the American Heritage Center at the University of Wyoming in Laramie for permission to peruse their photo and text files on Bushman and the scrapbooks of Beverly Bayne. We thank Debra and Lon Davis for their permission to use material donated to the American Heritage Center.

We also extend our thanks to the staffs of the Academy of Motion Picture Arts and Sciences, the American Film Institute–Louis B. Mayer Library, the American Museum of the Moving Image, the Chicago Historical Society, the Cleveland Public Library, the Library of Congress, the Lincoln Center Library for the Performing Arts, the Museum of Broadcast Communications, the Museum of Modern Art, the National Public Broadcasting Archives at the University of Maryland, the New York Public Library, the UCLA Film Archives, the UCLA Arts–Special Collections, the University of Michigan, the University of Wisconsin and the USC Film Library.

Contents

Acknowledgments	vii
Introduction	1

Part One. Biography

1. EARLY YEARS: FROM SCULPTOR'S MODEL TO FILM STAR	5
2. ESSANAY STUDIO STAR	21
3. THE QUALITY PICTURES–METRO PICTURES YEARS	43
4. STARTING OVER, COMING BACK	69
5. KEEPING IN THE PUBLIC EYE	88
6. EPILOGUE	102

Part Two. Filmography

FILM, RADIO AND TELEVISION APPEARANCES	105
Appendix I. Lenore Bushman Filmography	203
Appendix II. Francis X. Bushman, Jr., Filmography	206
Bibliography	235
Index	241

Introduction

In the beginning—before Clark Gable, before Douglas Fairbanks, and even before Rudolph Valentino—there was Francis X. Bushman. He was not only a lady's man and a man's man in the real sense, he virtually created a role model that later generations of male heartthrobs would seek to imitate.

In many ways, Bushman's achievements on the silver screen remain unsurpassed today. To be sure, the acting style of the early silent screen days seems stilted and exaggerated by today's standards however, his poignant portrayal of Messala in *Ben-Hur* carried the epic movie. In fact, Bushman upstaged the movie's headliner, Ramon Novarro, whom Louis B. Mayer was trying to cultivate into a star.

It is difficult to assess how high Bushman's rising star might have traveled had events in his personal life not interfered. At the peak of his fame, starstruck movie fans were unaware that Bushman was married and the father of five children. Fans were disappointed when they learned the truth—and shocked when Bushman left his wife to marry actress Beverly Bayne. The scandal all but ended Bushman's and Bayne's movie careers. Today, their escapades would barely raise an eyebrow, but at the turn of the century it was a far different story.

As reported in *Variety* in August 1918, the Mall and Alhambra Movie Theaters in Cleveland announced that they would not run any more pictures in which Bushman and Bayne appeared, clearly implying that Bushman's divorce and subsequent marriage to Bayne was the reason for the decision. Speaking editorially, the *Cleveland News* said, "Marital troubles and moral delinquencies on the part of some members of the acting profession have long been familiar facts." Other factors may have come into play in Bushman's decline, as we shall see later.

Despite the negative publicity and fans turning their backs on him for nearly a decade, Bushman did enjoy a brief comeback in the epic movie *Ben-Hur*, released in 1925. Subsequently, however, Bushman experienced a second downfall, resulting from a confusing encounter with Louis B. Mayer. Mayer virtually blacklisted Bushman, preventing him from acquiring any major roles in any Hollywood movie studio for decades.

While many silent screen film stars failed to make a successful transition from silents to "talkies," Bushman appeared in many talking films in the early '20s and later during the '50s and '60s. In addition, his voice and acting ability carried him through the blacklist years with stints on Broadway, radio shows and television.

Bushman starred in the genesis of moviemaking. Now, find a relaxing chair and transport yourself back to the dawn of film history. Meet Francis X. Bushman, the King of the Movies.

>Richard J. Maturi
>Mary Buckingham Maturi
>*Cheramie, Wyoming, 1998*

Part One. Biography

1

Early Years: From Sculptor's Model to Film Star

Francis Xavier Bushman was born on January 10, 1883, to John Henry and Mary Josephine Bushman, who lived on Argyle Avenue in Baltimore, Maryland (not Norfolk, Virginia, as early press releases stated to discourage fans from finding out about Bushman's wife and children). Francis Xavier was one of 12 children. Among his brothers and sisters with equally impressive names were Mary Magdalen, Bernadette Soubirous, Edith Philimena, Robert Aloysius, Samuel Milton and Merlin Valentine.

Bushman served as an altar boy for Cardinal Gibbons at the cathedral when he wasn't with his Engine House No. 13 gang throwing stones at a rival southwest Baltimore gang to which the young H. L. Mencken belonged.

Early Stock Theater

Bushman received schooling for eight grades at Immaculate Conception, associated with his family's Roman Catholic parish in Baltimore. He later attended Ammendale College, a school located between Baltimore and Annapolis, which prepared young boys for the Christian Brotherhood. He discovered a dislike for schooling and a love for the theater. At an early age, he garnered walk-on parts with a Baltimore stock company, appearing in *The Lady of Lyons* at Baltimore's Albaugh Lyceum Theater. In 1907 he launched his show business career via appearances with the George Fawcett stock company. He worked a variety of stock companies such as Casino, Lyceum and Temple in the Eastern cities of Baltimore, Boston, Buffalo, Camden, Philadelphia and Rochester to learn his craft. When the "At Yale" company played Baltimore, Bushman joined it for the balance of its tour. The casting director selected him for the juvenile role in *The Red Mill* (credited as his first New York appearance), followed by performances in *The Top*

Early photo of Francis X. Bushman

o' the World. His appearance in *The Queen of the Moulin Rouge* at the Circle Theater marked his first Broadway appearance. *The Queen of the Moulin Rouge* opened at the Circle Theatre on December 7, 1908, and ran for 160 performances. The show program listed him as Frank X. Bushman. He played the Broadway lead in the Shuberts' *Going Some*, which opened at the Belasco Theatre on April 12, 1909, and ran for 96 performances. After returning to traveling stock companies, Bushman gained the notice of an Essanay producer. The rest, as they say, is history.

"I loved the beauty of the theater all lighted up," said Bushman on one occasion. "Acting intrigued me right from the beginning. There was family opposition to the theater. I used to sneak out to work on the stage as a super when a play came to town. I picked up 37 such jobs in two years."

Bushman worked various jobs as he strove to break into the theater. He married Josephine Flauduene in 1902 at age 18. His wife sought out seamstress work to help support their growing family. Ralph Everly was born in 1903, Josephine in 1905, Virginia in 1906, Lenore Konti in 1909 and Bruce in 1911.

"Daddy fell in love with Mother at church. He served as an altar boy and noticed Mother. He followed her home after church and eventually asked her to marry him," says Virginia Bushman Conway Stuart, Bushman's daughter and wife of famous movie director Jack Conway.

"It was my father's wish that I be a doctor," Bushman later recalled. "My mother wanted me to be a priest. But most of all, she wanted me to be great. It must have affected me prenatally, for I too wanted to excel in everything I did. Before I was 12 I had read all the classics in my father's library."

It is only fitting that one of Bushman's early starring film roles was in *Romeo and Juliet* (playing opposite Beverly Bayne). Later, he set the standard for acting in the epic film *Ben-Hur*. He took his acting seriously, memorizing the lines from such great Shakespearean plays as *Hamlet* and *MacBeth*. He idolized the great English actor Sir Forbes Robertson. According to his daughter Virginia, he would run up the piano scale every morning to keep his voice in shape. He continued this practice, even after he left the theater to work in the silent movies.

1. Early Years

Mary Josephine Flauduene Bushman, mother of Francis X. Bushman, shortly after her 1902 marriage.

Lifelong Passion: Taking Care of His Physique

Bushman took great pride in his physique and avidly followed the bodybuilding exercise routines widely promoted by Bernarr Macfadden. He probably saved his money to purchase Macfadden's *Encyclopedia of Physical Culture*, with its promises to help "to possess exhilarating health every day in the year" and "build a powerful physique." Undoubtedly Macfadden impressed the young actor with his series of "Throbbing Dramas from Everyday Life," carried in "True Story

Pictures," and his philosophy that the sex lure is "divine, godlike." According to Macfadden, the "sex lure is God-given, God-made. It was sent for an ennobling and exalted purpose. Take it at its real value and the manhood or the womanhood in your very soul will expand. Your life will broaden and you will be a man or woman of greater power and possibilities because of this attitude."

Bushman developed his impressive physique by boxing, long distance running, weightlifting and wrestling. One night he sneaked away from home to enter a strongman contest at a burlesque house in East Baltimore, coming away with $25 in prize money.

"Daddy talked his mother into letting him use a portion of the basement for his weightlifting equipment in exchange for his getting up every morning at four o'clock to stoke the fires with coal," says Virginia.

According to newspaper reports, at one of his odd jobs as a laborer at the Baltimore brick manufacturing firm of Burns & Russell Company, Bushman could be regularly seen exercising, using bricks as dumbbells. At least once he picked up two railroad car wheels using the axle as the lifting bar. Another time, proving the strength of his physique, Bushman walked up to a solid wooden door and hit it, splitting the door right down the middle.

He worked hard to develop his body into that of a Greek god. The December 1916 issue of *Motion Picture Classics* called Bushman "an all-around athlete, a sculptor's model and one of the best wrestlers in the country." The article went on to say that

Bushman shows off his carefully tended physique.

1. Early Years

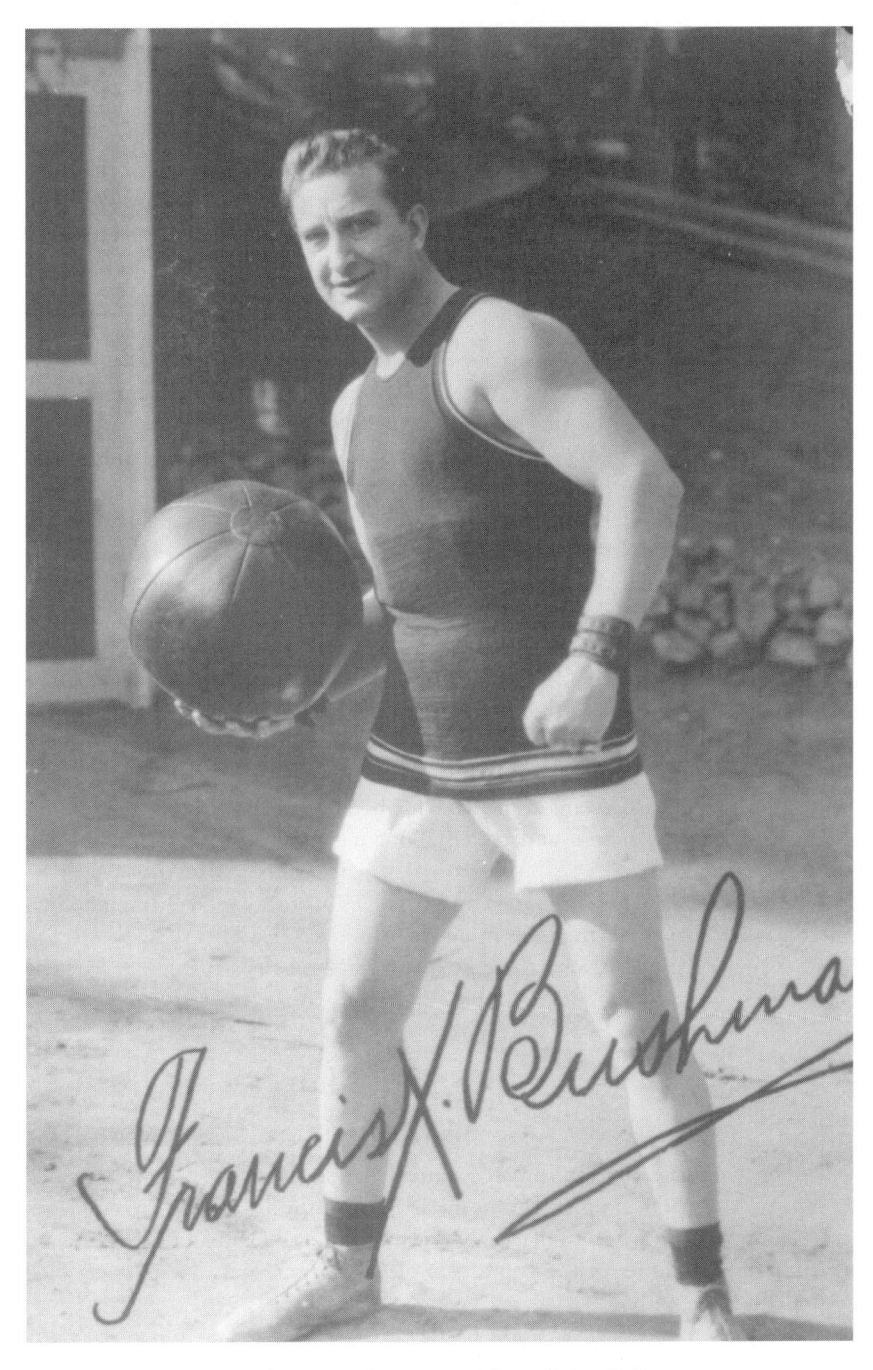

Bushman working out with medicine ball.

Bushman "cultivates every side of his physical self, and is as graceful as he is strong."

"I thought a sound body was important in anything a man planned to do. I took up boxing, wrestling, bike racing, distance running and weightlifting. I won a lifting match at the Maryland Athletic Club," Bushman once remarked. "While I have fads and hobbies, keeping in physical shape is not one of them. It is just as much a part of my life as eating and sleeping. In many ways, the ancient Greeks are my ideal of a people.... It is, you see, the application of the old Greek idea. The soul is contained in the body. Keep the urn bright and clean and the divine fire of the mind and soul glows more strongly."

Bushman's niece June Bushman Hannan recalls, "Uncle Frank was always very healthy and body conscious, constantly exercising to stay in shape. He was very strong. Whenever he traveled, he carried a small satchel. When the hotel bellman approached, Frank would hold the bag straight out in front of him and say, 'Would you take this bag please?', giving the impression that the bag was very light. When the bellman took hold of the bag, it would immediately pull him to the floor. Uncle Frank would laugh at the poor guy because it looked so comical to see the shocked expression on his face. He would open the satchel and show the bellman the weights inside, give him a big tip and thank him for the good laugh."

"Daddy was a natural," says Virginia. "He knew he was beautiful but he never fussed over himself. Other actors could not pass a mirror or plate glass window without admiring themselves. Daddy was not that way. He treated himself like the president of a company. He always wanted the company [himself] in the best order possible. He wanted to make his body and acting the best. He once came to talk at my school and talked about nature instead of about himself. That's the way he was."

"There were tours on the road and stretches in stock," said Bushman in an interview. "I learned all the lines of all the shows I suped in. I was ready to go on if they needed me. Always there was struggle, struggle, struggle."

Sculptor's Model

The work paid off as Bushman eventually landed leads in a New Jersey stock company. In order to supplement his meager actor earnings, Bushman took work as a sculptor's model. He modeled both at the Charcoal Club and the Maryland Institute in Baltimore for the grand sum of 50 cents an hour. He once recalled a modeling adventure:

> I had been posing at the Maryland Institute [1903] and went to the Fifth Regiment Armory one day to help set up an exhibition of sculpture.

1. Early Years

> In order to raise one heavy piece they had to use a block and tackle, and wanted somebody to climb up and fasten the rope to a girder. I volunteered to do it, and had no trouble crawling up the sloping steel beam and reaching the center of the network. I felt pretty proud of myself until, after tying the rope in place, I found my knees shaking so badly that I was sure I'd never be able to climb back down. A lot of people were watching, and I had some bad moments. Then, because there wasn't anything else to do, short of yelling for a long ladder, I slid down the rope, burning my arms and legs. Among those below were Daniel Chester French and other sculptors from New York. They found out about my work at the Institute, asked for a look at my physique and invited me to come to New York, promising enough steady posing work to make the offer quite attractive.

During his New York run on the stage, other artists and sculptors saw him and over the years he posed for such noted sculptors as Leyendecker, Wenzell, the Kinneys, Flagg, Alonzo Kimball, Isadore Konti and others. He modeled in New York from 1905 through 1908 in between working on various East Coast stage productions.

In a September 1916 article, Bushman stated that he had posed for some of the nation's leading sculptors including Augustus Saint Gaudens and Ulric H. Ellerhusen. Ellerhusen used Bushman for his 23-foot statue of "Conception" which was featured in the classic group in the rotunda of the Palace of Fine Arts at the Panama-Pacific Exposition in San Francisco. He also posed for a statue for the Public Library Building in New York City.

During an interview which appeared in the December 15-21, 1956, issue of *TV Guide*, Bushman related that he was also Nathan Hale in City Hall Park, George Washington's torso on Wall Street and Gov. Seward in Madison Square. He added that the Simon Bolivar statue in New York City that he posed for had been moved to an unknown location.

"New York sculptors kept me busy, that's how there are replicas of me all over the country, in parks and squares and on public buildings," said Bushman as a celebrity guest contestant on Groucho Marx's *You Bet Your Life*. "I'm on the cupola of the Fine Arts Building in San Francisco, and I'm on the Cuyahoga County Courthouse in Cleveland as a King, Pope and several famous lawmakers. I'm Nathan Hale and I'm an Indian on top of an Appalachian mountain."

A 1957 tribute to Bushman by the Motion Picture Costumers listed him as a model for Daniel Chester French (well-known for his portrayal of Abraham Lincoln in the Washington D.C. Lincoln Memorial) and Mrs. Harry Payne Whitney. In his hometown of Baltimore, Bushman modeled for no less than five public statues. In 1991, Bushman nephew Robert L. Bushman and the authors tracked down several of the Bushman statues still in existence.

"I remember as kids my father taking us down to see Uncle Frank's statues," said Robert.

In front of the Court House on St. Paul Street we located Albert Weinart's Lord Baltimore (Cecilius Calvert, second Lord Baltimore), erected by the Mary-

Lord Baltimore statue by Albert Weinart. (Photo: Clayton Davis.)

land branch of the Society of Colonial Wars in 1908. Weinart was born in Leipzig, Germany, and studied at the Ecole des Beaux-Arts in Brussels, Belgium. Other notable Weinart pieces of art include the McKinley Monument in Toledo, Ohio, an architectural sculpture for the Congressional Library in Washington D.C. and work for the 1915 Panama-Pacific Exposition in San Francisco (possibly using Bushman as a model). For Lord Baltimore, Weinart crafted a 17-foot bronze sculpture mounted on a marble pedestal inscribed "Cecilius Calvert 1606–1675."

When Bushman revisited Baltimore in 1951 to promote the new movie *David and Bathsheba*, he posed alongside the Lord Baltimore statue with Miss Maryland.

1. Early Years

The Maryland Daughters of the Confederacy commissioned Gloria Victus or "Glory" for location on Mount Royal Avenue in February 1903. Erected in honor of the soldiers and sailors of Maryland in the service of the Confederate States of America 1861–1865, the statue features winged Glory holding a wreath and standing alongside "Grief" in the form of a stricken soldier.

Another statue Bushman posed for, the Union Soldiers' and Sailors' Monument, was erected by the State of Maryland at the Mount Royal Avenue entrance to Druid Hill Park in 1909. Due to freeway construction, the monument was later moved; the authors have not been able to discover its present location. The sculpture by A. A. Weinman* included stone cannon posts, terminals of double wreaths in relief and bronze tablets around a bronze grouping consisting of a soldier turning from plow and anvil to buckle on a sword, attended by Victory and Bellona. The monument was "Erected by the State of Maryland to commemorate the patriotism and heroic courage of her sons whom on land and sea fought for the preservation of the Federal Union in the Civil War, 1861–1865."

As we drove up Eutaw Place, Robert L. Bushman exclaimed, "My God, it's just like seeing Uncle Frank."

***Gloria Victus* by Frederic Wellington Ruckstull, a statue commemorating the Confederate soldiers and sailors of Maryland. (Photo: Clayton Davis.)**

---

*Weinman was born in Germany and emigrated to America at age ten. He studied under Augustus Saint-Gaudens. Weinman is also credited with designing the relief work of the U.S. Mercury Head Dime (1916–1945).

Francis Scott Key memorial by Jean Marious Antonin Mercie. (Photo: Clayton Davis.)

Sure enough, of all the Bushman statues we have seen over the years, the 1911 Francis Scott Key statue at 1300 Eutaw Place is the spitting image of Bushman's familiar face. This statue features Key standing in a small boat and an adjacent marble columned monument topped with a figure of Liberty holding the United States Flag. The Francis Scott Key Memorial was presented to the City of Baltimore by Charles L. Marburg, a local tobacco merchant. The French sculptor Jean Marious Antonin Mercie created this work of art.

The final Baltimore Bushman statue is located at Charles Street and Wyman Park Drive near 29th Street and was erected by the State of Maryland to honor members of the Confederacy who fought in the Civil War. Bushman posed as a Confederate soldier dressed in full winter uniform including an overcoat with attached cape. Facing the monument from the front, a winged angle appears at Bushman's right while a figure wearing a helmet and brandishing a large shield stands to the left.

There's a lot of evidence to support Bushman's claims of statues of him all across the nation. Different newspaper accounts say that he posed for the Nathan Hale statue at Harvard while others cite the statue's location as Yale. Harvard lists no statue of Nathan Hale on its campus; however, according to "Buildings and Grounds of Yale," a Connecticut Hall statue of Nathan Hale was erected on September 30, 1914. Boston Sculptor Bela Lyon Pratt created the work of art. Since it undoubtedly took several years to complete, the time frame fits the period when Bushman could have modeled for it.

Cleveland, Ohio, sports several statues for which Bushman posed. As Bush-

1. Early Years   15

Statue honoring Confederate soldiers and sailors, Baltimore. Bushman posed as the soldier in this work. (Photo: Clayton Davis.)

man proclaimed (reported by the *Cleveland Press*), he posed for a number of the statues associated with the Cuyahoga County Court House. Bushman modeled for the statues of a number of important historical figures on top of the Court House including Roman Emperor Justinian by Isadore Konti, Pope Gregory IX by Herman Matzen and King Alfred the Great by Isadore Konti.

Other Cuyahoga County Court House figures that Bushman could have posed for include Moses by Herman Matzen; King Edward I and John Hamden by Daniel Chester French; Stephen Langton and Simon de Montfort by Herbert Adams; and Thomas Jefferson and Alexander Hamilton by Karl Bitter. The figures appear over the main entrance to the Cuyahoga County Court House.

Family history lends credence to the Bushman/Konti connection. Bushman named one of his daughters Lenore Konti Bushman in honor of Isadore Konti. According to Virginia, Konti lent her father money in order to provide needed medical treatment for her. "I had suffered a childhood illness and Mr. Konti con-

Isadore Konti's *Alfred the Great* adorns the Cuyahoga County Court House in Cleveland, Ohio. (Photo: Richard J. Maturi.)

vinced Daddy that I needed to go to a hospital and also paid the hospital bill," she said. "He lent Daddy money a number of times. By lending Daddy the money, he saved my life and in respect and gratitude Daddy named my sister Lenore after him."

The *Cleveland Plain Dealer* reported that Bushman posed for the bas relief of muscle-bulging figures located on the First National Bank building, which used to be located on lower Euclid Avenue in the '20s. (Unfortunately, the work of art has been lost to history.) When Bushman visited his brother Paul in Cleveland, he would stop to admire the bank's figures.

Robert A. Bushman, who grew up in Cleveland, remembers his father taking him to the First National Bank building and pointing to the large bas relief bronze plaque and saying, "That's your Uncle Frank."

Bushman's brother owned and operated the White House Candies, located in the B.F. Keith Building at the corner of Seventeenth Street and Euclid Avenue in Cleveland, adjacent to Playhouse Square where Bushman appeared numerous times.

Niece June Bushman Hannan remembers one occasion when both Bushman and Valentino were in town and the family went to see Valentino.

"Uncle Frank had a fit when he found out. But Mama said, 'We can see you anytime.'"

In front of the Federal Reserve Bank of Cleveland on Superior Avenue sits Henry Hering's "Energy in Repose," an imposing bronze upon a granite base.

1. Early Years

The sculpture portrays a man in the fullest development of his physical powers illustrating physical energy, intelligently employed to symbolize the industrial might of the nation's fourth Federal Reserve District. Hering also prepared works for the 1915 Panama Pacific Exposition, winning a silver medal for medals and a bronze medal for sculpture.

Without a doubt, Bushman's classic physique provided the ideal model for this sculpture. "A Survey of Public Monuments in Cleveland" reported that Bushman modeled for this bronze statue. Likewise, the booklet on the Federal Reserve Bank of Cleveland credits Bushman with modeling for "Energy in Repose."

The opening of Cleveland's Federal Reserve building took place in August 1923, after the actor had become famous. However, Bushman's fall from public favor in 1918 could have caused the star to revert to modeling for sculptors to earn additional cash. Newspapers reported that ladies "swooned" when the statue was unveiled and the manly physique with bare chest was exposed. Bushman would have certainly approved of their reactions.

Palace of Fine Arts: 1915 Panama-Pacific Exposition

The most impressive building sporting one of Bushman's statues is the Palace of Fine Arts, constructed for the 1915 Panama-Pacific Exposition in San Francisco. Bernard R. Maybeck served as the master architect for the Palace of Fine Arts, considered the most beautiful building at the 1915 Exposition. The Palace of Fine Arts is world-renowned for its architecture, coloring, lighting and lagoon setting. Not only is the Palace silhouetted against the sky but also reflected in the waters of the lagoon.

The Palace of Fine Arts stood next to the lagoon's edge with an attendant goddess guarding the flame of inspiration. Twin flanking peristyles traveled 1,000 feet with a great domed rotunda, rising 162 feet, fronting the encircling Corinthian colonnades. Concealed light shone through ground-glass shades, sending shimmering silvery moonlight onto the lagoon. Massive figures designed by Ulric H. Ellerhusen, including "Conception" for which Bushman posed, filled the spaces at the top of the rotunda.

Family photographs show Bushman and his wife Josephine on the grounds of the 1915 San Francisco Panama-Pacific Exposition. Bushman, decked out in white suit and straw hat, poses next to a Konti sculpture of a nude woman in one photo while another picture shows the rotunda of the Palace of Fine Arts with a handwritten "Bushman Statue" inked onto the photograph.

The Palace of Fine Arts is the only remaining building from the 1915

Henry Hering's *Energy in Repose*, Cleveland, Ohio.

Panama-Pacific Exposition and has been used for a variety of purposes over the years (including a stint as a motor pool during World War II and the site of the city's art festival in the 1950s). In 1964, the original structures were dismantled and models constructed to aid with reconstruction which continued until 1975.

Palace of Fine Arts, San Francisco.

The gallery area now contains the Exploratorium and the Palace of Fine Arts Theatre. After major restoration, the Palace of Fine Arts reopened to the public in 1996.

Incidentally, the following sculptors who used Bushman as a model all had sculptures or other artwork represented at the 1915 San Francisco Panama-Pacific Exposition: French, Hering, Konti, Pratt, Weinhart and Mrs. Harry Payne Whitney. Many of them won exhibition medals for their work.

A Daughter's Reflection

"The miracle of my father was that he created himself and his own image," says Virginia. "He was an original…there was no one for him to copy. He possessed a charm you don't see today. He had the most beautiful mouth. He did not have to pose. The grace, manner and way he carried himself were all natural. He enchanted you without doing anything. He was always his own man."

He lived by his motto, "Take things as they come, fear nothing and nobody." In 1997, Virginia gave us the following glimpses of Bushman:

> He was a dedicated man. "Acting" was a noble art to him. He told me that when great kings were unable to cope, the "Jester" was called in to entertain. Only an actor could distract the King so he could go on.
>
> Every day he spent time reciting Shakespeare to keep his voice "perfect." He loved Shakespeare and I picked that up from him. I am very much

"Daddy's Girl." I was an actress at age three and starred with him at the Temple Theatre in Camden, New Jersey, where he performed stock. That theater was torn down recently.

He was never idle, always either running, lifting weights or sitting at the piano exercising his voice. He would run the scale, starting low while going higher and higher. He kept his body in perfect shape. If he was called in the dead of night, he was always ready. The only time he sat down was to read or eat. He thoroughly enjoyed food. I used to watch him eat a big platter of fresh corn.

From the moment he could afford it, he owned a fine horse. His apartment at 435 Riverside Drive was located beside the bridle path and he rode every day. To prevent being recognized he donned a fake mustache and wore a wide-brimmed black hat. He named one of his horses "Nubian King." He always named his horses and Great Danes "Hamlet," "Marcus" or similar grand names. He liked everything *big*! Big horses, big dogs, big birds. He once gave his mother a parrot named Frank.

His proudest moment was purchasing wonderful, wonderful Bushmanor. Bushmanor was a "Gentleman's Farm" in Green Spring Valley, a heavenly area! When he moved to Bushmanor, they were still fox hunting across the property. He was horrified at the sport and put a stop to it immediately. His love of his animals and birds was one of his chief charms. He could not stand cruelty to animals. Bushmanor was everything to Daddy. It had a beautiful carriage house copied after Mount Vernon. There were many houses built of field stone on the property for the servants who worked at Bushmanor. Every morning he would visit them. He was genuinely interested in them and their lives, especially the children. He had presents for everybody, candy for the children, and even bones for their dogs. He wanted the rest of his world to share in his good fortune. He loved having his family at Bushmanor. He put his mother, father and Aunt May in a fine stonehouse at Bushmanor. My favorite building, located down by the stream, was busy with activity as they made butter. There were tall wild flowers there and the stream was dark and exciting to a young girl. I used to stand in the water and sing to Daddy. The water was extremely cold and I wanted to scream but instead I sang. That was the best acting I ever did.

In Daddy's day, movies were *magic*. You can't imagine the adulation! He was very much a part of the early *reverence*. If you possess something very fine, you take good care of it. That's the way he took care of himself, not of himself as a person but as a caretaker of a valuable asset.

If I were asked, "What was it about your father that impressed you the most?" I would have to think for a long time. It was just that Daddy wasn't like other people, he was *different!* He was many things to many people. ...To me, he was "Daddy."

2

Essanay Studio Star

Discovered

Not surprisingly, the same attributes that drew sculptors to Bushman also made him a perfect choice for the fledgling movie industry. The bodybuilding techniques he learned from Bernarr Macfadden stood him in good stead as the attractive and masculine romantic lead, as did his "Classic Roman" profile. Likewise, his natural acting talent and early years of experience on stage gave him eye-catching film presence. Bushman stood six feet tall and his wavy brown hair and blue eyes left women swooning in the theater aisles.

Years later, Bushman reflected, "I put all of my emotions in my jaw." The handsome actor rightfully claimed title to the role of the undisputed romantic screen idol of the day in the United States and in England (where his films listed him as actor Cecil Stanhope).

Prior to entering films, Bushman appeared in lantern slides to earn some extra money. The song slides were shown in nickelodeons and vaudeville houses. He received no billing for his early lantern slide appearances.

His movie career started in 1911. Bushman was playing Philadelphia stock theater in *The Bishop's Carriage* when Richard Foster Baker saw his work and asked him to join the Essanay Film Manufacturing Company as a leading man. Essanay already possessed a strong Western program featuring "Broncho Billy" Anderson and a talented comedy team with actors such as "Alkali Ike" and later Charlie Chaplin and Ben Turpin, but they lacked a strong leading man to compete for film audiences with the other studios.

Wallace Beery and Gloria Swanson also began their film careers at Essanay. Among other notable silent movie screen actors and actresses working there were Lily Branscombe, E.H. Calvert, Harry Cashman, Maurice Costello, Lester Cuneo, Helen Dunbar, Frank Dayton, Taylor Holmes, Max Linder, Dorothy Phillips, Marguerite Snow, John Steppling, Ruth Stonehouse, Bryant Washburn and, of course, Beverly Bayne. Essanay also attracted its share of quality directors with the likes of George Ade, E.H. Calvert, W. Christy Cabanne, Lester Totten,

Richard C. Travers and Theodore Wharton. Particularly noteworthy was humorist-turned-director, George Ade, who adapted many of his famous "Fables in Slang" into photoplays for the enjoyment of early movie audiences. Overall, 59 Ade Fables were made into Essanay films between 1915 and 1917. In addition, Ade's long story "The Slim Princess" was produced by Essanay as a four-reel movie starring Francis X. Bushman in 1915.

Gilbert M. "Broncho Billy" Anderson was the A of S & A from which Essanay took its name. His original name was Maxwell Aaronson. He appeared in the first film classic, the 1903 *The Great Train Robbery*. Anderson left Selig Polyscope Company to join forces with George K. Spoor and form the Essanay Film Manufacturing Company in 1907. Spoor provided the S in S & A (Essanay). Spoor previously managed the Waukegan Opera House and invested $100 in 1895 in the production of a movie projector designed by a local inventor. Spoor went on to own a chain of movie theaters.

Essanay established offices at 521 First National Bank building in Chicago and a main studio at 1333-45 West Argyle Street in Chicago. As can be seen from the Essanay Film Manufacturing Company photo, the studio entrance featured the company's trademark Indians with headdresses (the design reportedly taken from the Indian head penny) mounted on marble and flanking the golden letters of "Essanay." The building still exists and received historic landmark designation in 1990 from the Commission on Chicago Landmarks as an important historical reminder of Chicago's early filmmaking days.

Essanay later established movie studios in Niles, California, and Ithaca, New York, as well as shooting on location in Oakland, California, Denver and Golden, Colorado, and El Paso, Texas. Essanay was one of the first film companies to shoot Westerns on location out West, bringing authentic Western settings and real cowboys to the movie screens. "Broncho Billy" Anderson films were shot in locations near Denver as early as 1909. Essanay also created a British agency for its films in 1909 and opened branch offices in Barcelona, Berlin, London and Paris.

It did not take Bushman long to consider that the emerging film industry held greater promise than battling for stage roles. Besides, the starting film studio salary more than tripled his annual income. In an interview four years later, he stated that he joined Essanay because he believed that "the Motion Picture stage has a far greater power [to give pleasure and strengthen high ideals] than the speaking stage or even the pulpit."

The First Films

Present-day knowledge of the early Chicago filmmaking days is, at best, fragmentary. Films and their dates must be researched in quite a range of sources.

2. Essanay Studio Star

Entrance to the Essanay Studios building, Chicago. (Photo: Richard J. Maturi.)

These sources must be weighed for comparative reliability. The discussion that follows is based on the authors' findings.

By mid–1911, Bushman teamed up with Dorothy Phillips in a one-reel photoplay directed by R.E. Baker. In *His Friend's Wife,* Bushman portrayed an artist who marries a flower girl whom he soon discards only to discover later she has married his friend. His first Essanay movie was released on June 3, 1911. Some sources credit *Lost Years* as Bushman's first movie but that film was not released until September 23, 1911. Bushman reportedly went to George K. Spoor to buy his first film so he could destroy it because he felt it was so bad. Spoor, of course, said no, and they went on to make many more films together.

With each succeeding film, Bushman gained popularity among the moviegoing audience. Likewise, new industry magazines such as *Motion Picture Classic, Motion Picture Magazine, Motion Picture Story Magazine, Motography, The Moving Picture World, Photoplay* and *Picture Play Weekly* made the scene, feeding anxious fans tidbits and photos of their favorite photoplayers.

Bushman benefited from this media blitz as well as from other attempts to build fan interest in the movies and their stars. Movie patrons could purchase photo postcards of their favorite stars for five cents each, about the price of admission to the theater. National Stars Corporation advertisements in *Motion Picture Magazine* offered national film star spoons which were also sold in the lobbies of moving picture theaters.

One such ad showed a picture of Bushman and referred to the Francis X.

An early photo of Bushman.

Bushman Teaspoon as one of the most attractive. The ad copy read, "Girls, here is your chance! Take tea with Mr. Bushman, the matinee idol of filmland." The spoons were produced by the International Silver Company, the largest makers of silverware in the world. Actress Anita Stewart was honored with the first female film star spoon while Bushman carried the male honors with the first male film star spoon.

Movie patrons received a free coupon at their local theater that could be redeemed with 15 cents for a spoon. Fans also voted for their favorite movie stars for consideration for future spoon issues.

In an advertisement in *The Motion Picture News*, the General Film Company, Inc., Poster Department sold photograph posters of such major stars as Bushman, Carlyle Blackwell, Maurice Costello, Octavia Handworth and Crane Wilbur. The price of a 22" by 28" poster was 40 cents while the 11" by 14" size cost 20 cents, both postage prepaid. *The Motion Picture News* also carried advertisements offering Famous Star Series "postage" stamp sets. Movie exhibitors were urged to display the stamp sets in a handsome album and offer a free stamp with each movie theater patron admission to attract new fans.

In other efforts to build the star system, movie exhibitors held balls across the country, selling tickets to the public. Attendance by film actors was compulsory to attract attention. Mary Pickford and Bushman led the grand march at several of these gala events hosted by the Motion Picture Exhibitors' Association in New York. Bushman served on the reception committee at the January 31, 1914, Screen Club Ball held at Grand Central Palace in New York City.

On May 14, 1914, in excess of 8,000 people turned out for the first annual International Motion Picture Association Ball at the Coliseum Building in Chicago. Bushman, Beverly Bayne, Wallace Beery, Helen Dunbar, Ruth Stonehouse, Bryant Washburn and other Essanay favorites manned the Essanay Film Manufacturing booth and met with movie fans and exhibitors. *The Moving Picture World* reported that "Francis X. Bushman, Marc MacDermott, Billy Quirk and Harry Meyers were well nigh worn out by the ordeal." Bushman escorted Clara Kimball Young in the grand march.

In several interviews, Bushman later reflected on how films were literally churned out at Essanay. "We averaged a picture a week. This is inconceivable today... They didn't even turn off the studio lights between pictures. I would just change my costume and go right into a new role.... We didn't sit around between shots. We pulled this or moved that. The movie set was lit by Cooper-Hewitt arc lights, later on, Kliegs. We just turned on all the juice we had, and let it go at that. The heat was terrific. When you got Klieg eyes, the pain went right into your brain. During some scenes, instead of reading from the script, we would sometimes use profanity to try to break up the other actor. Only the lip readers knew what was going on."

Bushman circa 1912.

In the July 1914 issue of *The Photoplay Magazine*, Bushman summed up the appeal of movies to the audience: "It's romance ... just romance. We all know the ordinary ways of ordinary lives. We know that the peddler on Halstead Street and the bricklayer and the teamster have loves, and hates, and hopes, and disappointments. But unless these human feelings are set down in acting in a spirit of high romance or of moving pathos, we don't have any genuine interest in them.... It's not the world we know, but the world we'd like to know that we wish to see set in mimic. If it makes us forget for a little time our cares and worries, it is good. If it inspires us in an ambition to live with the spirit of nobility, of sacrifice, of aspiration that the heroes and heroines of the play possess—as heroes and heroines—then it is more good."

Bushman's love of the movies and his love for the audience guided his work. He remarked in the October 26, 1914, issue of the *Essanay News*, "I always feel the audience before me."

His appeal to the fans and romantic roles made him a favorite among women. Of course, along with his status as a leading man, Essanay demanded that his contract stipulate that his marriage and family be kept secret from the moviegoing public. That is why his birthplace is listed as Norfolk, Virginia, in early studio press releases and magazine articles. For example, the December 14, 1912, *Moving Picture World* carried an article about Bushman leaving for his home in Norfolk to spend Christmas with his mother and father.

Enter Beverly Bayne

While Bushman was teamed up with Dorothy Phillips for a number of his early Essanay pictures, he joined the ranks of top leading men when the studio teamed him up with young, brown-eyed beauty, Beverly Bayne in 1912. Their first picture together carried the appropriate title of *A Good Catch*, and hit the street on May 18, 1912. Bayne joined Essanay in early 1912, appearing in her first film, *The Loan Shark*, released March 12, 1912. She earned $35 a week for her first film performance.

Bayne was born Pearl Beverly Bain on November 22, 1894, in Minneapolis, Minnesota. She was raised in Chicago after her parents Jessie Pearl and Augustus R. Bain were divorced and her mother remarried and relocated to the Windy City. As a student at Chicago's Hyde Park High School, Bayne stopped by the Essanay studios and applied for a job. Director Harry McRae Webster had her test-read a script and she won the feminine lead part in *The Loan Shark* at the age of 16. Within months, Bayne and Bushman were making movie history as the first great love team.

A March 1912 actor popularity contest sponsored by *Motion Picture Story Magazine* placed Bushman fourteenth with Maurice Costello (Vitagraph) ranked first and G.M. Anderson second. *Moving Picture World* reported in April 1912 that Bushman suffered an injury during rehearsal for a detective drama when a revolver discharged and the wadding from the blank cartridge struck the actor in the fleshy part of his left arm. When the director decided to call off rehearsal for the rest of the day, Bushman refused, had the wound dressed and went back to work.

Looking to spotlight their new star, Essanay cast Bushman in an epic picture as Cortez, the conqueror of Mexico, in *The Fall of Montezuma*. The filming was announced as early as June 1912 with regular announcements to watch for the opening of "Essanay's Masterpiece of Film" all the way up to October 1912. *The Moving Picture World* reported that the three-reel picture in production "has already set the moving picture world agog with interest." We could not discover an actual release date

Beverly Bayne

2. Essanay Studio Star

Bushman in "Daydream of a *Photoplay* Artist," ca. 1912.

or review of *The Fall of Montezuma* and must conclude that Essanay never released the production.

While filming *The Romance of the Dells* on location at the Wisconsin Dells and Bayfield, Wisconsin, in 1912, Bushman gained notoriety by defeating six-foot-two, 215-pound John Pederson, champion wrestler of Buck McCarthy's lumber camp #9. Even though he was outweighed by nearly 30 pounds, Bushman won the match in straight falls, the first in 45 minutes, and the second in 26 minutes. *The Romance of the Dells* also fails to show up anywhere as a completed film. Production may have been halted, or the film may have been released under a different title.

During the filming of *Daydream of a Photoplay Artist* in 1912, Essanay used an intricate series of double exposures to enable Bushman to appear as two characters simultaneously. *Daydream of a Photoplay Artist* also failed to make it to the movie theaters.

Essanay also filmed out of its Ithaca, New York, studio and on location during 1912 and 1913. Essanay rented the home of Judge Clymer on the Cornell University campus during the summer of 1913 and featured the home and picturesque Cornell campus in a number of movies shot that summer. The September 20, 1913, *The Moving Picture World* commented that movies were helping to keep Cornell students sober, according to the report of Theodore Twestomn, a proctor at the university.

Director Theodore Wharton turned out a number of one- and two-reelers at Ithaca: *The Hermit (of Lonely Gulch)* (1912) with both Bushman and Bayne, *The Love Lute of Romany* (1913) with Beverly Bayne and *The Right of Way* and *Tony, The Fiddler* (both 1913) with Bushman. Wharton finished up the 1913 filming at Ithaca with Bushman and Bayne starring in *Dear Old Girl*. The one-reeler featured a realistic train wreck and was completed in just four days.

The Moving Picture World reported that the Essanay Ithaca Company returned to Chicago on September 1, 1913, and would remain there for five or six weeks. After completing their work in the main Essanay studio they were planning to head South to work around Jacksonville, Florida, for the winter. The article listed the company as consisting of William Bailey, Beverly Bayne, Otto Breslyn, Francis X. Bushman, Frank Dayton, Helen Dunbar, Juanita Dalmorez and Miss McClellan.

A follow-up article by writer Hugh Hoffman, entitled "With Essanay at Ithaca," told how Ithaca handed the Essanay people the keys to the city. Instead of being holed up in gloomy hotel rooms, the cast and crew were domiciled in "some of the finest residences in the most exclusive section of the town...living on Cornell Heights in the homes of college professors...." Bushman, Mr. and Mrs. Theodore Wharton and dog "Buster" took up residence in Judge Clymer's home.

By October 1913, Bushman had moved up to sixth place in *Photoplay Magazine*'s popularity contest (more than 7 million votes were cast). Bushman's oldest sister, Mary, remarked on her 100th birthday that no one in the family was surprised at Francis X.'s movie career: "He was always theatrical. One of his first Christmas gifts was a stage. Later on he worked all the time to develop his body. Papa made fun of him, but he had his ideas and he kept to them."

Essanay's 1913 Christmas greetings message carried in the movie picture magazines featured photos of the Essanay players with Francis X. Bushman featured right in the middle of the page, directly beneath the Essanay logo of an Indian in a headdress.

The Ladies' World Hero Contest

The romantic team of Bushman and Bayne was beginning to become inseparable. In January 1914, *The Ladies' World* invited its readers to vote for their favorite movie heroes. The contest introduction stated, "*The Ladies' World* wants you to pick the moving picture actor you would best like to see in Louis Tracy's tremendous romance, *One Wonderful Night*. The hero of this story is a fine, handsome, young American, full of the fire of youth, adventurous and romantic.... You can choose him...your favorite hero of photo-play, one of the seven leading men pictured on this page...the seven favorites of the silent drama."

"Will your vote be for King Baggot? for smiling Maurice Costello? or handsome Crane Wilbur? Or is your favorite the sterling actor Arthur Johnson, or Carlyle Blackwell of national fame? Perhaps you think that it should be for the cleancut Francis Bushman, or that Warren Kerrigan, the versatile, should be the man?"

As a contest incentive, the magazine offered a complimentary half life-size portrait of their favorite photo player in sepia brown ink on heavy India print plate paper suitable for framing. For ten cents, the contest voter received ten postcards showing the actor in a movie scene and the portrait. A number of these photos of Bushman survived the years and exist today. For some unknown reason, each ballot was worth ten votes.

The Ladies' World reported that the contest started out swiftly with a snowdrift of contest envelopes swamping the girls counting the votes. Bushman started out in the middle of the pack and by the March issue had accumulated 71,460 votes. Crane Wilbur led with a tally of 82,880. Votes were received from as far away as Alaska and Hawaii in the U.S. territories and on the international front from Australia, Bermuda, Cuba, France, Haiti, Ireland, Italy, Mexico, Panama, Puerto Rico and Scotland. Bushman carried great favor in the Canadian balloting.

In order to heat up the contest, the magazine announced in March 1914 that for the next 30 days each ballot would be worth 20 votes instead of the usual ten. By the March issue Bushman had moved up to third place (114,260) behind Maurice Costello (200,101) and contest leader Jack W. Kerrigan (222,290). The contest promoters again upped the ante in the April 1914 issue, making the value of each ballot 50 votes. They also increased their advertising revenues as the studios took out full page promotional ads for their stars in *The Ladies' World*.

For example, an Essanay ad urged fans to "Vote for Bushman of Essanay" and featured Bushman extolling his virtues and his ambition to play such parts as emphasized by his Americanism: the clean-living, clean-thinking, active-minded, athletic youth of our nation. He also mentioned being chosen by Daniel Chester French and Carl Bitter as the type of American man exhibited in their sculptures and his great heritage of ancestors, who settled in Virginia 300 years ago (the studio was still covering up Bushman's real hometown of Baltimore and status as a married family man). Adding to his exposure, Bushman appeared on the cover of the July 1914 issue of *Photoplay Magazine*.

Movie theaters also got into the act, initiating "Heroes Nights," special nights when movie patrons could cast their votes for their favorite actor. "Hero Clubs" also sprung up to help fans keep up with the latest news of their favorite film stars.

Bushman surpassed Costello by the May 1914 issue with 316,600 votes to 271,750 and was hot on the trail of Kerrigan with 338,750 votes. The May 23, 1914, issue of *The Moving Picture World* broke the news of the winner of the "Hero Contest": Francis X. Bushman's come-from-behind campaign brought victory with 1,806,630 votes, trouncing the nearest competitor (Kerrigan) with 1,262,740 votes.

The Moving Picture World declared that the contest "will long be remembered as a stamp of unqualified approval upon the moving picture industry, an infant only a few short years ago and now grown to lusty health and strength despite the contemptuous sneers and the unprincipled attacks of those who failed to recognize moving pictures of the kind that leading manufacturers have always meant to produce as the ideal entertainment for the masses." *The Ladies' World* presented the three highest vote-getters (Bushman, Kerrigan and Maurice Costello) with a solid gold, diamond-studded medal bearing the inscription "*Ladies World* Hero Contest."

The Motion Picture News of June 6, 1914, showed a picture of the medal won by Bushman. The medal was attached to a broad ribbon and featured a bas relief of a woman holding a palm branch in her outstretched left hand, her right hand resting on a shield decorated with a single diamond acting as a crest. The article quoted from Bushman's letter to his many friends: "My untiring efforts to please you in the future will attest my love for you and my gratitude to you for the great honor you have bestowed on me in selecting me to play the part of John Delancey Curtis, the typical American, in *One Wonderful Night*. Gratefully, sincerely, Francis X. Bushman."

The tabulated record in the magazine's offices indicated that Bushman's full-page advertisement (in strict conformity with the latest practices of candidates for public office) "did the trick" for him and boosted him from a poor third to a big winner. Ironically, his clean-cut image pushed him over the top in the contest. Tarnishing of that image in the public's eye later proved to be his downfall.

Bushman attributed a big part of his contest success to his personal appearance tour to theaters. In an interview after the close of the contest he said, "During my spare time, I talked at 250 theaters in and around Chicago. After the show I'd come out on the stage and say a few words. With these personal appearances my popularity soared. Now that I have won the contest, I shall strive to give the best that is in me."

As the contest winner, Bushman was featured as the leading actor of Essanay's elaborate production *One Wonderful Night*. The studio announced that an entire company of actors would be brought to New York from Chicago in order to film the picture in the spots made famous by John D. Curtis in the play. Bushman, as John Curtis, was supported by Beverly Bayne in the role of Lady Hermione. George K. Spoor, president of the Essanay Company, personally supervised the production of the photoplay.

> *The Ladies' World* described *One Wonderful Night* as follows: *One Wonderful Night* is just the story to give the best picture of a character like John Delancey Curtis. It is a story of breathless action, daring adventures, deep mystery and bold love-making. It is a story to stir the pulses and the sympathies. A charming and wealthy heroine matches with a rare hero. It is most remarkably adapted to moving pictures and as a photo-play it will demand and repay the best work of the man whom *Ladies' World* readers are choosing to take the part of Curtis.

Essanay Film Manufacturing Company wasted no time in placing advertisements in the major movie magazines proclaiming Bushman as "The World's Foremost Photoplayer," along with a statement from Bushman that he "wishes to express his sincerest thanks and appreciation to those who made this election possible."

The Moving Picture World covered departure of the Essanay cast on Saturday, June 6, 1914, for New York to begin filming of *One Wonderful Night*. The contest and Bushman's victory caused worldwide interest in the Essanay dramatic company and the upcoming production. The magazine proclaimed, "Bushman's lead in *One Wonderful Night* will mark his finest work."

The Ladies' World heightened interest in *One Wonderful Night* by publishing the story in serial form. The magazine continued its promotion of *One Wonderful Night* with an article in which it was proclaimed that 10,000,000 people were anxiously waiting to see the photoplay. Essanay released the four-reel film on July 18, 1914.

Essanay news releases declared that *One Wonderful Night* was a drama full of love and intrigue. An August 14, 1914, *Variety* review described the production as "well staged, well photoplayed and has sufficient action to keep the interest keyed up… splendidly directed, consistently woven together and the action sustained to the point relished by movie folks… The leads are capably taken and Bushman does some capital work throughout. There are several 'big moments' and for the camera interest are bound to help business at the box office."

Both Chicago newspapers and magazines throughout the country predicted that *One Wonderful Night* would be one of the biggest hits of the 1914 movie season. Critics proclaimed that Essanay spared no expense and that every detail of the story was faithfully portrayed in the film.

The collaboration between Essanay Film and *The Ladies' World* worked so well both to sell magazines and to create interest in films that the two teamed up again with short stories appearing in the magazine in conjunction with release of the films. For example, Essanay released the three-reeler *The Plum Tree* with Beverly Bayne and Wallace Beery on September 18, 1914. The photoplay derived from a short story featured in *The Ladies' World*. To spur both magazine and movie ticket sales, a crucial part of the storyline was intentionally left out of the magazine story but left intact in the film. A contest invited moviegoers to submit their portrayal of the missing information as they saw it in the movie. Another collaboration occurred with the Essanay release of *The Accounting* on February 18, 1915, in conjunction with the short story running in the March issue of *The Ladies' World*.

Songs By and About Bushman

Sheet music publisher Frank K. Root & Company of Chicago and New York also capitalized on the popularity of Bushman and *One Wonderful Night* with the issuance of sheet music for the waltz ballad "One Wonderful Night (You Told Me You Loved Me)," with words by E. Clinton Keithley and Joe Lyons and music by Clarence M. Jones. The cover featured a striking picture of Bushman.

Other Bushman song connections included a waltz ballad entitled "My Ship o' Dreams"; *Feature Movie* reported in April 1915 that Bushman had composed it. The sheet music distributed by Chicago publisher Will Rossiter featured lyrics written by Bushman and music by Frank M. Suttle. Rossiter promoted the song as "one of the catchiest songs of the year and sure to be immensely popular." One of Chicago's leading cabaret singers, Sayde Pearl, sang the ballad at the American Cafe.

The "My Ship o' Dreams" sheet music also featured a photograph of Bushman on the front. The cover text promised pleasant memories from Bushman's recent successful film *Dear Old Girl*. The May 23, 1915, issue of *Motography* also carried a story on Bushman's song, describing it as a beautiful waltz ballad. It described splendid poster cards available to exhibitors that are "decidedly attractive and in the center bear the title page of the song with a portrait of Mr. Bushman."

In 1917, another sheet music ballad, "Carry Round a Smile with You," appeared with words by Bushman and music by Carl Fique. F.J.A. Forster Music Publisher of Chicago released another piece of sheet music called "The Moving

Picture Hero of My Heart." This time Bushman did not write the words but was featured on the cover with other leading male actors of the day.

As a tribute to Bushman, Chryse Lenard composed the following verse:

Francis X. Bushman

From every clime and country,
Regardless where they are,
A host of friends give tribute
Now, to our beloved star.
Candid, upright, honest,
In all he undertakes,
Simple, unaffected,
Francis X. scintillates.

Bent on doing worlds of good,
Unheeding he strives,
Smiling ever happy,
He brightens other lives.
Master of his wonder art,
Alone he holds sway.
None can ever take his place,
Francis X., of Essanay.

Essanay wisely starred the successful love team of Bushman and Bayne for its August 29, 1914, release of *Under Royal Patronage*, directed by E.H. Calvert. The two-reeler also featured Calvert, Thomas Commerford, Lester Cuneo, Harry Dunkinson, Charles Hitchcock, Jane Paddock, Betty Scott and Bryant Washburn. The storyline was adapted from a short story appearing in *Munsey Magazine*. *The Moving Picture World* concluded that the film developed an interesting plot with Bushman playing his part "nobly and bravely. [Moviegoers will be] treated to a film story of love and intrigue that cannot fail to delight them."

The movie was filmed in Chicago, using the elegant home of one of the city's millionaires as the grand setting for love in high places. Princes and princesses and high state officials interact in the plot, bringing two pairs of lovers happiness in the end. The prince and princess, in order to avoid marrying, ask American friends to take their place. Although they do not know each other's identity, the royals proceed to fall in love. The Americans also fall in love. Both couples overcome seemingly insurmountable difficulties but Fate intervenes to bring them happiness.

The Moving Picture World characterized Bushman as "especially fitted for romantic roles. He is an athlete of no mean prowess and an adept swordsman." Likewise, the magazine heaped praise on Beverly Bayne as "altogether lovely as the Princess. There is an unaffected sweetness in her impersonation that fits the part admirably."

Sheet music for "One Wonderful Night" features Francis X. Bushman on the cover.

Rising Fame

    Winning the "Hero Contest" and co-starring in popular romantic films with Beverly Bayne sent Bushman's fame soaring. Bushman and Bayne were universally regarded as America's first authentic red-hot love team. It was reported that the heartthrob of millions of women received in excess of 7,000 letters per week. In order to have each letter personally answered, Bushman hired Louella Parsons

2. Essanay Studio Star

as his parttime secretary to supervise a roomful of other secretaries who wrote back to Bushman's adoring fans. Bushman claimed to have spent $40,000 a year answering fan mail with 13 secretaries. Parsons stated in a magazine article that the letters were from women from 12 to 80 years of age. Most of them spoke of love and a great many asked Mr. Bushman's aid in embarking on a moving picture career. All of them demanded an autographed picture.

Bushman insisted that every letter receive a personal, individual reply. Each letter was kept and filed under a card system. He looked over the letters every month to get a feel for what the public wanted. He said, "Parsons would look over all the replies to be sure I wouldn't get too involved. You see, I was getting passionate love letters—each one thought she was the one for me. We kept 'em interested."

Parsons already worked at Essanay as a scriptwriter. She earned the job by moonlighting movie scenarios while working daytime as a reporter for the *Chicago Tribune*. She wrote the script for such films as *Chains*, a November 2, 1912, release starring Bushman, Ruth Stonehouse and Bryant Washburn.

Parsons estimated that she read in excess of 20,000 submissions and crafted 125 one- and two-reel scripts during her years at Essanay. Sometimes her scripts called for a baby, and her own daughter Harriet earned billing as Baby Parsons in such films as the August 10, 1912, release *The Magic Wand,* directed by Theodore Wharton and starring Bushman, Beverly Bayne, Helen Dunbar and Billy Mason. The script revolves around a poor child who receives the role of a fairy queen in a *Cinderella* production. The child steals the wand in the hopes that its magic will help transform the poor circumstances of her mother. *The Moving Picture World* panned *The Magic Wand,* mainly due to Baby Parsons' performance. "A delightful and very promising situation was quite ruined by its treatment in this particular picture ... The great trouble with this picture is the child player, who never for a moment forgot the camera and was quite wooden throughout. The picture's story cannot help pleasing, but the production is almost without atmosphere."

Parsons' salary increased dramatically, from $18 a week to the grand sum of $45 per week before she parted company with Essanay. In 1914, Parsons initiated one of the first movie columns in the country for the *Chicago Record-Herald*, launching her lifelong career of reporting on the movies and their stars. She also authored the book *How to Write for the Movies,* which was published in 1915 and sold for one dollar a copy. She continued to move up with a position at the *New York Morning Telegraph* in 1919 and as movie editor of the Hearst-owned *American* in 1923. Impressed by her hard work and talent, publisher William Randolph Hearst promoted her to movie editor for Universal News Service in 1925. That move made her the undisputed journalistic queen of Hollywood. Her path and Bushman's would cross a number of times over the years.

This was about the time that Bushman started his lavish lifestyle—a lifestyle befitting the "Handsomest Man in the World," as he was advertised. He was

Here and on the next page, Bushman's famous amethyst ring is much in evidence.

renowned for the large amethyst ring he wore, the specially made eight-inch, monogrammed, lavender cigarettes he smoked from a cigarette holder, and the $100 tips he gave to bellboys and waiters.

He also traveled extensively and bestowed expensive gifts on family and friends. He traveled in style, driving a specially designed, 20-foot-long lavender Marmon with all the exposed metal work trimmed in gold plate. His name was spelled out in gold lettering. Bushman maintained that the Marmon Automobile Company gave him $2,000 off the $22,000 price of the car if he had his name painted in gold on the outside doors. It was reportedly one of the longest cars in America and could reach speeds up to 110 miles per hour.

Nephew Robert A. Bushman, a little boy in the '20s, recalls that when Uncle Frank arrived in Cleveland by train with his Marmon on a flat car, "the police blocked the street whenever he visited." Bushman once remarked, "I lived like a king and spent money like a Congressional committee."

Everywhere Bushman went, crowds followed. Salesgirls would leave their counters when Bushman showed up in their stores, giving shoplifters a field day. He received a letter from the Merchants Association requesting that he stay out of their stores to prevent pandemonium. If he desired anything, they would send it to him. On one occasion, Bushman and Mary Pickford were traveling to Boston via train for a benefit. President Taft was aboard and called for Bushman. He had watched the demonstration at the train station as mobs of fans descended on Pickford and Bushman. Pickford almost had her clothes torn off and Bushman looked like the wrath of God. According to Bushman, Taft remarked, "All the people love you and I can't have even the love of half the people."

During his time at Essanay, Bushman also met other actors and actresses who would grow to become famous stars. Wallace Beery starred in many films with Beverly Bayne at Essanay as well as several with Bushman. Beery met his short-term wife Gloria Swanson at Essanay before he left to join MGM. Swanson was only 15 years old when she joined Essanay as a $3.25-a-week extra, bit player and stock player. She appeared unbilled in some early Bushman and Bayne films, receiving billing in the January 23, 1915, release of *The Ambition of a Baron*. In her book *Swanson on Swanson*, she described her initial meeting with the great god of Essanay:

> The dressing room I shared first with Virginia Bowker and later with Agnes Ayres and two other girls had wall partitions that did not extend all the way to the ceiling. Next door Beverly Bayne had a star dressing room all to herself. Male performers were not supposed to come anywhere near the women's dressing rooms, but Francis X. Bushman, the biggest star in motion pictures, was of course a law unto himself. Whenever we heard whispering

in Miss Bayne's dressing room, we always knew Mr. Bushman was breaking the rules. We would climb on our dressing tables and try to hear what was going on. Beverly Bayne and Francis X. Bushman always starred together, and naturally the gossips said they were madly in love.

Mr. Bushman wore a large violet amethyst ring on his finger and he had a spotlight inside his lavender car that illuminated his famous profile when he drove after dark. Everybody at Essanay knew he was married and had five children, but to the public that was a deep dark secret. Studios felt that if word got out that stars were married and had children like ordinary people, it might destroy their image as romantic lovers.

One afternoon I was sitting on the wardrobe counter waiting for the wardrobe mistress to find a strip of elastic for my costume. Mr. Bushman came out of the men's costume department and walked over and stood beside me. Without saying a word, he confidently, casually, put his hand on my right knee. With no more conscious thought than I had been aware of the day I told Helen Dunbar I was going to be famous, I heard my hand colliding with his face. We didn't exchange a word.

On September 13, 1914, the *Buffalo Times* reported that Francis Bushman had been rescued from the sea. Further reading revealed that the "rescue" was actually a scene from a new film, *Sparks of Fate,* starring Bushman, Ruth Stonehouse, and Bryant Washburn. *The Moving Picture World* described *Sparks of Fate* as "a drama of absorbing interest and intensity ... with the photography, acting and directing deserving special interest."

Sparks of Fate was just one of a flurry of films that finished out 1914 for Bushman. Others included *A Splendid Dishonor* with Lester Cuneo, Ruth Stonehouse and Bryant Washburn, and *The Other Man* with Thomas Commerford, John Cossa, Lester Cuneo, and Lillian Drew. He also made a cameo appearance as a matinee idol in *Fable of the Bush League Lover Who Failed to Qualify,* starring Wallace Beery and Beverly Bayne.

In October 1914, Bushman, E.H. Calvert, Ruth Stonehouse and Wallace Beery returned from a trip to New York and Washington, D.C., where they spent a week shooting scenes for George Ade's *Slim Princess* for Essanay. The company spent two days in the capitol and scenes were shot at the White House and on the steps of the Executive Building. A number of high government officials were among the spectators watching the filmmaking.

The November 21, 1914, issue of *The Essanay News* carried a number of items about Bushman. While filming *The Prince Party* (released November 7, 1914), Bushman tumbles Lester Cuneo over a cliff. Cuneo found the experience a bit "too real" for comfort. Bushman suffered a cut with a surgeon's knife during the filming of *Scars of Possession* (released November 21, 1914). When Bushman arrived at Fort Sheridan for the showing of *The Private Officer* (partly shot at Fort Sheridan, and released October 17, 1914), the soldiers cheered. The December 7, 1914, *Essanay News* reported that Bushman led the Grand March at the Motion Picture Exhibition Association annual gala event at Grand Central Palace with over 30,000 people in attendance.

2. Essanay Studio Star

Bushman (center) in an early film of his Essanay years.

By 1915, Bushman ranked as Essanay's prime asset, especially when teamed with Beverly Bayne in love plots. An Essanay ad in the February 5, 1915, *The Moving Picture World* proclaimed to movie exhibitors that "Broncho Billy" Anderson, Bushman and Chas. Chaplin were the A-B-C of photoplay drama and film finance, designed to make money for the exhibitors. The ad described Anderson as the face known around the world, Bushman as the man voted the world's most popular photoplayer and Chaplin as the world's funniest comedian. "The A-B-C of photoplay drama and comedy, who never fail to attract immense throngs.... Their popularity is a known quantity.... Book the photoplays with the A-B-C trio and insure your own success."

The next week, Essanay followed up the A-B-C campaign with a full-page spread with a large photo of Bushman under the heading, "The Man Voted the World's Most Popular Photoplayer."

Two notable 1915 Essanay productions were spinoffs from a popular novel and a popular story. Both George Barr McCutcheon's novel *Graustark*, and George Ade's story *The Slim Princess* placed Bushman and Bayne in royal settings perfect for their romantic interludes.

In *Graustark*, Bushman falls in love with the princess (Bayne) of a Balkan country and winds up winning both the princess and the country's crown. The December 19, 1914, *Essanay News* reported that *Graustark* scenes were shot on a

Bushman as a priest in an early film from his Essanay years.

New York wharf, and in California, Chicago, and Washington, D.C. One of the most spectacular shots showed the Potomac River at sunset from the top of the Washington Monument. The July 17, 1915, *Essanay News* proclaimed *Graustark* "the most powerful and thrilling love romance ever screened. It holds every spectator tense with its gripping interest." From a performance standpoint, *Graustark* ranks along with *Romeo and Juliet* and *Ben-Hur* as some of Bushman's best work.

While McCutcheon's *Graustark* combined drama and love to command attention, *The Slim Princess* effectively employed a combination of comedy and love. Bushman played an American millionaire, and again he was in love with a foreign princess, though this time the roles in the royal court were played for laughs. In a letter to Essanay president George K. Spoor, reprinted in the May 29, 1915, *Motion Picture News*, George Ade said, "In order to prove that female loveliness is whatever we choose to admire, I wrote a story for *The Saturday Evening Post* and called it 'The Slim Princess.' Later I amplified the story and put it into a little book published by the Bobbs-Merrill Co. Then Henry Blossom made the book into a play, with music by Leslie Stuart, and Elsie Janis starred in the play for two seasons. To prove the unbounding vitality of the princess, I must say that she seems livelier than ever in the pictures just made by the Essanay Company. I like Mr. Blossoms' photoplay and I like Ruth Stonehouse as Kalora

Bushman (center) in an early film from his Essanay years.

and I doubt your company has ever turned out cleaner and truer specimens of photography. I am writing to thank you for letting me see the pictures and to thank you for having such dandy pictures for me to see."

The July 17, 1915, *Essanay News* described *The Slim Princess* as "one of the most delightful and pleasing comedy-dramas ever presented. Its humor is irresistible. Thousands are laughing with George Ade daily." Not all of the critics loved Bushman—*Variety* accused him of "monopolizing the spotlight" and said his "ambitiousness" was a handicap to Ruth Stonehouse's performance—but that didn't stop millions of fans from idolizing him.

In 1915, Essanay joined forces with Vitagraph, Lubin and Selig to form a new distribution group for their pictures. *Graustark* was the first Essanay film to be distributed by the new distribution group, V.L.S.E.

Bushman Departs Essanay

Despite the growing popularity of Bushman and his films, his salary continued to trail that commanded by Charlie Chaplin. Around the same time, film stars were angered by stage stars receiving higher billing than their film counterparts. Both irritants finally resulted in Bushman leaving Essanay. The May 1, 1915, *Moving Picture World* reported that Bushman terminated his association with Essanay on May 1, 1915, and signed a long-term contract to appear exclusively for Metro Pictures Corporation under the brand name of Quality Pictures. An average of one production per month was projected.

This signaled the beginning of the end for Essanay. Bayne followed Bushman to Metro and Quality in 1916 and in that same year Chaplin left the studio after his contract with Essanay lapsed. Also contributing to Essanay's decline, a 1915 Supreme Court decision ruled that the Motion Pictures Patent Company (formed by Essanay and the other major motion pictures companies) violated the Sherman Anti-Trust Act by monopolizing film production. The Court ordered the company to disband. The final nail in Essanay's coffin was the shift of the industry to California headquarters and production. In efforts to maintain an audience, Essanay re-released a number of its popular films starring Bushman and Bayne in 1916 but the writing was already on the wall. For all practical purposes, Essanay exited the production of major motion pictures in 1917.

3

The Quality Pictures– Metro Pictures Years

Quality Pictures–Metro Pictures Partnership

Metro Pictures Corporation was formed in February 1915 as a closed corporation capitalized at $300,000. Metro established offices at 1475 Broadway in New York City to distribute the pictures of five small production companies: Columbia Pictures Corporation, Dyreda Art Film Corporation, Popular Plays and Players, Quality Pictures Corporation and Rolfe Photoplays, Inc. Metro's goal was to release one picture a week. Corporate officers included Richard A. Rowland of Pittsburgh as president and Louis B. Mayer of Boston as secretary. Virginia Bushman Conway Stuart says that her father rented offices in New York City to Mayer and Metro when they first started out. Metro went public in 1917 with a capitalization of $2.5 million, absorbing many of its production affiliates at that time.

The company got off to a great start, signing up such stars as Bushman, Ethel and Lionel Barrymore and Mary Miles Minter. Metro's first four releases (announced in the March 27, 1915, *Motion Picture News*) included *Satin Sanderson* starring Orrin Johnson, *The Shadows of a Great City* with Adelaide Thurston, *The Heart of a Painted Woman* featuring Olga Petrova and *The Cowboy and the Lady* with S. Miller Kent.

Also in March 1915, Fred J. Balshofer launched Quality Pictures Corporation. Balshofer affiliated his new company with Metro Pictures Corporation for distribution. Balshofer sported extensive industry experience as the former head of the Bison Company. Quality Pictures' studios were located in the Nestor Plant at Sunset Boulevard and Gower Street in Hollywood. Quality began producing films featuring Bushman and Marguerite Snow. William Bowman served as director and William Adler handled the camera for the early Quality Pictures Corporation productions.

The May 1, 1915, issues of *The Moving Picture World* and *Motion Picture News* carried photos of Bushman and Balshofer signing the historic contract making Bushman a Metro star. The agreement called for Bushman to appear exclusively on the Metro program under the brand name of Balshofer's Quality Pictures. A number of major film manufacturers had been courting Bushman to lure him away from Essanay. Bushman's contract was reportedly the most lucrative ever offered a male star. As reported in *Variety* on May 21, 1915, one of the reasons Bushman left Essanay related to the flap over film manufacturing companies hiring legitimate stage actors for movie picture roles and giving them top billing over photo players. The other reason was purely financial. Balshofer signed Bushman for the princely sum of $750 per week plus a percentage of the profits. Balshofer also included a $10,000 advance against Bushman's future earnings and royalty payments. According to Balshofer in *One Reel a Week*, Bushman used the advance to buy a brand new purple Marmon.

In *One Reel a Week*, Balshofer told of the lengths he went to sign Bushman:

> When I learned that [Bushman] was in New York and available, I went after him. Others had the same idea in mind. On the last day he planned to be in the city, Bushman finally consented to talk with me a couple of hours before his train, the Twentieth Century, was due to pull out for Chicago. I remember very well watching Carl Laemmle as he talked with him like a Dutch uncle in the lobby of the hotel while I stood on the sidelines impatiently waiting and getting nowhere. Suddenly I decided the only way to be alone with Bushman so that I could present an offer was to get on the train and go with him to Chicago, even if I had no luggage... The night following our arrival in Chicago, I signed him to a contract while he, Beverly Bayne, his leading lady at Essanay, William Aranson, his manager, and I were having dinner together at the College Inn, a night club in the Sherman Hotel... My partners were jubilant over my success in acquiring Bushman, and Harry Reichenbach started at once to turn out stories publicizing Francis X. Bushman as the "Woman's Choice"...

It took a train baggage car to haul Bushman's menagerie of animals, two motor cars and personal possessions to Hollywood. Taking advantage of the baggage car as a traveling billboard for its new star, Reichenbach posted a large canvas banner on its side, announcing Bushman's new studio affiliation "Francis X. Bushman...Star of Quality Pictures Corporation."

Ever since he was a young boy, Bushman had collected all sorts of pets. He moved four horses, several hundred singing canaries and his prize Great Danes to California. In 1915, he rented a residence on Riverside Drive in New York City where his birds flew freely around the penthouse apartment.

"Daddy always had lots of animals," said his daughter Virginia. "Birds appeared as if by magic. They nearly drove Mother crazy. When we lived in Camden, New Jersey, very early on, there were bird cages from floor to ceiling. Later, when I went to live with him in Hollywood, you could have called his home 'Parrot Place.' He absolutely loved parrots."

3. The Quality Pictures–Metro Pictures Years

In a recording made by Bushman, he discussed his early life and attraction to pets. "I wanted to be surrounded by things that loved me.... I had hundreds of pets—beetles, frogs, lizards, birds, dogs, cats... I rose at 5:00 A.M. every morning to go to Lafayette Market to get food scraps to feed my pets. I earned money for my pets by running errands for all the neighbors and selling newspapers...."

Metro anticipated the release of one Bushman feature production per month. The studio declared, "Nothing but the biggest and most powerful of dramatic pieces will be selected for Bushman's use."

At the time of the contract signing, Metro was actively interviewing a number of prominent movie actresses and stage stars to play the leading lady opposite Bushman.

Bushman and two of his beloved parrots.

Balshofer also lured other stars from a variety of other film manufacturers to join Quality Pictures. Among those enticed to make the move were James Cruze, Lester Cuneo, Mr. and Mrs. Sydney Drew and Marguerite Snow. *Photoplay* reported that Snow left New York for Los Angeles on May 6, 1915, to become Bushman's leading lady, having won out over more than 60 other actresses interviewed for the position. Like Bushman before her, Snow arrived in California with a full load, including her Mercer runabout, 18 trunks and her Belgian seamstress.

According to *Photoplay*, Snow's own stature as one of the most popular movie actresses made her an ideal choice to be the leading lady for the Apollo of the screen: "Bushman is an actor whose work reflects his own physical bigness and power in every detail. It was felt that he should have a leading lady with equal magnetism and strength of personality combined with what the untranslatable screen expression terms 'facial strength.' Miss Snow has long been an admirer of Mr. Bushman's work before the camera, and has expressed great satisfaction at the opportunity which has been presented to her to play opposite him."

Metro Pictures wasted no time in promoting its new star. A full page advertisement in the May 1, 1915, *Motion Picture News* featured a large profile photograph of Bushman and announced that he is "appearing exclusively in Quality

Pictures." "Metro Pictures Corporation will include among other magnificent features, at an early date, the exalted, soulful, superb screen star FRANCIS X. BUSHMAN in a series of sterling and appealing dramatic documents of moment and vitality, breathing and pulsing the triumph of artistry." The ad also described Bushman as "Sovereign of the silent drama and idol of all photoplay lovers throughout the universe."

A week later, another Metro Pictures ad in *Motion Picture News* proclaimed Bushman "the most important screen star in the history of motion pictures," and featured a telegram from Bushman to Balshofer:

> Fred Balshofer, since signing up with you, my enthusiasm has assumed boundless proportion. Metro and success are synonymous. I could not wish to be associated with greater champions of excellence in photoplay. I predict Metro will be the world's guide in moving pictures productions. Delighted to hear *The Second in Command* will be my first picture and also that you have secured *The Silent Voice*. Am impatient to get started.
>
> Regards
>
> Francis Bushman

Bushman also took a high profile in a two-hour meeting with Chicago Mayor William Hale Thompson, discussing moderation of Chicago's censorship laws. *The Moving Picture World* quoted Bushman, "The Mayor...had long recognized the fact that a better method of dealing with the 'passed' and 'ban slips' were surely necessary and that the corrective methods were already being considered."

Photoplay featured Bushman, along with other photoplayers, in its impressions segment of the magazine with the following description: "Francis X. Bushman: an ancient Greek *a la* Hart Schaffner & Marx; your wife's first husband; imaginary Faust to two million Marguerites; a candidate's picture of himself."

Early Quality Pictures–
Metro Pictures Releases

The first Quality Pictures–Metro Pictures production featuring Bushman and Marguerite Snow was *The Second in Command,* released on July 26, 1915. Bushman portrayed Lt. Col. Miles Anstruther, who vied for Muriel Mannering (Snow) against Major Christopher Bingham (William Clifford). The film is notable for innovative use of the mobile camera and garnered excellent coverage with a photo scene on the cover of *Moving Picture World.* Balshofer said,

3. The Quality Pictures–Metro Pictures Years

It was a British war story that just suited Bushman's type and allowed him to display his best qualities while dressed in the tailor-made British officer uniforms he wore in the picture... The film was previewed in Chicago (where Bushman was well known)...nearly 90 percent of the audience consisted of women who aahed, oohed and sighed throughout the picture and swarmed around Bushman when the screening ended, buzzing like bees. The picture, plus Reichenbach's eye-catching publicity campaign, put Bushman over with a bang....

Reviewer Peter Milne of *Motion Picture News* stated, "*The Second in Command* will result in the producer's name being firmly established in the minds of the public... The extreme popularity [of Bushman and Snow] and their marked ability for the parts of the two lovers well recommends the choice of the producers to feature them in the picture."

Bushman was loved by fans of all sorts. One woman wrote in to *Photoplay* that her five-year-old son gave a whoop and yelled, "Here comes Bushman!" whenever his name appeared on the screen. Knowing that her son could not read, she inquired how he knew Bushman would be in the film. "Don't you think I know a big 'X' in the middle spells Bushman?" he replied.

In August, Bushman attended the Exhibitors' Field Day Carnival at Brighton Beach, New York. More than 2,000 photoplayers attended the event, which included a grand parade with elaborate floats, sporting events and a band concert.

Bushman and Snow next teamed up in *The Silent Voice*, released on September 25, 1915. The film was shot mainly in the Big Bear Lake region in California. An ad in the August 14, 1915, issue of *Motion Picture News* showed Bushman playing piano in a scene and read, "To all my friends: I am now with Quality Pictures and my mail address is: Gower and Sunset Boulevards, Hollywood, Cal., Francis X. Bushman." Balshofer and Bushman personally delivered *The Silent Voice* for its New York showing.

Cameraman William F. Adler utilized some innovative shooting with a number of different cameras used for the dynamite scenes in the picture. *The Moving Picture World* reported in July 1915 that "Quality Pictures director William J. Bauman was portraying Bushman in roles other than the juvenile leads he has been known for to date."

Balshofer and Bushman were often at loggerheads over film production, money, filming in California (Bushman wanted to return to New York) and obtaining Beverly Bayne from Essanay as Bushman's leading lady. As early as June 1915, *Photoplay* predicted, "Miss Bayne, who has been Mr. Bushman's very effective as well as beautiful leading woman in the Essanay studios, will probably accompany him in his Western progress."

About this time, movie industry trade magazines were reporting that Bushman and Snow were preparing for an eight-reel production of the famous historical play *Richard Carvel* by Winston Churchill. By September 1915, Bushman succeeded in getting Bayne a contract at Quality Pictures. *Motion Picture News* reported, "The addition of Miss Bayne's name to the list of stellar lights of the stage and screen already under contract with the companies who release through the Metro program is in line with the progressive policies of President Rowland...making Metro one of the biggest factors in filmland in the few short months since its organization...." Other Essanay defectors to Quality Pictures included Lester Cuneo, Helen Dunbar and director and photoplayer E.H. Calvert.

Motography reported in September that the arrival of Beverly Bayne, "the star with the $50,000 wardrobe," caused a stir in the local Hollywood motion picture social circles and that early evidence indicated that she would be a leading favorite.

Rosemary was scheduled to be Bushman's third Quality film, but trouble between Bushman and Balshofer resulted in Lester Cuneo playing the lead instead. Likewise *Richard Carvel* fell through for Bushman; it either never started production or was scrapped before completion. For all practical purposes, this ended the relationship between Balshofer and Bushman. He still made pictures under the Quality Pictures umbrella but they were filmed at locations other than Balshofer's California studio. The October 23, 1915, *Moving Picture World* reported that Bushman would now make New York headquarters for his picturemaking. Bushman, Bayne and other cast members set up shop in the Rolfe Photoplays Inc. production facilities in New York. Balshofer later wrote,

> In a way, I liked Bushman and he seemed to like me, but he was getting too temperamental for me to lose any sleep over, so I arranged to send him to my partners in New York to worry about. We had already spent considerable money getting ready to do *Rosemary*, so I produced it with Marguerite Snow, William Clifford, Lester Cuneo and Frank Bacon....

Pennington's Choice, released November 8, 1915, came next and featured Bushman, Bayne and former world heavyweight champion, Jim Jeffries in a story of love in the Canadian Northwest. It ranks up there with *Graustark, Romeo and Juliet* and *Ben-Hur* as one of Bushman's better films.

The December 1915 *Motion Picture Magazine* carried an 11-page synopsis of the film along with scene photos.

Bushman's physical conditioning and strength came into play during the filming of *Pennington's Choice*. As reported in the October 9, 1915, *Motography*,

> Bushman and Jeffries were going full tilt in a final rehearsal of the scene in the Los Angeles studio when the ex-champion gave Bushman a sharp blow to the mouth. Bushman received two or three more jabs that could hardly be called "love taps," and it somewhat ruffled his temper. Ducking a vicious swing, Bushman came up and let go with a straight arm punch to Jeffries' chest. Jeffries countered with a glancing blow off Bushman's left eye. Both men were sparring in earnest when Jeffries stepped back a few feet and came forward, his head down, in one of his furious rushes. Bushman squared

himself and met the ex-champion with a healthy, full sized right hand swing to the jaw. Jeffries straightened up, reeled and pitched forward on the floor. It required several minutes and a bucket of cold water to bring the former champion back to his feet.

The *Motion Picture Magazine* Great Cast Contest

In late 1914, *Motion Picture Magazine* launched the Great Cast Contest featuring a number of categories in which movie patrons could vote for their favorite actors and actresses. By the end of the first month, Bushman led in the leading man category and held second place in the handsome young man contest, trailing Warren Kerrigan. He also placed in the top six rankings in the old gentleman and character man categories. Through the next several months, Bushman and Earle Williams engaged in a seesaw battle for top position in the Great Cast leading man category.

Just before Bushman made the switch to Quality Pictures–Metro Pictures from Essanay, he led in the leading man vote getting with 609,905 to Williams' 580,915. Beverly Bayne ranked fourth in the leading woman designation with Mary Pickford taking the top honors at that point. After the announcement of Bushman's departure from Essanay, he dropped to second place in the leading man race in May before recapturing the lead position in July. At the close of the contest, Earle Williams won the leading man Great Cast voting with 1,571,655 to Bushman's 1,355,090. Bayne also placed in the Great Second Cast as leading lady with 1,524,330 votes. Bushman came in third as handsome young man and fourth as character man while Bayne captured eighth place as beautiful young woman.

Many letters to the editors of the movie magazines inquired about Bushman's marital status. The *Motion Picture Magazine* October 1915 issue carried the following poem by one of its readers:

> Is He Married?
> The Essanay Star, Francis X.,
> Continues the maidens to vex;
> So long as 'tis said
> This Apollo's unwed
> His image will haunt the fair sex.

Another letter foreshadowed Bushman's fate in the movie business: "The reasons why stars flit about the sky of filmdom and never become fixed planets can only be learnt by asking them.... If [Bushman] has made a mistake we shall soon know it, for the great movie public has an unmistakable way of making its wishes and grievances known at very short notice...."

One lady wrote in to question Bushman's popularity. "Won't someone take the trouble to explain to me why Francis X. Bushman is considered such a wonderful actor? His physical and personal charm I admit. I consider him the handsomest man on the screen. But I have seen him in many, many plays and have yet to see him do any *real acting*. Is he considered so fine an actor because he is always so plainly *acting*, because it is all so upon the surface and ever-present that it cannot be forgotten? Certainly, I have never been able to convince myself that he *felt* one emotion he tried to portray.

"Mr. Bushman has possibilities. I always feel that he should do well and am disappointed because he doesn't. *Sincerity, depth of feeling, naturalness* are the first requisites of good acting. Has Mr. Bushman these, and am I too blind to see? Or does he really lack sincerity, and is he acting entirely upon the surface? I do not deny that I am a Wilburite, or that Wilburites generally do not admire Bushman.... I am open to conviction...."

In response, another reader wrote, "We Bushmanites consider our favorite 'great' and that he has 'personal charm.' He has *more* than that. He has a *wonderful* personality—a personality whose bigness and fineness and cleanness grips one in spite of himself. And added to this 'charm' is the easy, graceful manner of the *true* gentleman... He seldom plays anything but the big, clean American man, and being big and clean and fine himself, how can he help putting some of himself into his parts? I know a tiny theater way off from nowhere which seats about 400. Its audience is the coldest, most critical, fault-finding crowd I have ever seen. They never applaud a picture—not even a Williams feature. But listen! I have heard them cheer Francis X. Bushman until the house shook. I have seem them laugh and cry with him. And let me tell you that people do not cheer a lead who has only 'physical and personal charm.' People do not weep at surface acting. We love Francis X. Bushman because he is real!"

The remarkable thing about these two letters is that they were written by two sisters. Another moviegoer came to Bushman's defense: "As a stage lover Mr. Bushman is, to my mind, unequaled. There is none of the inane mush in his acting that is so common with others.... Bushman is one of the manliest actors America has, also one of the most artistic; he is beautiful without being effeminate...."

The last letter also referred to another Bushman brouhaha. He was well-known for the large amethyst ring he wore, reportedly sent to him from an admiring fan. Some people wrote in to comment on the ring, complaining that it made the actor appear "affected." The September 11, 1915, *Motion Picture News* showed a photograph of the famous amethyst ring.

Panama-Pacific International Exposition—Metro Day/Bushman Day

One of the premier attractions of 1915 was the Panama-Pacific International Exposition with events held in both San Diego and San Francisco. As mentioned in Chapter 1, Bushman posed for figures in the Exposition's Palace of Fine Arts in San Francisco but that was just a small part of the impact the exposition had in launching Bushman and Bayne into film stardom.

On July 4, Metro Pictures unfurled the largest national flag in the world in New York City's Times Square. The flag stretched across Broadway and 42nd Street, hanging between the eighteenth floor of the Heidelberg Tower, holding Metro's offices, and the nineteenth floor of the Times Building. The flag was shipped to San Francisco for unveiling at the July 15 Metro Day/Bushman Day at the Panama-Pacific Exposition. Bushman performed the flag-displaying honors. The day featured marching bands, fireworks, 50-foot likenesses of Bushman and Marguerite Snow and the enactment of a silent drama starring Bushman, Snow and other Metro stars. Bushman and team performed in a one-act playlet written by Robert W. Service, famous for *The Shooting of Dan McGrew* and other famous stories.

As reported in the August 7, 1915, *The Moving Picture World*, "Shortly after arriving at the Fillmore Street Entrance, Francis X. Bushman, Marguerite Snow and others of the Metro party made their appearance and, headed by Exposition guards and a band of music, marched through the dense crowds that filled the Avenue of Palms to the Court of the Universe, where preparations had been made for their reception."

The Exposition Board of Directors presented Bushman with a bronze medal, "The Reward of Merit," as a special award for the best picture shown during competition. Metro entered the Quality Pictures–Bushman production *The Second in Command*. An estimated 76,000 people attended the presentation and cheered. Bushman also participated in some medal-presenting of his own. The day was capped by a night flight in an illuminated biplane which etched "Metro" into the sky with "let-

Another shot of Bushman with the famous ring.

ters of fire." At the end of the flight, Bushman presented the aviator, Art Smith, with a gold medal. Following the aerial display, 40 photoplay stars attended a Grand Ball in the exposition's largest hall. Overall, nearly 97,000 people passed through the exposition gates on Metro Day/Bushman Day, over 60,000 people more than any preceding weekday of the exposition.

In *One Reel a Week*, Fred Balshofer, recalled how publicity agent Reichenbach created a stir around Bushman.

> Harry had arranged to have Bushman make a personal appearance at the fairgrounds, as well as act in several scenes which I directed… The stunt…was planned for the cocktail hour… The entire company, consisting of Bushman, Marguerite Snow, Lester Cuneo, Efe Asher, Bill Adler, Harry Reichenbach and I arrived at the St. Francis Hotel. Back in those days the cocktail hour at the hotel was something to see, and during the height of it a smartly dressed, beautiful woman in black bedecked with sparkling jewels pushed her way through the crowded lobby toward the hotel desk. From under her wrap, she produced a parcel the size of a cigar box which she shoved toward the desk clerk, saying breathlessly, "See that Francis X. Bushman gets this right away," and vanished. A ticking sound caused the clerk to beckon a nearby house detective who put the parcel to his ear and then held it at arm's length as he gingerly marched toward the elevator, talking loudly about a damn bomb and Bushman. "Top floor," he barked to the elevator boy, "And make it fast."
>
> Harry Reichenbach, of course, had the reporters lined up to the bar bending their elbows when the excitement of a bomb having been delivered to Bushman reached them…. The morning papers went to town with the story of a mysterious woman in black who had tried to bomb Bushman. When we arrived at the fairgrounds that afternoon, the place was overflowing with women, young and old, who had flocked in droves just to see the virile and handsome Bushman. To protect him from any possible harm, Harry, always alert to the publicity angle, talked the officials of the fair into providing a guard. Flanked by a couple of dozen uniformed fairgrounds police, we paraded Bushman in all his glory through the jam-packed fairground, said to be the largest crowd the fair attracted during its run….

Metro wasted no time in capitalizing on the successful exposition events. The August 7, 1915, *Motion Picture News* carried a full-page ad depicting the bronze Reward of Merit Medal received by Bushman and the Metro representative. Several weeks later, *The Moving Picture World* featured a Metro ad promoting Bushman, Madame Olga Petrova, Mary Miles Minter and William Faversham as "The Biggest 4"—the most formidable quartet of stars ever offered as permanent attractions on any program.

King and Queen of the Movies

The great success of Metro Day/Bushman Day convinced exposition officials to declare a Motion Picture Day to be held on Saturday, September 11, culmi-

3. The Quality Pictures–Metro Pictures Years

nating with the crowning of the King and Queen of the movies. *Motography* covered the historic event:

> In a formidable field of starters that included the foremost artists of the screen, Francis X. Bushman and Beverly Bayne, Quality-Metro stars, were respectively crowned king and queen of the great carnival, their selection being made after a hotly waged popularity contest conducted by the newspapers of Los Angeles and San Diego....

Bushman beat out Charlie Chaplin, J. Warren Kerrigan, Roscoe "Fatty" Arbuckle, Victor Moore and other actors for the title of King. This was the second time in several weeks that Bushman was crowned 'King of the Movies,' having earned that honor in San Francisco just a few weeks earlier. Bayne bested Mary Pickford, Dorothy Gish, Mae Marsh, Blanche Sweet, Marguerite Clark, Theda Bara and others for the designation "Queen of the Movies."

Bushman and Bayne donned regal robes and crowns befitting royalty. They ruled over the festivities, rode in state throughout the exposition grounds (led by the Thirteenth Artillery Band) and participated in the coronation ceremony at the Spreckles Organ Pavilion. Exposition President G.A. Davidson presented large golden keys to the exposition grounds and San Diego to them. That evening, Bushman and Bayne presided over a dinner at the Café Cristobal and an open air ball at the Plaza de Panama. Cannons were set off and the Metro Girls, dressed in white, sang songs.

The November 1915 *Motion Picture Magazine* summed up Bushman's escalating popularity perfectly. "B stands for Bushman—Francis—erstwhile struggling actor, now hailed as Filmdom's Perfect Man, whose amazingly meteoric rise to fame and affluence is discussed in the press and magazines to an extent no stage star, past or present, has been honored...."

False Starts and Successes

Bushman and Bayne finished out 1915 with a number of false starts. As mentioned earlier, *The Red Mouse, Richard Carvel* and *Rosemary* failed to develop as Bushman movies or, in some cases, at all. In addition, the movie trade magazines carried Metro Pictures announcements in the final quarter of 1915 discussing upcoming Bushman features such as *The Man Without a Conscience* and *The Yellow Dove*, both of which never materialized. By October 1915, Quality Pictures and Bushman were advertising in *The Moving Picture World* and other industry publications for "scenarios for Francis X. Bushman... Good, strong subjects suitable as vehicles for the greatest star of the screen. Stories of romance and stories of adventure are especially desired in two and five reel lengths. Subject and treatment must be clean and wholesome...."

In January 1916, Metro announced an innovation for the company with 14 planned pictures, two reels in length, in which Bushman would star, Beverly Bayne appearing with him. Each individual film would comprise a story in itself but all 14 taken together would constitute a completed long story. The announcement mentioned that a celebrated author had completed the series and more details would be forthcoming. The series turned into the 18-episode *The Great Secret* discussed later in this chapter.

The January 15, 1916, *Motion Picture News* reported that a Metro company including Bushman and Bayne left for Jacksonville, Florida, to film exterior shots for *Man and His Soul*. The cast and crew returned to Florida and other southern locations again in February to film scenes for *The Wall Between* and *Boots and Saddles*. *Motion Picture News* reported that Bushman almost lost three fingers while filming *The Wall Between* on location near Savannah, Georgia. Film production was halted for three days while he healed.

Man and His Soul hit the theaters on January 31, 1916, and received good reviews. It was followed by *The Wall Between*, *A Million a Minute* and *A Virginia Romance,* all starring Bushman and Bayne. There was no further reference to *Boots and Saddles.*

Movie fans continued to be divided about the quality of Bushman's acting. The February 1916 issue of *Photoplay* published the first two letters while the third appeared in the July 1916 issue:

> I am going to unburden my mind. First, the ambitiousless F.X. Bushman was once a real actor, qualified to play opposite the beautiful Beverly Bayne, but now he seems content to be stationary and expressionless. I was formerly an ardent Bushman fan, but *The Silent Voice* was the last straw.
>
> It is not alone the earnest and forceful portrayal of character given by Mr. Bushman that impresses me, but the absolute cleanness of every act and gesture, his innate refinement which is so gratifying to right thinking spectators. There is room for improvement along this line in a few of our so-called screen stars. A star sheds a pure light
>
> How anyone can criticize Francis X. Bushman in *The Silent Voice* is more than I can understand. Unless they have never witnessed any real legitimate acting. In *The Silent Voice* Francis X. Bushman competed with any Broadway Star that's on the screen. I know people that travel many miles to see Bushman pictures, because they love his innate refinement and recognize good acting....

A Collection of Bushman Limericks

By March 1916, the word was out on Bushman's marriage. He was a favorite topic for the limerick section of *Motion Picture Magazine* as illustrated by the following entries by readers during 1916 through 1918.

3. The Quality Pictures–Metro Pictures Years

      Francis, How Could You!
Since Francis has gone and got married,
The women are very much harried;
To the movies they go,
But they cry "They're s-o s-l-o-w-!"
I wish that the news had miscarried.

      They'll Get Him Yet!
We all love you strong, Francis Xavier,
For the nicety of your behavior.
This is on the level,
You charming young devil,
From bach'lordom I'd like to saveyer!

      Watch Out for Your Aorta, Girls!
There's a Francis whose middle name is X.,
But he's there with the looks,
Like the "guys" in the books,
And of the girl's hearts he makes wrex.

      With the Right Girl, Oh, Yes
Say, Bushman, I've tried to decide
What the "X" in your name signified.
With your salary so high,
Does it mean *multiply*?
Could you add, and subtract, and *divide*?

      And She's Paid to Do It, Too!
You're the luckiest one of our sex,
Your job I would love to annex…
Pretty soft for you, dear,
To be kist and held near
The heart of that sweet Francis X.!

      A Delayed Valentine
Francis X. Curlilocks,
Wilt thou not be mine?
Not one more time,
But sit on a cushion, Love,
Thou handsome dream!
And imbibe cold bottles, Love,
And birds that steam!

      Her Joy in Hymn
All should know that a lady in Lynn
Deemed movies a cardinal synn,
Till Fate swept her one day
To see Francis X. play…
Now at home she is rarely found ynn.

Bushman garnered additional fame when named by Robert Grau as one of the "Twenty Greatest of Filmdom." In the May 1916 *Motion Picture Magazine*, Grau wrote, "Francis Xavier Bushman, the screen's most ingratiating personality, combined with an almost irresistible charm of pantomimic expression; a photoplayer not always well cast, but who, it is hoped, will one day penetrate the maze of neglected romance...."

Romeo and Juliet

Metro announced its summer 1915 plans with fanfare: "Among the notable Metro productions of the year will be the pretentious six-part feature *Romeo and Juliet* with Francis X. Bushman and Beverly Bayne in the stellar roles. This production will be apropos of the Shakespearean tercentenary, which is being celebrated throughout the civilized world.... Mr. Bushman and Miss Bayne believe the picture will mark the greatest achievement of their career in the silent drama...." The June 1916 *Photoplay* stated, "Greater honor still, is to be paid the Bard of Avon! Francis X. Bushman is to give to the world, in connection with

Bushman and Bayne are *Romeo and Juliet* (1916).

the Tercentenary celebration, a film version of that deathless romance, *Romeo and Juliet*."

The *Romeo and Juliet* set constructed at Brighton Beach was destroyed by a terrific storm that blasted the area on July 13. Several hours of nature destroyed weeks of work by set construction crews.

In an interview with Tom Fulbright for the *Classic Film Collector* in 1966, Beverly Bayne revealed, "The most interesting shopping I have ever done was for Juliet. Not only did I buy all the materials used in the seven costumes but I helped Mr. Bushman [she frequently called him either Mr. Bushman or Francis X. Bushman] shop for Romeo, and you've no idea how difficult it was in those war years to find the velvets we needed. Not only did we search the department stores, but we forced our way into the wholesale establishments...."

The movie trade magazines devoted whole articles to the "magnificent garments" for the Bushman and Bayne screen classic. One of Bushman's costumes sported a tunic of gold tissue, with a raised floral design in pink velvet. Long tassels in pink and gold descended from the sleeves.

Metro advertised the elaborate production with a cast of 600 and produced at a cost of $250,000, an enormous sum in those days. "Stars of the Greatest Popularity with Motion Picture audiences in the most magnificent spectacle drama in the history of the screen... Francis X. Bushman, crowned King of the Screen, and Beverly Bayne, Queen of Motion Pictures, in the Titular Roles..."

Bushman also took an active role behind the cameras, assisting in the direction of this epic romance. He not only made a study of his own role but, as an active student of Shakespeare, researched the classic drama in order to deliver the most artistic effort of his career.

In the November 4, 1916, *Moving Picture World*, George Blaisdell commented, "*Romeo and Juliet*...is a great production, one that easily will rank with the best kinematographic efforts that have gone before.... Artistically and clearly presented are these gems of the world's best literature.... Francis X. Bushman and Beverly Bayne head the cast. It is an ideal combination. Mr. Bushman, above all else, possesses the physique ... Miss Bayne is a rare Juliet... Supporting these two is a splendid cast...."

Fox Film Corporation also produced its *Romeo and Juliet* starring Theda Bara in 1916, reportedly a pirated version of Metro's production. Julian Johnson reported in the January 1917 *Photoplay*, "While Metro's is the one entertainment worth perpetuity.... Mr. Fox, despite his copy-cat propensities, is in this instance a benefactor... He will present a highly satisfactory and reverently handled Shakespeare film before thousands who would not otherwise see it...."

Decades later, Robert Hamilton Ball confirmed the dramatic success of the Bushman-Bayne *Romeo and Juliet*. In his highly regarded scholarly text *Shakespeare on Silent Film*, Ball concluded, "Of the two productions, it was the Metro one which, quite rightly, received the critical acclaim, and which must be regarded as the most auspicious American film version of a Shakespearean play in the teens. It boasted sumptuous sets, sincere and intelligent acting from its principals...and it also claimed a number of Shakespearean acting names from the stage...."

Bushman and Bayne attended the film's grand opening at the Broadway Theater in New York City. A tremendous ovation greeted the romantic couple of the screen. To quiet down the crowd, Bushman and Bayne briefly addressed the audience before the showing of the film. Helen Dunbar, who portrayed Lady Capulet in the film production, accompanied them. Signalling things to come, Bushman was quoted as saying, "Don't you think I have the easiest task, after all? Who couldn't make love to Beverly Bayne. I know you love her, I do."

Undoubtedly, *Romeo and Juliet* was a crowning achievement for the Bushman and Bayne team. Looking back, with the exception of *Ben-Hur,* the Shakespearean classic represented the pinnacle of Bushman's film career.

The cover of the September 1916 *Motion Picture Magazine* featured Bushman decked out in full Shakespearean garb. Inside, Bushman discussed the tremendous challenges of acting in a Shakespearean production: "In essaying to play Romeo on the screen, I am putting into execution an ambition, and I hope a laudable ambition, which I have had for many years, for Romeo is one of the greatest parts to which every actor aspires, just as he aspires to play Hamlet.... I do not think I am essaying too great a flight of imagination if I say that it is my very firm belief that if Shakespeare were alive today he would rejoice at the opportunity of seeing *Romeo and Juliet* on the screen...."

Metro released *Romeo and Juliet* in October 1916 to both popular and critical acclaim. *Photoplay* gave the following appraisal of Bushman's performance: "This department found Mr. Bushman not only in the best role of his career, but doing the best acting he has ever shot into the transparencies. Medically, we might term Mr. Bushman the acting hypochondriac. He has always been thinking of himself and his pretty clothes and his sweet biceps and grand smile—and forgetting his character. He may have been 'scairt' into doing a superb Romeo by the overwhelming splendor and tradition of the woeful Italian lad; nevertheless, the fact remains that he *is* a super Romeo, performing with discretion, dignity, an unusual amount of reserve and astounding sincerity. As Romeo, Mr. Bushman fills the eye...."

Bushmanor

It was during the filming of *Romeo and Juliet* that Bushman established his own personal estate and kingdom, Bushmanor. The July 1916 issue of *Photoplay* reported that the actor purchased a 115-acre estate in the fashionable Baltimore suburb of Green Spring Valley for $65,000. He later added to the size of the prop-

3. The Quality Pictures–Metro Pictures Years

Interior of Bushmanor.

erty (it grew to anywhere from 280 to 500 acres). In a newspaper article, Bushman described Bushmanor as having 280 acres with eight inside servants and 20 outside staff. The original part of the house was constructed in 1820. Bushman furnished it with antiques from his travels abroad. The limestone entrance cost Bushman $7,500 to construct.

As before, he surrounded himself with multitudes of animals, including a stable of riding horses, a large bird aviary and a world-famous kennel of prize Great Danes. Among his noted Great Danes, which wore dog collars studded with rubies, were King and Romeo. He sold Great Danes to Harold Lloyd and Rudolph Valentino. *Time* magazine reported in 1957 that Bushman's Great Danes cost $10,000 each. Other animals at Bushmanor included cattle, chickens, hogs, pheasants and sheep.

Years later, looking back over his fame and fortune, Bushman commented that of all the glory and appurtenances of fame and wealth bestowed upon him, he favored Bushmanor and all that it stood for. "When we first moved into the place, none of our neighbors would have anything to do with us…. Within a few weeks, practically everybody within 15 miles had come to call or left their cards…." In other words, Bushman had arrived. In addition to Bushmanor, he maintained a large and lavish apartment at 116th Street and Riverside Drive in New York City and another apartment in Baltimore. The Baltimore apartment, now occupied by a law office, was located above a Packard dealership on East

Bushman in front of Bushmanor with Great Danes and other canine friends.

Mount Royal Avenue. It was classic Bushman. An outside elevator delivered visitors to a Gothic, cathedral-like portico with columns. The main area was decorated with rich oak wood paneling imported from Italy and containing an inset diamond design. A large fireplace with carved mantle grapes gave a feeling of warmth. Outside, a second story patio with glazed tile flooring, terra cotta and brick walls, and a fountain provided a grand vista of Mount Royal Avenue. The apartment reportedly later served as an intimate speakeasy during Prohibition.

Bushman loved to entertain and celebrate. In the March 1917 *Motion Picture Classic*, writer Elizabeth Reid described a lavish 1916 Christmas House Party hosted by Bushman at Bushmanor for friends away from their homes during the holiday season:

> Actress Helen Dunbar served as a chaperone and valued friend for the party, which was quite a gay one.... There was a wild clamor, a hurtling dash, and our host almost went down under the onslaught of several perfectly huge dogs. He greeted them with boyish pleasure.... Miss Bayne arrived as the guest of honor and her mother and grandmother joined the festivities.... There was Mrs. Bayne, stately and gracious in her frock of dull blue satin.... Miss Bayne looked about 16, dressed in simple, girlish white, with not a jewel to detract from the effect of simplicity.... Then there was Mr. Bushman at the head of the table—not a successful actor, the hero-idol of a world of movie-mad girls—but a Southern gentleman, the ideal, hospitable host,

Josephine Bushman (wife of Francis) with some of the children. Left to right: Daughter Virginia, niece Barbara, Josephine, grandson Michael, daughter Lenore.

> low-voiced and courteous, yet with a keen wit.... The evening was spent dancing in a huge hall. Maids attended to the lighting of candles in old-fashioned silver candlesticks, to assist the guests in finding the way to their rooms, despite the modern conveniences of electricity in the house... The next day, the host and guests piled into a sleigh and, to the merry jingling of bells on the frosty morning air, started off in high good spirits to find a suitable Christmas tree for Bushmanor. Miss Bayne struck the first blow with the ax, after which two servants completed the task. Bushman ... played the part of Santa and distributed the presents to the servants.... We said goodbye to our host the next day, in the little den where all letters from his admirers are answered—a pretty, cozy room, not small except in comparison with the other 28 rooms that make up the house. The walls are covered with gifts from the people who write to him.... It is the man's favorite room.... Long live Bushmanor and the man who has made it what it is!

In the January 1917 *Motion Picture Magazine*, Bushman placed the following New Year's greeting:

> Here's a health and New Year greetings;
> And may you have good luck, good health
> and no defeatings!

Less than two years later, Bushman and Bayne would spend their honeymoon at Bushmanor.

Around the end of 1916, *Motion Picture Magazine* asked Bushman for advice on how to break into the movies.

> I say make yourself as talented as possible before you seek a picture career. You must have certain natural qualifications to begin with. An actor will always be less than half a player without a vivid imagination, strong sympathy, and one who is in touch with his fellow man and knows their frailties and their strength.... You must have personality too, or rather, personality plus, which is the ability to shape your own personality that it radiates through and enhances that of the role represented.... Physical attributes are also of emphatic importance. A good figure, expressive eyes, preferably regular features and, above all, good habits are prime requisites.... I would read and try to analyze the greatness of famous plays, novels, and even go a step farther and read the scenarios of some of our strongest photoplays to find out just what sentiments, ideals and actions made them live.... A pictureplayer must have supreme command of his nerves and muscular system, so I would therefore go in for a thorough course of athletic training.... I believe that every actor, big or little in his profession, should have an uplifting hobby which complements the work of his profession. Reading, music, sculpture, painting, any or all of these broaden the artistic soul and reflect the refinements upon screen work....

Motion Picture Magazine Photoplayer Contests

Beginning in 1916, the *Motion Picture Magazine* conducted several new photoplayer and film contests. The Screen Masterpieces Contest by *Motion Picture Magazine* kicked off in January 1916. When the contest concluded, Bushman placed a respectable third place for his performance in *Graustark* with 18,240 votes. Earle Williams took first place honors with 19,920 votes for *The Christian*, followed by Henry Walthall with 19,760 votes in *Birth of a Nation*. Bushman also garnered ninth place for *The Silent Voice* and Beverly Bayne came in tenth for *Graustark*.

The magazine also initiated a Popular Player Contest early in 1916. Marguerite Clark and Mary Pickford started out in the lead for female photoplayers while Bushman and Warren Kerrigan battled for the top male spot. Kerrigan lead from May 23 through September 11 with Bushman capturing the male lead on September 24 by a slim margin, 127,015 votes to 125,130 for Kerrigan, but still trailing both Mary Pickford (186,345) and Marguerite Clark (146,100) in overall votes. At contest's end, Pickford took top honors with 462,190 votes with Bushman placing second with 411,800 votes, besting Kerrigan with 358,320 and Earle Williams with 251,610. Beverly Bayne captured 147,140 votes for nineteenth place. Farther down the ranks were such notable actors and actresses as Crane Wilbur (135,825), Mary Miles Minter (138,430), Marguerite Snow (132,020), Olga Petrova (125,940), Lillian Gish (113,130) and Charlie Chaplin (105,325).

The *Great Secret* Debacle

Bushman's association with Quality Pictures and Metro Pictures marked the beginning of his ill-fated dealings with Louis B. Mayer. Mayer, a movie exhibitor out of Boston and secretary of Metro Pictures, entered the movie production end of the business in 1916. Mayer pressured Bushman and Bayne, against their better judgment and over staunch protests, into making *The Great Secret Serial*. Both Bushman and Bayne rightfully believed that making a serial was below their stature as romantic leading stars. In addition, despite the popularity of serials, they attracted a different audience than the romantic photoplays which made the Bushman/Bayne team famous. However, Mayer's persistence won out and production of *The Great Secret* began after the completion of *Romeo and Juliet*. Metro announced the start of production and stated that the serial "promises to be one of the greatest triumphs of their screen career...." Fred de Gresac created the original story and William Christy Cabanne directed the production.

In a 1971 *Classic Film Collector* interview with Tom Fulbright, Beverly Bayne remembered their consternation at doing the serial: "Under great misgivings we started the first two-reeler.... After we did the first two-reelers, we never went into the projection room to see the 'rushes'—we were trapped by our contract for 26 of these horrible segments and were forced to go along to the bitter end...."

The storyline consisted of a young woman inheriting a fortune and the attempts of crooks to separate her from her legacy. Of course, her boyfriend successfully comes to her aid. The serial opened in Mayer's hometown of Boston on January 8, 1917, with great fanfare, but barely recovered its production costs.

Metro carried a $250,000 life insurance policy on Bushman with special provisions insuring his hands for $25,000 and a similar amount for his feet. According to the March 18, 1917, *New York Telegraph*, the $250,000 policy represented the largest life insurance policy on any actor in the motion picture world.

Francis X. Bushman snatches Beverly Bayne from peril as the train thunders toward them in *The Great Secret*, 1917. (Photo: Cleveland Public Library.)

Beverly Bayne was covered by a $50,000 policy with $15,000 coverage on her feet and $10,000 coverage on her hands.

According to contract provisions, the insurance company had to be notified in advance of any special risks. When notified of an impending train rescue scene, the insurance company refused to approve the filming and said that Bushman would have to assume the risk himself. When the insurance company would not budge from its position, Bushman went ahead with the filming anyway.

While Bushman and Bayne were paid handsomely, reportedly $15,000, for their work in *The Great Secret*, the debacle most probably started the falling-out with Louis B. Mayer and cost them their careers in the long run. The *Motion Picture Magazine* review of *The Great Secret* spared no criticism: "Unfortunately based on improbabilities and trick thrillers. There is an air of cheapness to the production. We are painfully aware that the rooms are wallboard scenery...."

Likewise, movie viewers responded unfavorably to the production. Excerpts from letters appearing in *Motion Picture Magazine* clearly illustrate the great disappointment felt by fans of Bushman and Bayne. One letter read,

> This gentleman [Bushman] has lost much of his charm and favor through too much interference from outside influence. He used to represent

to us, in the days when he carved that niche in picturedom's Hall of Fame, the virile, athletic type of American, of either humble or higher rank, with the truth and highest principles as his assets. His best work was of the true love, but melodramatic order, in which he triumphed over his adversaries through physical force backed by these same true principles. Today, they have practically ruined his art with experimental ideas...and by not paying enough attention to the main elements of his success in winning a place in our hearts.... I advise our friend and his Metro managers and directors to see some of his old works and note the difference—and here's hoping they awake. Give the gentleman more constant work and less outside suggestion ...let him be Francis X. Bushman again.

Despite Bushman's success in *Romeo and Juliet*, Metro took out some advertisements naming William Nigh "the screen's greatest actor." By May 1917, Bushman and Bayne hinted that upon expiration of the Metro contract, they would either start their own film company or associate with another major studio. Bushman appeared on the cover of the May 1917 *Motion Picture Classic,* and inside he announced to friends, "To avoid delay in the delivery of my mail, will not my friends address me at my home, thus: Bushmanor, Riderwood, Green Spring Valley, Maryland."

Bushman and Bayne did sign another contract with Metro by August 1917 but the ill feelings and dissatisfaction with the way Metro was handling their careers continued. Several Bushman–Bayne features were released during the second half of 1917 including *Their Compact* (September 17, 1917), *The Adopted Son* (October 29, 1917), *The Voice of Conscience* (November 14, 1917) and *Red, White, and Blue Blood* (December 18, 1917). *Photoplay* pinpointed the nagging problem: "The stories have not been up to the mark...and either Mr. Bushman insists upon posing interminably, or his director gets him to do it...." *Motion Picture Magazine* described *The Voice of Conscience* thusly: "No story, no action, and Bushman does not appeal...."

Francis X. Bushman Club

All of this led to the launching of the Francis X. Bushman Club. As described in a full-page advertisement in *Motion Picture Magazine,*

> The Bushman Club...founders believe that there are many persons who will welcome an opportunity to bring concerted pressure to bear on the producers of photoplays, so that their preferences will be considered and their ideas developed.... Francis X. Bushman and Beverly Bayne were chosen as the logical persons to cooperate in this endeavor to raise the photoplay to a higher standard, because of the sincere desire shown by them to make their productions something more than a vehicle for a display of their mastery of

the mechanics of the emotions.... The officers of the club seek the cooperation of those who believe that it is the public, and not the manufacturers, who must determine the future of the photoplay, and that through the work of Mr. Bushman and Miss Bayne their ideals can be carried out.

In his Winter 1971 interview with Beverly Bayne for *Classic Film Collector*, Tom Fulbright mentioned the Francis X. Bushman Club and concluded that its formation played a large role in the demise of Bushman's and Bayne's film careers. It was not the fact that the public found out that Bushman was married and had a family that caused their screen downfall, because by then his marriage was already well known to the moviegoing public. In fact, the July 1917 *Photoplay* carried a photograph of Bushman and his wife automobiling and the August issue pictured Bushmanor with Mr. and Mrs. Bushman astride their riding horses in front of the main house. Fulbright wrote,

> Bushman...had overestimated his power, which he hoped would be more potent than the people at the top of the studios, who would stop at nothing, in their rule, over people working for them.... I am reminded that this same studio tried hard to destroy another of their big stars, Madame Olga Petrova, when she showed signs of resistance and going on her own. ...This was before the Bushman affair. If they could control them, they could destroy them. Both Bushman and Bayne would find this out later. But meantime the studio heads waited for Bushman to make the wrong move so they could have at him....

Bushman's divorce from his wife Josephine and subsequent marriage to Beverly Bayne provided his adversaries with just the ammunition they needed to torpedo the career of the romantic team.

Mrs. Bushman Files for Divorce, and Romeo Weds His Juliet

On February 5, 1918, Mrs. Josephine Bushman filed for a partial divorce. She stated that the star's earnings topped $60,000 yearly. Previously, Mr. Bushman had agreed to pay his wife $100 a week in addition to defraying her expenses, but he was more than $1,000 in arrears on his payments. Mrs. Bushman requested custody of her children and asked that she be allowed to make her home at Bushmanor. She also requested that Bushman be restrained from disposing of any of his property.

When the divorce proceedings finally concluded in July, Maryland required Bushman to pay $40,000 in alimony as well as turn over the custody of their five children to the former Mrs. Bushman. After payment of the alimony, Mrs. Bushman had no further right, interest or title in any property that Bushman owned then or thereafter.

As reported in *The New York Times*, "He must pay $4,000 a year for the support of the children plus pay for 'suitable' schooling for them. He was permitted to have the children in his care for a period of 14 weeks annually. Bushman was also ordered to pay the court costs and his former wife's legal fees. Under the terms of the decree, Bushman was ordered to pay five percent interest on the alimony from the date of his alleged abandonment. Of the entire alimony amount, he had to pay $10,000 immediately, another $10,000 within eight months, another $10,000 within 14 months and the final $10,000 within 20 months...."

The *Sunday Leader Magazine* ran a story entitled *Not the Way Francis X. Bushman Makes Love in the Movies*, featuring a scene from *Romeo and Juliet* with Bushman embracing Beverly Bayne. The article cited a number of Mrs. Bushman's grounds for divorce: "After the purchase of Bushmanor...Mr. Bushman rented a large and expensive apartment in New York City and has continued to reside there for the greater part of the time, occupying the said apartment, as your petitioner avers and charges, with another.... He from time to time insisted upon coming to Bushmanor and bringing with him this person...."

While the divorce was being finalized, *Photoplay* ran a story on Bushman under the heading *More About Bushman Than You Ever Knew Before*. The article discussed the launching of the Francis X. Bushman Club and its drive to bring pressure to bear on manufacturers to produce better pictures. It stated that the actor had never been in a photoplay which was "not absolutely above-board morally." The article concluded with the question, "Now, don't you know more about this favorite of the screen than you ever did before?" After the divorce proceedings coverage in both the popular and movie industry press, the public certainly did know more about Francis X. Bushman.

Within days of his divorce from Josephine, Bushman wed Beverly Bayne on Monday, July 31, 1918. They honeymooned at Bushmanor, vacated by Josephine Bushman three weeks earlier.

Repercussions began to be felt almost immediately. On August 14, 1918, *Variety* reported that the Mall and Alhambra theaters in Cleveland, Ohio, announced that they would no longer run pictures in which Bushman and Bayne appeared, clearly implying the recent marriage of the two was the reason for the decision. The *Cleveland News* coverage of the story said, "Marital troubles and moral delinquencies on the part of some members of the acting profession have long been familiar facts.... It may be said that so far as the speaking stage is concerned, the rule has been that scandal attracts patronage and makes good business.... Can it be that the masses supposed to constitute the cinema's clientele are more sensible to matters of decency than the patrons of higher-priced amusement?"

Whether or not the Metro Pictures studio heads were behind the supposed public backlash against Bushman and Bayne is open to speculation. But at the end of 1918, Bushman and Bayne's contract with Metro Pictures expired without renewal.

God's Outlaw

Ironically, many of the movies in which Bushman and Bayne appeared in 1918 were received well by the theatergoing public and reviewers. Likewise, movie fans continued to vote Bushman and Bayne at or near the top in movie magazine contests. For example, both Bushman and Bayne fared well in *Motion Picture Classic*'s Kings and Queens of the Screen Contest, which ran from June 1917 to Coronation Day on June 15, 1918. Bayne was crowned top Beauty Queen and also placed fourth in Charm (behind Mary Anderson, Marguerite Clark and Mary Pickford) and fourth in Portrayal. Bushman earned King of Portrayal honors, came in third in Charm and fifth in Handsomeness.

Motion Picture Classic described Bushman as "the man with the universal popularity.... Young girls sigh as they watch him in his heroic action; maiden ladies dream of what might have been as they watch his love-making; and old ladies thrill as they gaze at this star of athletic build and think of their own sons. Even the male portion of any local theater wring their hands in ecstasy as he delights them with such wrestling as would put a champion to shame. Oh, it's great to be popular, and mighty nice to see at least one of the so-pampered seemingly unconscious of his good fortune."

It appears unlikely that the public turned its back on these stars in such a short time period. We agree with Fulbright's evaluation that the studio heads came down hard on Bushman and Bayne. To quote Fulbright, "Personally, I think it was a brutal crime; the cold-blooded murder of two careers, for the most sordid of motives: greed and malice."

Bushman and Bayne made only one movie in 1919, *Daring Hearts,* produced by Vitagraph Company of America. It proved to be a disaster with poor reviews.

Metro Pictures released a Bushman–Bayne picture under the title *God's Outlaw,* reworking a serious film with outlandishly ridiculous subtitles, turning the popular romantic team into a farce. We believe the mean-spiritedness of this release indicates the lengths to which the studio heads would go to destroy Bushman and Bayne.

4

Starting Over, Coming Back

Return to the Stage

With movie offers coming few and far between and major roles virtually nonexistent, Bushman and Bayne returned to the vaudeville circuit in the early 1920s. They did comedy sketches with such operations as the Keith-Orpheum Vaudeville circuit and Whitman Bennett Productions. Bushman and Bayne toured the nation with the successful Oliver Morosco production *The Master Thief.* They also appeared in *Marry the Poor Girl* plus appeared at the Palace Theater in New York in the 1921 production of *Poor Rich Man.*

Scattered Parts

Both Bushman and Bayne appeared in the film *Smiling All the Way* in 1920 as well as *Modern Marriage,* released in 1923. They employed a unique bit of promotion with *Modern Marriage,* which was produced by their own company, Bushman Pictures. Along with the showing of the film, they incorporated a personal tour during which the film would be stopped midway and Bushman and Bayne would narrate the rest of the film.

In its June 1923 issue, *Motion Picture Classic* ran an article on Bushman and Bayne, "The Return of a One-Time Idol." It featured several pictures of Bushman and Bayne separately plus one of the two of them with their son, Richard.

The article discussed their return to movies after several years absence. The author described Beverly Bayne as follows:

> There is about her slight person an air of pensive calm, a magnificent— a tremendous serenity. One immediately senses that this girl has suffered, has been through the mill that grinds out bitter years, but it has not destroyed

Left to right: Sam Bushman (brother of Francis), Beverly Bayne, Francis X. Bushman, Stella Bushman (wife of Sam).

> her. Quite the contrary. Here for once, were the uses of adversity sweet. Hers is the peace of painfully acquired wisdom. Beverly Bayne has come through.
> Francis X. Bushman is another story, another type. He is big and blond and ruddy, bristling with good health and unbelievably fit. He is robust, vigorous, aggressive. He is like a strong clean wind blowing. He really believes that all is right with the world, but what is more remarkable, makes you think so too, no matter how deep rooted your pessimism may be. He is wholesome, with a vitality that keeps that sanity and sense he possesses in so brave a measure, from ever being dull....

The article captured one of Bushman's premier qualities. No matter how bleak his career options, he never worried about the future. He remained ever the optimist.

The article continued,

> We remembered this pair.... Francis X. Bushman had a vogue then comparable to that of Valentino's now. He was the romantic hero of the day. The unfortunate circumstances that forced them to abandon pictures for a time are universally known. There is no need of going into that again. They went on the vaudeville stage and stuck to that, although a little unwillingly, for nearly four years. They had tried to come back to their first love several times, but richer and richer contracts were thrust upon them and vaudeville claimed them with such a loud voice that there seemed to be no denying it. Now they are back and we shall see. The public is a fickle jade and the outcome is at best, mere speculation.... The romantic youth has become the worthwhile man...the eager look of the adventurer in life that years can never take away. The return promises to be interesting.

Harrison's Reports said of *Modern Marriage,* "No doubt the erstwhile large following of [Bushman and Bayne] will welcome them back to the screen in this exceedingly good domestic drama." *Modern Marriage* did not immediately relaunch Bushman's career but it did keep him in the public eye and in the minds of casting directors. Bayne made three films in 1924 without Bushman, *Her Marriage Vow, The Tenth Woman* and *The Age of Innocence,* and two more in 1925, *Who Cares* and *Passionate Youth.*

Exemplifying how far some earlier stars had fallen from grace, the July 1924 *Photoplay* ran an article entitled, "Unwept, Unhonored and Unfilmed," discussing the magazine's search for the "Stars of Yesterday." In the article, writer Frederick James Smith discussed the circumstances of former film greats such as Lottie Briscoe, Mary Fuller, Gene Gauntier, Florence Lawrence, Marion Leonard and Florence Turner, the famous "Vitagraph Girl," who was quoted, "I want so to work…and it was taken from me before I am thirty years old!" The article mentioned that Bushman was now back at work in Italy filming *Ben-Hur.*

Bushman's *Ben-Hur* Comeback

No one in the movie industry rose to such lofty heights in such a short period as did Francis X. Bushman. Nor did any star fall from grace so swiftly. In the same vein, no movie star ever experienced as dramatic a comeback as Bushman did with his portrayal of Messala in the epic movie *Ben-Hur.* Unfortunately, the comeback proved extremely short-lived.

The May 1924 *Motion Pictures Story* magazine reported, "Cinematic circles were surprised when Francis X. Bushman was announced as the man chosen from the large aspiring ranks to play Messala in *Ben-Hur.* True, Mr. Bushman returned to the screen where he was one of the first premier matinee idols, over a year ago, but this is the first prominence he has enjoyed since his return."

At first, Bushman was not overjoyed at playing the villainous role of Messala. Reportedly he went to see Bill Hart, who had played Messala for years on stage.

"Bill, do you think I ought to play this filthy Roman?" asked Bushman.

"Frank, that's the best goddamned part in the picture," Hart responded. That sold Bushman on the part and he took the role.

The February 9, 1924, *Moving Picture News* announced that Goldwyn would begin filming *Ben-Hur* March 1, 1924, in Italy. Goldwyn took over the Cines Studio in Rome for the express purpose of making *Ben-Hur* under the direction of Charles Brabin. A miniature model of Jerusalem, as it existed at the time of Christ, was constructed after prolonged research by a team headed by archaeologist Diego Angli. Goldwyn commissioned famous Italian painter Camillo Innocente to design and color authentic costumes for the production and engaged

Francis X. Bushman as Messala in *Ben-Hur*, 1925.

Vatican architect Signor Brazini as consulting art director to aid in preparation of the sets, buildings, galleys and chariots.

Noted Hollywood scenarist June Mathis, hired as editorial director, proved instrumental in hiring Brabin as director and hand-picking George Walsh for the role of Ben-Hur, Bushman as Messala and Gertrude Olmsted as Esther. Kathleen Key came on board as Tirzah and Carmel Myers as Iras. The March 15, 1924, *Motion Picture News* reported that Bushman sailed for Rome to join Brabin, Mathis, and fellow actor George Mathis. Beverly Bayne stayed back in the United States since she would soon begin filming of *Her Marriage Vow*, her first film without Bushman since her days at Essanay.

4. Starting Over, Coming Back

Bushman as Messala.

When Bushman arrived in Italy, director Brabin told him they weren't ready for filming and to do some traveling. By the time they summoned him back to the location, Bushman and a sister had traveled through several dozen countries, including the Holy Land.

While the production of *Ben-Hur* was initiated to bolster the slumping stature of Goldwyn, within months the studio had to merge with Metro to form MGM Corporation. In the wake of the merger, Louis B. Mayer took the position of vice-president in charge of all production for the new corporation, once again bringing Bushman and Mayer into contact. MGM released a list of stars who would be seen in upcoming productions of the new studio. The list included Bushman, indicating that his work at MGM would continue beyond the completion of *Ben-Hur*.

By the time of the Metro-Goldwyn-Mayer merger, the *Ben-Hur* production in Italy was already plagued with costly delays. Mayer and Irving G. Thalberg took over the reins and halted production for two months while they reorganized. They scrapped much of Brabin's footage as useless. They also made wholesale changes in the cast and crew. Fred Niblo took over as director, Bess Meredyth and Carey Wilson replaced Mathis, Ramon Novarro moved into the role of Ben-Hur and May McAvoy became Esther. Of the original cast, only Bushman and Carmel Myers remained. Brabin sued MGM for $575,000 for damage to his reputation but dropped the suit when he was offered the director's job on the production of *So Big*.

Filming resumed but labor problems, sea scene casualties, the death of a stunt man in a chariot race and more cost overruns bedeviled the filmmakers. In an interview, Bushman said that he had been asked to take over the direction of *Ben-Hur* but he refused because he did not want all the troubles.

MGM dispatched Mayer to Italy in September 1924 to assess the situation. Mayer tore into director Niblo for the lack of progress. In response, Niblo promptly resigned.

"You're not resigning. As of this moment, you're fired!" said Mayer. Bushman also received Mayer's wrath for upstaging his protégé, Ramon Novarro.

"Mayer gave me absolute hell. He said, 'You have stolen every scene, you are an absolute pickster. I have millions of dollars tied up in that fella [Novarro], he's another Valentino. I want you to quit it,'" recalled Bushman.

Mayer ordered that filming cease and he moved the entire production back to MGM's Culver City, California, lot. MGM reconstructed Circus Maximus there at a cost of over $250,000 for the great chariot scene. It proved to be the biggest movie set erected up to the time. The set brilliantly used deception in the form of miniatures and 10,000 movable puppets for the upper stands to create the illusion of size. Thousands of extras, including movie stars such as Douglas Fairbanks and Mary Pickford, packed the life-size lower stands.

Bushman performed all his own chariot racing. A chariot crash threw him to the track once, resulting in his knee being treated for a laceration. In order to capture the action, he raced past the cameras more than 40 times in the reeling Roman chariot.

"I have more chariot experience than any man alive," Bushman proclaimed.

As reported in *The New York Times* on November 1, 1925, MGM employed 42 cameras and 10,000 extras to film the chariot race, which featured 48 horses pulling 12 chariots for seven laps of mad galloping around the track. The studio shot 53,000 feet of film on that day alone. Stunt men drove ten of the chariots

4. Starting Over, Coming Back   75

Ramon Novarro (left) and Francix X. Bushman square off in *Ben-Hur,* 1925.

while Bushman and Novarro handled their own. MGM contended that no horses were killed in the filming of the final crash scene where Messala gets buried beneath the wreckage and Ben-Hur rides on to victory, but Bushman recalled that at least five horses died.

Young William Wyler served as an assistant for the chariot racing scenes. Ironically, years later he would direct his own version of *Ben-Hur* (1959), starring Charlton Heston and Stephen Boyd.

"The last day we raced. I was anxious to get home for Christmas. The horses

Bushman (left) and Novarro in *Ben-Hur*.

were all wet, and we were all pretty exhausted. All of a sudden, smoke bombs went off, pistols were fired, and all hell broke loose. It was our farewell. We shook hands all around and, do you know?...there were tears in our eyes," said Bushman.

Overall, approximately 2,000,000 feet of film were photographed for the 12 reels finally shown on screen. *Ben-Hur* opened on December 30, 1925, at the George M. Cohan Theater in New York City. Bushman, May McAvoy and Fred Niblo attended the New York debut and were greeted by enthusiastic applause. Ramon Novarro had traveled to New York for the premiere but became ill during the train trip and was confined to bed upon arrival in New York. *Photoplay* reported in its March 1925 issue that "the blasé Broadway audience forgot itself so far as to cheer madly during the chariot race...." *Ben-Hur* received both popular and critical acclaim and ran for a year on Broadway. It was voted one of the Ten Best Films of 1925 despite being released on the next-to-last day of the year. It also garnered second place, behind *Variety*, as the second best picture in 1926 by *The Film Year Book*.

The New York Times called *Ben-Hur* a "magnificent pictorial conception" and *Variety* proclaimed, "This is the epic of motion picture achievement to date and don't let anyone tell you otherwise...."

It was also well-received overseas, with the exception of Italy, which banned

Top: Bushman (left) and Novarro in *Ben-Hur*. *Bottom:* Ben-Hur (Ramon Novarro) fights with a soldier while Messala (Francis X. Bushman, at left) points out a handy exit in *Ben-Hur*.

Left: Bushman as Messala in *Ben-Hur*.
Above: Bushman in chariot for *Ben-Hur*.

it after Mussolini discovered that the Jewish Ben-Hur defeated the Roman (Bushman) in the chariot race. In 1931, MGM reissued *Ben-Hur* with sound and music because by then the new technology of talking films were all the rage.

Originally budgeted at $750,000, *Ben-Hur*'s final production cost came in around $4,000,000. Goldwyn's original agreement called for a 50 percent royalty to go to the Erlanger syndicate, owner of the rights, leaving only 50 percent for the studio. The movie grossed over $9.3 million; after distribution costs totaling over $3 million, the studio received net earnings of around $6.1 million. After paying the 50 percent royalty, MGM's share remained a net loss.

The 1925 *Ben-Hur* remains one of the classic film productions of all time. Bushman performed admirably in the epic film, as evidenced by the reviews:

Variety: "Francis X. Bushman does a comeback in the role of the heavy (Messala) that makes him stand alone. Don't let Bushy ever go back to the heroic stuff...."

The New York Times: "Bushman, a man of mighty muscle, well-suited to the character of Messala, is effective in his acting...."

Bioscope: "Bushman is a fine figure as Messala...."

Photoplay: "Bushman, as Messala, is very fine indeed, and screens magnificently...."

Film Daily: "Bushman outstanding as Messala...."

Bushman exerts his will and his whip against Ramon Novarro in *Ben-Hur*.

Bushman was now solidly on the road back to stardom and commanding $2,000 a week.

In an interview, Bushman reflected on the *Ben-Hur* premiere, "During the chariot race, people stood on their seats and screamed for Bushman. You see, I had always been the hero. My God, when the race was over, there was absolute dead silence...."

The Masked Bride

In between his shots on *Ben-Hur*, Bushman worked on another Metro-Goldwyn-Mayer production, *The Masked Bride* with Mae Murray. He played an American millionaire in love with a dancer who has been coerced to steal a valuable necklace by her former partner. At this time, MGM promoted Bushman in advertisements such as the one which appeared in the *1926 Film Year Book*. A full-page ad featured a large profile photo of Bushman with the following copy:

Bushman with Mae Murray in *The Masked Bride,* 1925.

Francis X. Bushman
"Messala" in "Ben-Hur"
also with
Mae Murray in **"Masked Bride"**
Metro-*Goldwyn*-Mayer

MGM's focus on Bushman provides further evidence that the studio planned to showcase Bushman in his movie career comeback. *The Masked Bride* was released on December 13, 1925.

Blacklisted

Stories abound concerning Bushman being blacklisted by Louis B. Mayer. Peter and Pamela Brown in *The MGM Girls* reported, "When the silent film star Francis X. Bushman failed to accept a dinner invitation with Mayer in Rome during the late '20s, Mayer didn't even wait until his return to Hollywood. That night he dictated a 25 page telegram to studio executives, stating that the actor's contract would not be renewed and that he wanted him blackballed throughout the industry.... It had all been a mistake. Bushman's valet, a new servant, had taken it upon himself with misguided zeal to trash the Mayer message and refuse for his boss. Mayer was on the boat for America before Bushman could determine what had happened. He cabled apologies immediately. No answer..."

This scenario simply does not wash with the facts. Bushman and the rest of the *Ben-Hur* cast and crew returned to America in January 1925 to finish filming in Culver City through most of that year. If the snubbing of Mayer occurred in Rome, MGM would not have put him in a starring role in *The Masked Bride*. Nor would Mayer have featured Bushman prominently in advertisements for both movies. And Mayer would have prohibited Bushman from attending the *Ben-Hur* grand opening in New York City on December 30, 1925.

In *All the Stars in Heaven*, Gary Carey stated that Mayer disliked Bushman not only for upstaging Novarro but also "because of an earlier incident that occurred when [Bushman] was appearing in a play called *Midsummer Masquerade* in Los Angeles. Mayer and his wife had then gone back stage to pay a courtesy visit, but because of an oversight on the part of his valet, Bushman was never informed they were waiting to see him. This unintentional snub, the actor insisted, was the reason that Mayer later had him blacklisted...."

Another rendition of the blacklisting appeared in Samuel Marx's book *Mayer and Thalberg: The Make-Believe Saints*. Marx has Mayer going to see Bushman, "who was portraying the villainous Messala. The actor's dresser, Johnny Powers, informed Mayer that Bushman was too busy studying his role to receive him. Red-faced, Mayer departed. He would never be friendly to Bushman after this, although the actor apologized and claimed his man failed to recognize the studio boss and didn't identify him properly...."

Bosley Crowther, in *Hollywood Rajah*, recounts an incident similar to this one, this time taking place in Los Angeles but occurring during the showing of *Ben-Hur* and not before. In this case, Bushman does not find out until years later.

To be sure, Mayer was capable and had the power to destroy actors' careers and did so without any afterthought. Bushman referred to the incident in the January 1931 issue of *Photoplay*. In an article called "Ex-Millionaire," Bushman stated, "Ever since *Ben-Hur*, I've been blacklisted. Only a few independent producers with courage have used me. I've never been with a major studio since then. Perhaps I could have lifted the blacklist, but I wouldn't crawl. I'm not the crawling kind. Rather than do that, I'll become a flagpole sitter. Other stars and the public may feel pity for me. The deuce with that! I don't want pity or sympathy. I'm happy. All I want is a chance to entertain my public. They've been sweet to me, and their applause is still sweet to my ears. They haven't forgotten me. I learn that every time I step on a stage, even if the producers have forgotten.... I've done all that could be done in pictures.... I've had my share of adulation and success, and the fans still love me, I believe. The way they show it is a matter of personal gratification to me far above what money could buy...."

Bushman repeated the story several times through the years. It appeared in a 1944 *Baltimore Evening Sun* interview about his role as Bernard Baruch in the 20th Century-Fox production of *Wilson*, in an October 1957 interview with Hedda Hopper and later on a November 1957 George Fisher Close-Up show.

The most plausible account is the snub of Louis B. Mayer after a Los Angeles theater performance. As for the timing of the snub, it probably occurred after the wrap-up of the *Ben-Hur* and *The Masked Bride* productions and the *Ben-Hur* New York opening. Up to that time, Bushman appeared to be in good favor with Mayer and MGM. However, some time in early 1926, Bushman disappeared from MGM advertisements. A ten-page-plus spread on MGM in an early 1926 *Film Daily* made no reference to Bushman among the listing of the studio's star performers despite great mention of the blockbuster *Ben-Hur*. Within a few short weeks, Bushman had gone from an actor making a great comeback in an epic film to the status of *persona non grata* in the industry.

It's easy to see how the snub of Mayer may have happened. According to his daughter Virginia, "Daddy used to always tell me to never go back stage to visit an actor or actress after the performance. They give their all during the performance and are thoroughly exhausted upon its completion. Their privacy must be respected."

Bushman and Bayne Split

The pressure of scrambling for work and the separation of Bushman and Bayne during the filming of *Ben-Hur* were less than ideal conditions for any marriage. Bushman arrived back from Italy in January 1925 and *The New York Times* announced on January 21, 1925, that Bushman and Bayne had separated.

Bushman with Anna Q. Nilsson in *The Thirteenth Juror*, 1927.

The Times quoted Bayne, "Mr. Bushman and I just decided it would be more agreeable for us to live apart." Bayne filed for divorce in April 1925, charging desertion. She was granted an interlocutory decree of divorce on June 2, 1925. Bayne received the final divorce decree on September 15, 1926. She obtained custody of their six-year-old son, Richard, with the agreement that he not appear on the stage or screen before he turned 15.

Bushman's marital troubles were not over yet. In September 1927, his first wife, Josephine, filed suit for $52,000 for payments in arrears on their divorce settlement. The Superior Court of Los Angeles found in favor of Mrs. Bushman in May 1928. Bushman had to appear in the Circuit Court of Towson, Maryland, in October 1928 to show cause why he should not be held in contempt for failing to pay the back alimony.

Universal Pictures and Other Productions

If Louis B. Mayer did order Bushman blacklisted, it did not take hold throughout the industry. Universal Pictures picked up Bushman for a series of

Left to right: Einar Hansen, Corinne Griffith, and Francis X. Bushman in *The Lady in Ermine*, 1927.

pictures beginning in 1926. He played the leading role of Barry Townsend in *The Marriage Clause*, in which he starred with the popular Billie Dove. The movie earned good reviews as did Bushman and the rest of the cast. His next Universal picture *The Thirteenth Juror* came out in September 1927 and was followed by *The Grip of the Yukon* in July 1928. Neither production drew raves from the critics. It would be decades before Bushman appeared in another Universal film, *Hollywood Story* (1951).

Bushman appeared in the First National Pictures production of *The Lady in Ermine*, released January 9, 1927. He was again teamed up with one of the screen's most beautiful leading ladies, Corinne Griffith. However, instead of playing the romantic lead, Bushman portrayed the villain Gen. Dostal. *The New York Times* found favor with the film: "To make any comments upon Corinne Griffith's looks is almost superfluous.... If one shuts one's eyes to the episodes wherein Miss Griffith is absent, one has to be satisfied with Francis X. Bushman...."

Bushman even made a film for MGM during this period. It was a two-reel historical production about the making of the American flag. Bushman played the role of George Washington in *The Flag*, released on September 14, 1927. The role was a far cry from leading romantic leads and Mayer may have thrown this

4. STARTING OVER, COMING BACK   85

Top: Corinne Griffith and Francis X. Bushman in *Lady in Ermine*, 1927. (Photo: Cleveland Public Library.) *Bottom:* Intoxicated by burgundy, General Dostal (Bushman) dreams of Countess Mariana (Corinne Griffith) who is watching him from the door. *Lady in Ermine*, 1927.

Corrine Griffith, *The Lady in Ermine*, 1927 (*Movie Herald*).

bone to Bushman to humiliate him. *Variety,* which often took pot shots at Bushman's acting style, commented, "Bushman makes a splendid Washington...."

The last major work of the decade for Bushman was his appearance in *Say It with Sables* for Columbia Pictures. He starred opposite Helen Chadwick and received good reviews from *Harrison's Reports* for his portrayal.

Bushman worked sporadically with a variety of minor studios, appearing in *The Charge of the Gauchos* for Ajuria Productions (September 16, 1928), *Midnight Life* for Gotham Productions (August 28, 1928), *The Call of the Circus* with Pickwick Pictures (January 15, 1930), *The Dude Wrangler* for Sono-Art Productions (June 1, 1930) and *Once a Gentleman* for James Cruze Productions (September 1, 1930). Bushman won the role of Gen. Belgrano for *The Charge of the Gauchos* due to his popularity in Latin America. The picture was produced by Ajuria Productions, which owned 300 theaters in Latin America. *The Call of the Circus* represented Bushman's debut in talking pictures.

Despite finding choice roles few and far between, Bushman kept busy. He traveled to Japan in 1927 to take a look at the Japanese film industry. Also in 1927, he attended the christening party for the Garden of Allah, a famous hotel-apartment complex built in 1921 by the popular actress Alla Nazimova. Incidentally, when the Garden of Allah was to be torn down in 1950, a large party was thrown. Bushman was the only person in attendance at the bash who was present at the original christening. In December 1927 Bushman announced his intention to return to the Keith and Orpheum vaudeville circuits in a skit called *Passengers*. Bushman also made *New York Times* headlines in 1929 over the Actor's Equity Association's efforts to force an Equity contract upon the motion picture industry. Clark Silvernail verbally attacked Bushman, George Jessel and Charles Chase for statements they made at a previous Equity meeting. Bushman rushed on stage and responded, "I fear no man or body of men. I am not a catspaw for the producers or a groveling beggar for Equity."

As always, Bushman stood his ground for what he thought was right. He was not about to back down to anyone...be it Equity or Louis B. Mayer.

Second Generation Stars

The December 29, 1926, *Variety* listed a number of second generation movie stars taking after their film industry pioneer parents. Included in the listing were such newcomers as William Collier, Jr., Dolores and Helen Costello, Douglas Fairbanks, Jr., Tim Holt, Lincoln Steadman, Richard Walling, Virginia Bushman and Ralph Bushman, later known in film credits as Francis X. Bushman, Jr.

According to *Photoplay*, Virginia met her future husband, director Jack Conway, on the set of the 1926 production of *Brown of Harvard*, in which Ralph Bushman appeared. *The New York Times* announced the engagement of Virginia Bushman and Jack Conway on August 24, 1926. Conway became a prominent director in his own right over the years, directing the 1935 classic *A Tale of Two Cities* as well as *Too Hot to Handle* (1938), *Boom Town* (1940) *and Honky Tonk* (1941) for MGM. Conway began his movie career as an actor in 1909 and learned his director's craft as an assistant to D.W. Griffith.

Although not mentioned in the *Variety* article, Ralph and Virginia's sister Lenore also appeared in some movies during the late 1920s and the early 1930s. Filmographies for Lenore and Ralph (Francis X., Jr.) Bushman follow their father's filmography at the end of this book.

5

Keeping in the Public Eye

From Stage to Radio

The stock market crash wiped out what cash and investments Bushman had put aside. He recalled how he found out he was broke in a taped interview. "I traveled with three Great Danes in the back seat of my Marmon. I sat up front with the driver. We stopped at a brokerage firm and looked at the stock prices. When I saw the stock prices I said, 'Isn't that a mistake.'"

At one point, Bushman called upon his good friend William Randolph Hearst for a loan. He offered to put up his Great Danes as collateral. Hearst refused the collateral and gave Bushman a blank check, telling him, "Make it out for $10,000 to tide you over and then when you get in the money again you can pay it back." Bushman cashed it for $600 and later repaid Hearst.

In January 1931, *Photoplay* ran an article on Bushman titled "Ex-Millionaire." It mentioned that over the years Bushman earned $6,000,000 but that he was now broke. Even his chauffeur sued him for back salary. Bushman promised the judge to pay off the chauffeur in installments. When asked about losing all his money in the stock market crash, he once remarked, "Everybody else committed suicide, I went into radio."

On March 12, 1931, Bushman said in a Chicago newspaper interview that "he would marry any woman who could support him in the manner to which he was accustomed." The article went on to say that Bushman would wed the woman who would pay the most for the privilege...and it must be a million or more. While the publicity ploy did little to advance Bushman's career or find him a wife, he did get briefly engaged in 1934 to Carmela Ponsella, a soprano of the Metropolitan Opera Company. The two were betrothed on February 9, 1934, but a week later Bushman called off the wedding, stating that he and his first wife, Josephine, might reconcile. That reconciliation never took place. Bushman and his third wife, Norma, tied the knot in 1936.

The lack of any meaningful movie parts led Bushman back to stock theater in the early '30s. He appeared in the leading role of *Thin Ice* in Pacific Coast stock theater. From there he went to Chicago. While appearing in 1932 at the Kedzie Theater, the first step on the ladder to success for stage hopefuls and the last step on the way down for those less fortunate, he was offered a job in radio. He jumped at the new opportunity to place himself before the public. He started in radio first as a narrator and then as a serial actor.

In addition to appearing on Chicago radio for a number of years, Bushman also had other ties to Chicago. In 1933, he opened a wholesale liquor business which failed. On April 25, 1933, Bushman filed a voluntary petition for bankruptcy at the United States District Court in Chicago. He listed his assets as $100 in clothing versus $107,084 in liabilities. That same year, Bushman appeared in the *Chicago Daily News* dressed in his *Ben-Hur* armor, kneeling and surrounded by young dancing girls from the second All Chicago Chanukah Festival.

Bushman in 1952.

The liquor business was not Bushman's only foray into the entrepreneurial world. On October 28, 1934, the Associated Press carried a story on Bushman the inventor. The story pictured a revolver he invented to aid police in capturing fleeing criminals. The revolver/camera took a photo of the criminals' car as the officer shoots at it. In 1936, he opened a drive-in restaurant near the major studios in California. Newspapers carried a photo of him sharing a meal with movie star Madge Evans. He later sold out. In 1937, he collaborated with Elmore J. Andre on a book, *So You Want to Act, Do You*. The book offered his advice on personal appearance, voice and characterization. Bushman dedicated the book as follows:

> To the young and hopeful in the world of the theater—I dedicate this book with the wish that in some way it will help them to fulfill their most cherished dreams.
> F.X.B.

Francis X. Bushman was not a man who feared new horizons. In addition to his radio appearances, in the 1950s, he turned his attention to the new medium of television. After all, this was a man who graduated from lantern slides to legitimate stage to vaudeville and to the motion pictures before radio and television beckoned. While other stars fell by the wayside as new entertainment media emerged, Bushman put his professionalism to work learning the nuances of the business, making the transition appear easy. Beginning as the master of ceremonies of a local late television movie show, he went on to make a number of appearances on television programs ranging from detective shows to situation comedies and from dramatic anthologies to medical dramas.

Bushman's third wife, Norma, died in February 1956, and Bushman married Iva Millicent Richardson in August of that year in Las Vegas. A wire service photo shows the 73-year-old Bushman and Iva being congratulated by Nevada Lt. Gov. (and former silent film star) Rex Bell. Bushman also demonstrated his famous kissing technique for the photographers. Iva, herself a widow, charmed Bushman into a marriage proposal within three hours of their meeting. As a Hollywood agent, Iva knew the ropes of getting work. No doubt she played a prominent role in the amount of television and other work Bushman picked up in the years after their marriage.

Iva Bushman, fourth and last wife of Francis X. Bushman.

Cameo Movie Appearances

Although major roles were off limits to Bushman after the mid–1920s, he managed to obtain sporadic parts in movies, establishing a record of acting in films for six straight decades (from his first film with Essanay Film Manufacturing in 1911 until the year he died, 1966).

Bushman traveled to Great Britain to make *Watch Beverly* (released 1932), an interesting title considering the fact that Beverly Bayne was enjoying a vibrant stage career while Bushman's own career had floundered. Clips of Bushman from an early Essanay film appeared in *The Film Parade* (released 1934) while he played a bit part as a movie director in *Hollywood Boulevard* (released 1936) and as a

5. Keeping in the Public Eye

race track official in *Thoroughbreds Don't* Cry (released 1937). His major 1930s role was featured in the serial *Dick Tracy* (released 1937). Ralph Byrd starred as Dick Tracy and Bushman portrayed Chief of Police Anderson. The March 1937 issue of *Picture Magazine* featured a photo of Bushman at his police chief's desk discussing how to battle the underworld. The *Dick Tracy* serial consisted of 15 episodes.

The 1940s saw Bushman in a horse racing movie, *Mr. Celebrity* (1941), the Western/gold mining drama *Silver Queen* (1942) and the biographical *Wilson* (1944). Bushman put forth an admirable portrayal of Bernard Baruch, head of the War Industries Board during World War I. Bushman bore a remarkable resemblance to the stately man himself. He also appeared in clips in the cavalcade of silent films *The Good Old Days* (1945).

In an interview with the *Cleveland Plain Dealer*, Bushman commented about his role in *Wilson*, "It's only a small role in a big picture. But it's one more proof that there's a lot of life in the old boy yet. I don't have anything to mope about. I've still got my health. I've still got a living in show business, and I'm happy."

In 1951, Bushman appeared with other silent film stars portraying themselves in *Hollywood Story*. On the Universal-International set, Bushman gave lead actor Richard Conte a lesson in love-making on the screen. He gave silent movie siren Betty Blythe a lingering kiss, then faced Conte and said, "How did we do it, my boy? The formula is still the same today. Just render them helpless."

"Amen!" added Blythe, "And he's the boy who knows."

That same year, he exhibited his vitality at age 68 by going on a 30-city tour to promote *David and Bathsheba*. Bushman appeared as King Saul in the movie starring Gregory Peck and Susan Hayward. Taking pride in his craft, he applied his own makeup and researched his historical costume. An estimated 500 plugs on network and local shows resulted from the nationwide tours by actors from the movie. In connection with the tour, Bushman received the key to his native city from Baltimore Mayor D'Alesandro at a reception at the Sheraton Belvedere Hotel on August 20, 1951. The mayor also presented him with a scroll declaring Francis X. Bushman Day in honor of "the first great motion picture idol of the American people…a native Baltimorean who has brought entertainment and pleasure to untold millions of citizens, both young and old, whose memory will live as long as motion pictures endure." While in Baltimore, Bushman also stopped to have his picture taken next to the statue of Cecilius Calvert (Lord Baltimore), for which he posed decades earlier. In Milwaukee, a Bushman Fan Club presented him with a plaque which read, "Whereas no other actor has ever attained his pinnacle of success…we hereby claim him still to be the number one matinee idol…."

The 20th Century-Fox press release preceding Bushman's *David and Bathsheba* tour read, "Forty years have been extraordinarily kind to Francis X. Bushman, whose profile once earned him the title, the Handsomest Man in the World. The sexagenarian star, greatest matinee idol in the history of films, recently

Bushman as Moses in *The Story of Mankind*, 1957.

completed an important role with Gregory Peck and Susan Hayward in the 20th Century-Fox Technicolor film *David and Bathsheba*.... Studies of his profile reveal only small ravages of time in the face that once launched a thousand hits."

After Bushman finished the tour, he told United Press correspondent Aline Mosby, "In every city, loyal ladies from 40 to 85 told me they still loved me. It was an amazing reaction. Imagine, to go to the public after all this time and find such astonishing loyalty.... I was always the symbol of triumph, chivalry, and true love.... What a glorious privilege an actor has been given.... More actors ought to go out on the road and meet the people."

In the Gene Autry Western, *Apache Country* (1952), Bushman portrayed Commander Latham. In correspondence to us, Gene Autry commented on Bushman and his role in the movie: "He was a very nice man trying to make some sort of a comeback.... He was very effective in it. He was an important part of Hollywood history...."

Next, he joined the star-studded cast of *The Bad and the Beautiful* (1952) headed by Kirk Douglas and Lana Turner. This represented Bushman's first appearance in an MGM production in many years. In an article appearing in the January 11, 1963, *Chicago Herald Tribune*, Bushman discussed coming back to MGM: "Everything happened to make me feel welcome. A few minutes after I arrived on the set, I met an MGM advertising man, Frank Whitbeck, who in 1911 gave me my first job as a leading man [at Essanay].... A lot of fellows remem-

Bushman as King Saul in *David and Bathsheba*, 1951.

bered me and yelled, 'Hi, Francis! It's great to have you back again.'" The role came about after Louis B. Mayer saw Bushman on a TV show with Walter Pidgeon and Greer Garson.

A reference to Bushman was included in the 1952 movie *Million Dollar Mermaid* starring Esther Williams, Victor Mature and Walter Pidgeon. In one scene, in reference to a prize German Shepherd riding on a train, the conductor says, "I don't care if he's Francis X. Bushman, he doesn't belong in this car."

Bushman finished out this rather productive decade with roles in *Sabrina*

(1954) and *The Story of Mankind* (1957), which received the dubious honor as one of "The Fifty Worst Films of All Time" in the book of the same title by Harry Medved and Randy Dreyfuss.

The '60s saw Bushman appearing in such low-budget films as *Twelve to the Moon* (1960), *The Phantom Planet* (1961) and the haunted house comedy *The Ghost in the Invisible Bikini* (1966) with Nancy Sinatra and oldtimer Boris Karloff as the Corpse. The movie was also known under the pre-production title of *Pajama Party in a Haunted House. The Phantom Planet* was shot in eight days with a budget of $150,000.

Bushman's voice was heard in the new production of *Peer Gynt* (released 1965). The film was originally shot in 1941 as a silent film project of Northwestern University. It includes Charlton Heston's first screen appearance at age 16 as Peer Gynt. Bushman was heard as Boyg, a voice in the darkness.

At the time of his death in August 1966, Bushman was once again preparing to work in a Western film. He was to portray a saloon proprietor in the A.C. Lyles production *Huntsville*, which was eventually released in 1967 under the title *Hostile Guns*. Donald "Red" Barry, a veteran of many Westerns, took over the role.

Bushman Firsts

Francis X. Bushman claimed a number of firsts in the film industry, among them:
—First great lover.
—First matinee idol.
—First great star.
—First photoplayer to have his name featured before the title of a film.
—The first star to use a personal secretary (Louella Parsons).
—The first star to have a fan club.
—The first to introduce mood music on a set.
—The first to be crowned "King of the Movies."
—The first millionaire actor.
—The first to own a large estate, Bushmanor.
—The first actor to actively engage in business: Bushman Kennel, Great Danes imported from Germany.
—The first movie star to make a personal appearance.
—The first star to tour the country.
—The first star to carry the load of "Block Booking."
—The first star to popularize a style of clothing, the Buster Brown collar.
—The first star to make a major comeback.

5. Keeping in the Public Eye 95

Top: Bushman with family members. Left to right, back row: Great niece Marjorie Anthony holding great-great niece Mary Beth Anthony; William Anthony, Bushman, and great-great nephew John Marano. Seated in front: Kathleen Hannan, great niece, and Frank P. Bushman, great nephew. *Bottom:* Left to right: Myrtle Bushman, sister-in-law; Thelma Smith, niece, holding great-great niece Mary Beth Anthony; Bushman; Pauline McManamon, niece; Henrietta Jabs.

—Only star who appeared in lantern slides, stock theater, vaudeville, movies, radio and television. A career that spanned six decades.

—One of the first stars to campaign for the war effort. He not only purchased Liberty bonds and helped sell them to others, he contributed crates of cigarettes with Bushman on them to the boys fighting in Europe. *Motion Picture Classic* carried an ad by the Francis X. Bushman Tobacco Fund requesting dona-

Left to right: Myrtle Bushman, sister-in-law; Norma Bushman, third wife; Bushman; James Smith (partially obscured); Marie Hannan; Evelyn McGovern, niece.

tions of ten cents and up to help buy pipes, smoking tobacco and cigarettes for our soldiers in France: "Give as much as you can afford. The happiness and comfort resulting from your gift cannot be measured by dollars and cents." The ad featured a picture of Bushman at Bushmanor.

—The first star with a star grandson (Pat Conway in *Tombstone Territory*) on television.

—First star swimming pool in Hollywood.

—Held the all-time high for number of film appearances.

—Met four United States presidents: Theodore Roosevelt, William Howard Taft, Woodrow Wilson and Herbert Hoover.

Bushman Awards and Recognition

Bushman received a number of awards over the years. In addition to winning several movie magazine photoplayer contests in the early years of his career and being named "King of the Movies" at the Panama-Pacific International Exhibition in 1915, he received the following accolades and honors:

In 1951, the *Chicago Daily News* ran an article on Bushman with a photo showing him hammering a golden spike into Stage A at 1345 Argyle in Chicago, which housed the Essanay Film Manufacturing Company when he began his movie career in 1911. It was the first time in more than four decades that Bushman stood on that historical stage which launched such stars as Wallace Beery, Beverly Bayne, Charlie Chaplin and Gloria Swanson. Bushman was in Chicago with his wife to make a personal appearance at the Chicago Theater, which was showing *Hollywood Story* in which Bushman played himself.

The Motion Picture Costumers featured Bushman as its Guest of Honor at its Ninth Annual Costumers Ball held at the Beverly Hilton Hotel on October 25, 1957. The Motion Picture Costumers presented awards on the basis of the stars' artistry in the wearing of costumes. Keenan Wynn served as the Master of Ceremonies. Seated at Bushman's table were Mike Todd, Elizabeth Taylor, Glenn Ford, Shirley MacLaine and Keenan Wynn. The program included a special tribute to Bushman and photos from the 1916 *Romeo and Juliet* and *David and Bathsheba*. The program read, "In Hollywood where legends come in all sizes and descriptions, Francis X. Bushman is a genuine 14-karat legend ... a romantic idol who captured the imaginations of millions of women.... His magnificent physique has been immortalized in bronze, stone, canvas, as well as pictures.... His physical prowess as Messala in Metro's two-year long production of *Ben-Hur* ... still makes exciting conversation.... So it is that the Costumers...salute Francis X. Bushman for the glory he has achieved as an actor and for the distinction he has brought the many-faceted art of theatrical costuming." Other actors who have been awarded the top honor by the Costumers included Fred Astaire, Humphrey Bogart and Laurence Olivier.

In 1959, Bushman and others read a poem selection in a tribute to Carl Sandburg held at UCLA. Afterwards, the participants sat in the Vine Street Brown Derby. Bushman glanced around at the caricatures on the walls of the greats of Hollywood such as Doug Fairbanks, Wally Reid and Wallace Beery and said, "So many dead. Dead. Yes, they're all dead but Bushman."

Back row: June Hannan, niece, with Bushman. Front row: Kathleen and Joseph Hannan, great niece and great nephew.

Francis X. Bushman (center) at Mary Pickford's party.

Ramon Novarro and Bushman received the "Special Award to Famous Silent Film Stars" in the 1960 Golden Globe Awards for their portrayals of Ben-Hur and Messala in *Ben-Hur.*

In 1963, Bushman received two gold scrolls presented by the Los Angeles Senior Citizen Committee for his untiring efforts, including over 200 appearances a year for senior citizen events. Mayor Sam Yorty, who appointed Bushman to the committee, called the actor "a good leader." The year before Bushman joined, a senior citizen club in Redondo Beach had 41 people come to its meeting. The next year, with Bushman on the program, over 500 people showed up. Bushman was named Mr. Senior Citizen of Los Angeles in 1957 and Mr. Senior Citizen of California in 1960.

Some time during this period, Mary Pickford hosted a party at her home, Pickfair, for the titans of the early movies. Among the 200 guests were Bushman, Betty Blythe, Buster Keaton, Marion Davies, Ramon Novarro, May McAvoy, Claire Windsor, "Broncho Billy" Anderson, Anna Q. Nilsson, Marguerite Snow and Dorothy Phillips.

The Masquers Club hosted a Francis X. Bushman Testimonial Dinner on April 26, 1963. Among the dignitaries attending and speaking were Charlton Heston, Bob Hope, Mayor Sam Yorty, Raymond Burr, Ramon Novarro, Louella Parsons, Joel McCrea, Cesar Romero and June Allyson. Yorty presented Bushman with a scroll declaring him "Hollywood's Number One Senior Citizen."

5. Keeping in the Public Eye

A month after Bushman's death in August, A.C. Lyles, the producer of the movie Bushman was making when he died, was awarded the first FXB Trophy for his efforts in providing movie roles to older persons. The trophy was sponsored by National Shows, Inc., and presented in conjunction with the September 1966 "Over 50 Fair in San Diego."

In October 1996, a Francis X. Bushman room was dedicated at the Knickerbocker Hotel and on November 17, 1970, a bronze plaque was placed on the West wall of Grauman's Chinese Theater: "To the Memory of Francis X. Bushman: Noted Motion Pictures Star Whose Home Occupied This Site Prior to the Construction of the Grauman's Chinese Theater." Iva Bushman attended the dedication ceremonies.

Final Words About Bushman

There is no better final recognition for Francis X. Bushman than this letter to the editor which appeared in the *Cleveland Plain Dealer* shortly after his death:

Praise for Bushman

> Francis X. Bushman never had to depend solely on his matinee idol looks as a performer. He was a very competent and versatile actor. I still recall his Messala from my childhood, so thoroughly did he portray the role, proving with it that he could play villains as expertly as heroes.
>
> There were always people sympathetic to him in the industry, so he kept coming before the public time and again. After *Ben-Hur,* he was Corinne Griffith's leading man in a 1927 film [*Lady in Ermine*]. In radio, he revealed a fine speaking voice, emoting convincingly without the need of personal appearance. In the talkies he held his own, and on television he made the transition to character parts with no difficulty.
>
> He was magnificent and handsome and healthy all his life, finishing out as an outstanding senior citizen.

Francis X. Bushman passed away on August 23, 1966, following a fall in his Pacific Palisades home. He was 83. Newspapers and magazines around the world carried variations of the headline, "Francis X. Bushman, King of the Movies, The World's Handsomest Man, Filmdom's First Heartthrob, Dies."

Newsweek carried a four-column feature on his career under the heading "The First Movie Star." *The New York Times* ran a front page special on September 2, 1966, reviewing Bushman's remarkable career. The article quoted Charlton Hes-

Francis X. Bushman

ton, president of the Screen Actors Guild and star of the later film version of *Ben-Hur*. "His passing marks the fall of one of the landmarks of Hollywood history. He represented all that was best in the tradition of Hollywood as well as of his own profession." *Variety* wrote, "Of the many-generations ago silent film idols, few have lingering impact in memory as Francis X. (for Xavier) Bushman...known as the handsomest man in the world. ...Bushman's death at 83...saw him still actively engaged as a professional thespian.... For the annals, Bushman is one of the pioneer Hollywood great marquee names."

Ironically, Bushman died 40 years to the day after another great film idol,

5. Keeping in the Public Eye

Rudolph Valentino, passed away. Services for Bushman were held in the Church of the Recessional at Forest Lawn Memorial Park in Glendale, California. Pallbearers included Ramon Novarro, Leigh Silliphant, Dr. Frank Baxter, Victor Jory, Jackie Coogan and Don DeFore. He is entombed in the Freedom Mausoleum, Sanctuary of Gratitude, Corridor of the Patriots.

From the unparalleled thrilling chariot race in *Ben-Hur* to the hundreds of movies in which he appeared to the thousands of radio broadcasts to the numerous statues around the nation for which he modeled, Bushman has left us a rich and lasting legacy.

Within the Sanctuary of Gratitude is the following Biblical verse:

> "...Let the peace of God Rule in your Hearts...and be Ye Thankful."
> Col. 3:15

Life somehow has a way of coming full circle. Francis X. Bushman began his movie career partly due to his modeling for statues in his hometown of Baltimore. The statue that bears the closest resemblance to Bushman is the Francis Scott Key monument on Eutaw Place. With that in mind, it is only fitting that at the end of the Hall of Patriots, not 15 feet from where Bushman lies entombed, is a stained glass portrayal of Francis Scott Key.

Bushman's plaque is simple but proud. It reads:

Francis X. Bushman
King of the Movies
1883-1966

6

Epilogue

In an interview with Peter Martin, Bushman reflected on his life and career. "I have no regrets. I loved every minute of it. If I had to do the same thing over, I'd do it the same way. I spent it as fast as it came. When you have the capacity for enjoyment, that's the time to enjoy life...."

Niece June Hannan remembers her Uncle Frank: "I'll never forget the time when I was down home visiting my grandmother and aunt. There was a loud pounding on the door. Aunt May told me to see who it was. I opened the door and Uncle Frank and two Great Danes came bounding in (he always loved a grand entrance). He picked me up, held me in the air like a bag of chips and roared, My God June, how you've grown! It was a surprise visit by him to see Grandmother on her birthday. He loved to talk to the young children in the family and, just as much, he loved to listen to them. He was so full of life."

Part Two. Filmography

Film, Radio and Television Appearances

Films are listed in order of release date. If two or more films were released on the same date they are listed in alphabetical order. Films whose release dates could not be determined are grouped alphabetically at the end of the most likely year of production.

1911

His Friend's Wife

Release Date: June 3, 1911. Essanay Film Manufacturing Company. 1,000 feet. Director: R.E. Baker. Cast: Francis X. Bushman, Dorothy Phillips. The first known Francis X. Bushman film.

An artist tires of his wife and discards her only to discover later that she has since married his best friend. After a dramatic scene in which the husband and former wife meet again, he dies of heart disease.

The Moving Picture World found the film's pictorial beauty its "most commendable quality."

The Rosary

Release Date: July 15, 1911. Essanay Film Manufacturing Company. 1,000 feet. Director R.E. Baker. Cast: Francis X. Bushman (Young Payne), Dorothy Phillips (Ruth Martin).

Father Grant raises a young boy after his mother dies. Years later, Young Payne (Bushman) is on the verge of becoming a priest when he meets Ruth Martin (Phillips) and falls deeply in love. He decides to leave the church and marry the girl but she convinces him that she would only be happy if he returns to the church.

The Moving Picture World: "The acting is strong and well sustained, each of the principal characters interpreting his or her part admirably. The film is certain to make a deep impression since its subject is unusual and the actors perform their parts sympathetically."

God's Inn by the Sea

Release Date: July 22, 1911. Essanay Film Manufacturing Company. 1,000 feet. Director R.E. Baker. Cast: Francis X. Bushman (Captain Crandal).

Commodore Leighton's ship "Petrel" is lost at sea with his five-year-old daughter Dora aboard. He offers a reward for her return but no one with her unique tattoo can be found. Ten years later, a friend of the Commodore's, Capt. Crandal (Bushman), meets a young woman with a tattoo living on an island. She is confirmed as the Commodore's longlost daughter and a happy reunion ensues. Crandal and Dora fall in love and marry.

Her Dad the Constable

Release Date: July 22, 1911. Essanay Film Manufacturing Company. 1,000 feet. Director: R.E. Baker. Cast: Francis X. Bushman (Tom Thornton), Harry Cashman (Constable), Dorothy Phillips (Mary Perkins).

Mary Perkins (Phillips) and Tom Thornton (Bushman) fall in love and plan to marry. The young man is delayed and speeds to arrive in time for their wedding. The constable (Cashman), Mary's father, is alerted about the speeder and arrests Tom, whom he has not yet met. The situation is finally straightened out and the marriage proceeds.

The Motion Picture World called *Her Dad the Constable* a classy, well-acted comedy. "Thanks to F.X. Bushman and Dorothy Phillips, who represent the happy pair in the story, we are given a valuable lesson in the art of making love without indulging in uncouth 'bear' methods." The magazine also revealed that Bushman had not yet learned to drive a car and that the car in the movie was driven by a chauffeur, kept out of sight of the camera.

Bushman must have picked up some driving skills later in order to maneuver his famous lavender Marmon around town.

The New Manager

Release Date: August 5, 1911. Essanay Film Manufacturing Company. 1,000 feet. Director R.E. Baker. Cast: Francis X. Bushman (Philip Carlton), Howard Messimer (Samuel Gorman), Dorothy Phillips (Nellie Gorman), Bryant Washburn (New Manager).

Philip Carlton (Bushman) inherits his father's business and gets rid of an old faithful manager, Samuel Gorman (Messimer). However, Gorman also inherited $5,000 from Carlton's father. He invests it wisely and becomes very wealthy. Gorman's daughter Nellie (Phillips) is educated in Europe and returns home to fall in love with Carlton. Her father forbids her to marry Carlton because of their earlier dealings. Carlton subsequently goes bankrupt and the man he discharged purchases the business at the sheriff's sale. The older man forgives the young man for firing him, returns the business to him, and offers his daughter's hand in marriage.

The Moving Picture World found *The New Manager* exceptionally well-cast: "The acting in all parts is discriminatingly subdued, yet played with a quiet fervor and sincerity which is thoroughly convincing."

The Gordian Knot

Release Date: August 12, 1911. Essanay Film Manufacturing Company. 1,000 feet. Director: R.E. Baker. Cast: Francis X. Bushman (Harry Robbins), Dorothy Phillips (Marion Walters).

After her older sister elopes, Marion Walters (Phillips) breaks off her engagement with Harry Robbins (Bushman) in order to take care of her father. Playing the matchmaker, the father concocts a plan to reunite his daughter with Robbins. He feigns a serious illness and on his apparent deathbed asks Marion to marry Harry right away. A preacher is summoned and the two marry at the old man's bedside. After the ceremony, the father jumps to his feet and tells them of his deception. After Marion's anger subsides, the happy couple is congratulated by everybody.

Fate's Funny Frolic

Release Date: August 19, 1911. Essanay Film Manufacturing Company. 1,000 feet. Director: R.E. Baker. Cast: Francis X. Bushman (Richard Malcolm), Dorothy Phillips (Alice Trevor).

A society matron tries her hand at matchmaking by inviting two friends to a party. The two first meet en route to the party, at the railway station and on the train. Richard Malcolm's (Bushman) actions annoy Alice Trevor (Phillips) during the trip. They are later surprised to encounter each other at the party. Alice, at first angry, is eventually persuaded to let bygones be bygones. The two hit it off and fall in love. Their matchmaker is rewarded six months later with the receipt of a wedding invitation.

The Dark Romance of a Tobacco Tin

Release Date: September 2, 1911. Essanay Film Manufacturing Company. 700 feet. Cast: Francis X. Bushman (George M. Jackson).

George Jackson (Bushman) learns that his uncle died and left him a fortune but only if the young man marries within a week. Jackson finds a love note in a tobacco tin and writes to the girl who wrote the note, requesting her to come immediately. The girl, Grace Williams, arrives on the last possible day, but to Jackson's surprise she is a colored girl. At first she is put out, but then Jackson proposes and takes her to the marriage license bureau to get married and salvage his inheritance.

The Burglarized Burglar

Release Date: September 9, 1911. Essanay Film Manufacturing Company. 1,000 feet. Director: R.E. Baker. Cast: Francis X. Bushman (Charley Fortune-Hunter), Dorothy Phillips (Dorothy Willard).

Charley Fortune-Hunter (Bushman) apprehends a burglar and uses the burglar's loot, a pearl necklace stolen from the Willard household, as a present for his girlfriend, Dorothy Willard (Phillips). Dorothy's father recognizes the necklace and summons the police to arrest Charley. Charley leads the police to the closet where he locked up the burglar, only to discover that he has escaped. The policeman is about to take Charley away to jail when the father relents. Dorothy still believes Charley is the thief and will have nothing to do with him.

Live, Love and Believe

Release Date: September 16, 1911. Essanay Film Manufacturing Company. 1,000 feet. Cast: Francis X. Bushman (Harry Ainsworth).

Young Harry Ainsworth (Bushman) succumbs to drink but is influenced to mend his ways by a mission worker, with whom he falls in love. Knowing they are from different social circles, he joins the army and rises to second lieutenant. At a military ball, he meets the daughter of Col. Chalmers, the father of the mission worker, Dorothy. He and Dorothy reunite with the Colonel's blessing.

Saved from the Torrents

Release Date: September 16, 1911. Essanay Film Manufacturing Company. 1,000 feet. Cast: Francis X. Bushman (Arthur Chester), Dorothy Phillips (Katie Carrington).

Katie Carrington (Phillips) hampers police from stopping a train because they are after her criminal (but repentant) brother, who is on the train. When she learns of impending flood danger and that her brother may die in a train wreck, Katie and her sweetheart Arthur (Bushman) race on a rail hand-car to stop the train before it crosses an endangered trestle.

Lost Years

Release Date: September 23, 1911. Essanay Film Manufacturing Company. 1,000 feet. Cast: Francis X. Bushman (James Brown). This is often listed as Bushman's first Essanay film, but the release dates indicate that *His Friend's Wife* was his first.

After an altercation, a worker falls into a river, is swept under the docks and then shanghaied. Another worker, James Brown (Bushman), is accused of his murder, convicted and sentenced to life imprisonment. After 30 years, a pardon request is refused and reported in the newspaper. The supposedly murdered man reads the story and obtains his former fellow worker's release.

The Moving Picture World: "There are too many impossibilities in the picture for it to be a great picture, but it gives a chance for some remarkably human acting that is surely well worth seeing."

A False Suspicion

Release Date: October 14, 1911. Essanay Film Manufacturing Company. 1,000 feet. Cast: Francis X. Bushman, Mabel Moore.

A spendthrift (Moore) borrows money from a gentleman friend to pay for her expensive clothes. Her husband (Bushman) discovers the receipts signed by the friend and demands an explanation from his wife, whom he unjustly believes has engaged in intimacy with the friend. The unpleasant situation is cleared up and the wife vows to never again be extravagant.

The Moving Picture World reported, "The audience seemed to like it and it gave the reviewer much pleasure."

Bill Bumper's Bargain

Release Date: October 29, 1911. Essanay Film Manufacturing Company. 1,000 feet. Cast: Francis X. Bushman (Mephisto), Harry Cashman (Bill Bumper), Dolores Cassinelli (Marguerite).

A tramp, Bill Bumper (Cashman), discovers a book containing the libretto of Faust. He falls asleep reading it and dreams that the Devil appears and offers him a chance to exchange his soul for 12 hours of worldly pleasure. Bill accepts and spends his allotted time with Marguerite (Cassinelli) in a cafe and the theater and taking a joy ride. At the end of the 12-hour period, Bill revisits the Devil and pays dearly for his 12 hours of gaiety.

He Fought for the U.S.A.

Release Date: November 4, 1911. Essanay Film Manufacturing Company. 1,000 feet. Cast: Francis X. Bushman, Bryant Washburn.

A Civil War drama in which brothers fight for different sides and meet on the battlefield and later at the old homestead. Frank fights for the North and spares his brother's life but only after Frank's former sweetheart Virginia pleads for Bob's safety. Upon returning from the war, Frank discovers that Virginia has always loved him and not his brother, who has become engaged to Virginia's sister.

The Madman

Release Date: December 2, 1911. Essanay Film Manufacturing Company. 850 feet. Cast. Francis X. Bushman.

A young man (Bushman) escapes from an insane asylum by impersonating his father. He goes to his father's house and overpowers him. A chase ensues and he once again escapes by commandeering a balloon from a military camp. The balloonist overpowers the madman and casts him to death on the rocks below.

The Goodfellow's Christmas Eve

Release Date: December 9, 1911. Essanay Film Manufacturing Company. 1,000 feet. Cast: Francis X. Bushman (James Sawyer).

A Scrooge-type character, wealthy bachelor James Sawyer (Bushman), lives a lonely existence at his club. On Christmas Eve he refuses to join other club members in distributing food baskets to the poor. He later finds an abandoned baby on a doorstep, evoking feelings of sympathy from the crusty Sawyer. As a result, he moves to help his fellow man, discovering that true happiness stems from good deeds.

The storyline took its name from the "Goodfellow Movement" started in Chicago in 1908 by an unnamed benefactor. Other cities followed Chicago's lead and started goodfellow movements of their own.

The Moving Picture World called Essanay's production a film that will be "a potent factor in making the movement world-wide."

1912

The Mail Order Wife

Release Date: January 2, 1912. Essanay Film Manufacturing Company. 1,000 feet. Francis X. Bushman (John White).

Two young men, Bob Strong and John White (Bushman), acquire land in Dakota under a government land grant. When ordering supplies from a mail order catalog, Bob jokingly writes on the bottom of the order form that he would like the mail order company to send him a wife. To Bob's surprise, May, the mail order company stenographer, responds that she would take up the man's offer of marriage. When May arrives on the wedding day, she discovers that John is her former boyfriend. Bob graciously steps aside and John and May renew their love and get married.

The Count and the Cowboys

Release Date: January 14, 1912. Essanay Film Manufacturing Company. 1,000 feet. Director: G.P. Hamilton. Cast: Broncho Billy Anderson, Francis X. Bushman, Marguerite Clayton.

In this comedy, a French count arrives in the Western town of Rawhide looking for mining properties. An altercation between the count and a cowboy results in a duel. The cowboys arrange a ruse: The count's challenger first engages in another duel in which he guns down six men. The count witnesses the scene with horror and catches the next stage out of town.

The Moving Picture World: "The story is told with a clarity that leaves nothing to be desired.... A comedy which possesses all the crisp and attractive qualities that are usually present in the comedies from this house [Essanay]."

Alias Billy Sargent

Release Date: January 20, 1912. Essanay Film Manufacturing Company. 1,000 feet. Cast: Francis X. Bushman (Mr. Weston).

A wife's forgetfulness saves diamond broker Mr. Weston (Bushman) from making a large deal with a potential customer. It turns out the man was a thief. Instead of losing a big sale, Weston is saved from financial ruin. He is grateful to his wife.

The Moving Picture World: "A good story and well acted."

The Melody of Love

Release Date: February 3, 1912. Essanay Film Manufacturing Company. 1,000 feet. Cast: Francis X. Bushman (Maurice Eaton), Lily Branscombe (Isobel McIntyre).

Composer Maurice Eaton (Bushman) falls for society belle Isobel McIntyre (Branscombe). To show his love, he composes the music for their upcoming wedding. On the eve of their marriage, Eaton is stricken with fever that leaves him blind. He breaks the engagement and several years pass by while Isobel enjoys the social scene. On her wedding day to another, the church organist is taken ill. Not knowing whose wedding it is, the blind Eaton agrees to play. Isobel recognizes Eaton's playing but goes through with the wedding. After the ceremony, Isobel asks to be taken to the organ loft to meet the organist.

Tracked Down

Release Date: February 10, 1912. Essanay Film Manufacturing Company. 1,000 feet. Cast: Francis X. Bushman (Jim Ford), William Walters (Detective Walters).

Swindler Jim Ford (Bushman) passes himself off as an English lord in order to gain entrance to the home of a wealthy family and rob them. His plan is foiled by alert Detective Walters (Walters) who recognizes Ford from a previous encounter.

The Moving Picture World said *Tracked Down* possessed a "virile plot, thrilling climax and a carefully selected cast, who interpret the story's splendid situations with telling effect.... [Bushman and Walters] both render splendid portrayals."

The Little Black Box

Release Date: February 17, 1912. Essanay Film Manufacturing Company. 1,000 feet. Cast: Francis X. Bushman.

Bushman plays a jewelry store clerk who steals a pearl necklace from his employer. Other clerks also fall under suspicion.

The Moving Picture World called *The Little Black Box* "a cleverly conducted and fresh picture of the 'third degree.'"

Out of the Depths

Release Date: March 3, 1912. Essanay Film Manufacturing Company. 1,000 feet. Cast: Lily Branscombe (Marjory Lawton), Francis X. Bushman (James Grey), Bryant Washburn (Dan Matthews).

James Grey (Bushman) is a reformed ex-convict who had been convicted of stealing from his employer in order to get his mother medical treatment. Grey is elected mayor but blackmailer Dan Matthews (Washburn) threatens to expose his past and ruin his upcoming marriage to Marjory Lawton (Branscombe). Grey and Matthews scuffle and Matthews leaves to go to Marjory's house to tell her about Grey's dark secret. Fortunately, the blackmailer is killed by a bolt of lightning before he can carry out his threat.

The Moving Picture World raved, "The entire cast has been selected with great care, and the production is a corker in every way.... *Out of the Depths* ... is a vital, gripping melodrama replete with poignant thrills and unfolding to a smashing big climax that hits straight from the shoulder.... Francis X. Bushman plays Grey, and gives the character a splendid portrayal, while Lily Branscombe is charming in the role of Marjory Lawton. Bryant Washburn is Matthews and performs villainish enough to satisfy the most ardent lovers of melodrama."

At the End of the Trail

Release Date: March 23, 1912. Essanay Film Manufacturing Company. 1,000 feet. Cast: Francis X. Bushman (Tukish).

Bushman plays a Northwest Indian half-breed in need of help. The film centers on the interaction between the half-breed, a bad man, a good Samaritan and the Northwest Mounted Police officer on the trail of the bad man.

The Moving Picture World said *At the End of the Trail* kept the audience's attention with some interesting scenes: "We enjoyed it and think it a desirable filler."

The Laurel Wreath of Fame

Release Date: March 25, 1912. Essanay Film Manufacturing Company. 1,000 feet. Cast: Francis X. Bushman (Guido Marcello), Dolores Cassinelli (Marie Medici).

Composer Guido Marcello (Bushman) is in love with Marie Medici (Cassinelli), a singer who prefers to concentrate on her career instead of getting involved. Guido falls on hard times while Marie's career blossoms. They meet years later and Marie agrees to sing one of Guido's compositions, which becomes very popular. When Guido learns of his success after many years of hardship, he dies. Marie is grief-stricken.

Essanay called *The Laurel Wreath of Fame* "a tragic page from the empty life of one of the world's greatest musicians. Superb in splendid plot-strength and beautifully portrayed by Francis X. Bushman and a select cast."

Lonesome Robert

Release Date: April 5, 1912. Essanay Film Manufacturing Company. 1,000 feet. Cast: Francis X. Bushman (Tom Morris), Richard Carroll, Harry Cashman, Frank Dayton, Helen Dunbar, Thomas Shirley, Bryant Washburn.

Tom Morris (Bushman), a wireless operator, teaches a crippled boy, Robert Woods, telegraphy. Each night Tom and Robert exchange messages. One night, Tom is attacked by crooks who intend to rob the company's safe. Tom manages to send a help message to Robert, who alerts the police. The young boy wins a reward for his help in apprehending the thugs.

The Rivals

Release Date: April 13, 1912. Essanay Film Manufacturing Company. 1,000 feet. Francis X. Bushman.

Two sisters fall in love with the same man. *The Rivals* was described by Essanay as a film that runs "the entire gamut of human emotions, love, jealousy and hate.... A superb production with a moral that strikes deep and true. Interpreted in the fresh, vigorous way that always characterizes Essanay photoplays."

Napatia, the Greek Singer

Release Date: April 27, 1912. Essanay Film Manufacturing Company. 1,000 feet. Cast: Frances X. Bushman (Billy Arnold), Dolores Cassinelli (Napatia). Essanay used the Chicago Fire Department in the filming of this movie.

A young fireman, Billy Arnold (Bushman), rescues a beautiful Greek singer (Cassinelli), from her mean foster father and the two fall in love. Essanay declared about *Napatia, the Greek Singer*, "You want the best, and this is par excellence!"

Out of the Night

Release Date: May 4, 1912. Essanay Film Manufacturing Company. 1,000 feet. Cast: Francis X. Bushman, Dwight Mead.

Millionaire Howard Moore loses his fortune in a bank crash and his girlfriend rejects him. Distraught, he is contemplating killing himself when a stranger, Joe Brown, "out of the night," knocks on his window. The stranger's own tales of woe give courage to the millionaire.

The Moving Picture World review said, "The thread of the story is kept clear and is pretty well acted. The camera work is good."

The Eye That Never Sleeps

Release Date: May 11, 1912. Essanay Film Manufacturing Company. 1,000 feet. Cast: Francis X. Bushman (Howard Mayne), Harry Cashman, Frank Dayton, Charles Hitchcock, William Mason, Howard Messimer, Bryant Washburn.

Sleuth Howard Mayne, on the trail of a counterfeiting gang, disguises himself as a common thief and penetrates the gang. After getting the goods on the counterfeiters and having them arrested, Mayne reveals himself as a super sleuth for the Secret Service Bureau.

Essanay announced *The Eye That Never Sleeps* as the first release of a great melodrama series centering around adventures of the Secret Service Bureau. "Subtle and thrilling, the premier Secret Service melodrama ... in which Francis X. Bushman is featured in the role of Howard Mayne, the greatest sleuth of two continents! Startling adventures! Marvelous interpretation! Photography worthy of highest comment! The last word in photoplay excellence!"

A Good Catch

Release Date: May 18, 1912. Essanay Film Manufacturing Company. 1,000 feet. Cast: Beverly Bayne, Francis X. Bushman. Recognized as the first teaming of Bayne and Bushman.

A photoplay featuring slapstick physical comedy. *The Moving Picture World* said, "The players are pleasing in themselves ... good camerawork. The audience liked part of it and got some good laughs."

The Mis-Sent Letter

Release Date: June 8, 1912. Essanay Film Manufacturing Company. 1,000 feet. Cast: Francis X. Bushman (Isaac Silverman).

Jeweler Isaac Silverman marries a beautiful young woman who is jealous of stage ladies. A letter from his niece, an actress, provokes his wife's jealousy. Other mix-ups complicate the situation before it gets cleared up to everyone's satisfaction.

Essanay characterized *The Mis-Sent Letter* as "one of those long, lingering, laughing gems that starts your chuckles at the very first foot and carries you through a series of complex comic situations that calls for roars—positively shrieks of mirth! Absolutely guaranteed to bring joy-tears to a pair of glass eyes!"

The Passing Shadow

Release Date: June 8, 1912. Essanay Film Manufacturing Company. 1,000 feet. Cast: Francis X. Bushman, Eleanor Kahn.

A little girl shows affection to a tramp who has been beaten by her family. The tramp later enjoys good fortune and returns as the holder of the family's mortgage, which is about to be foreclosed. But he does not hold a grudge and refuses to foreclose on the family of the little girl.

The Return of William Marr

Release Date: June 15, 1912. Essanay Film Manufacturing Company. 1,000 feet. Cast: Francis X. Bushman (William Marr), Frank Dayton (Husband Number Two), Martha Russell (Mrs. Marr).

Drunkard William Marr (Bushman) deserts his wife (Russell) and swaps clothes with a tramp in exchange for a bottle of hooch. The tramp is killed in an accident that badly mangles his body, which is mistaken for Marr's. Years later, Mrs. Marr is happily married to a wealthy man (Dayton). She is confronted by Marr who demands money to keep quiet about her marriage to him. She runs out of money to pay blackmail and threatens Marr with a gun. When Marr grabs the gun from her, it accidentally discharges and kills him. She lies that the dead man was a burglar she killed in self-defense.

Essanay's ads called the film "a splendid dramatic subject ... of vital plot-strength, affording this popular actress [Martha Russell, making her screen comeback] a superb role. Your feature bill will not be complete unless headed by this pippin!" *The Moving Picture World* agreed: "Miss Russell especially shows a careful study and sure grasp of the role assigned her.... The acting of the principal characters is commendable."

Billy and the Butler

Release Date: June 22, 1912. Essanay Film Manufacturing Company. 1,000 feet. Cast: Joseph Allen, Francis X. Bushman (Billy McGrath), Harry Cashman, Dolores Cassinelli, Helen Dunbar, Walter Hitchcock, William Mason, Dwight Mead, Martha Russell, John Steppling.

Billy McGrath (Bushman) recognizes a crook hired as a butler at a friend's house. He moves to thwart a robbery only to be arrested himself in the confusion. Once Billy's real identity is discovered, an auto chase after the real thief and his accomplices ensues.

The Butterfly Net

Release Date: June 29, 1912. Essanay Film Manufacturing Company. 1,000 feet. Cast: Beverly Bayne (Beverly), Francis X. Bushman (Lord Roxbury), Howard Messimer, John Steppling. An early pairing of Bushman and Bayne.

An English naturalist, Lord Roxbury (Bushman), rents a summer place incognito in order to pursue his studies uninterrupted. However, several young women learn his true identity and vie for his attention. A young American woman, Beverly (Bayne), ignores him and pushes him down a bank. Naturally, he falls in love with her and she consents to marry him.

Essanay advertised the film as "light, airy, and altogether charming! A summer idyll that involves international complications deliciously captivating and featuring Miss Beverly Bayne and Mr. Bushman in wonderfully attractive roles." *The Moving Picture World* said, "It is all very cleverly done."

White Roses

Release Date: June 29, 1912. Essanay Film Manufacturing Company. 1,000 feet. Cast: Beverly Bayne (Mary Fuller), Francis X. Bushman (Convict and Mr. Loring).

Mary Fuller (Bayne), en route to meet her sweetheart, encounters a convict (Bushman) near the train station. She feels compassion for the handcuffed man and places a bouquet of white roses in his hand, whispering in his ear to keep the flowers as a symbol of hope. Years later, Mary is widowed and about to be evicted by her landlord per the instructions of the building owner, Mr. Loring (Bushman). She goes to see Loring to plead for additional time to meet her rent payment. She does not recognize him until the man removes a faded white rose from his wallet. As a gesture of good faith, he allows her to stay in her room forever without paying rent. In the final scene, Loring sends Mary a beautiful bouquet of white roses accompanied by a card which reads, "White Roses for Hope."

Essanay proclaimed that *White Roses* provided Bushman with "another of those exquisite roles that have won Bushman such sweeping popularity! A wonderfully appealing heart-interest drama that runs the gamut of love and tenderness. Extraordinary in plot, beautiful in point of production...."

Signal Lights

Release Date: July 6, 1912. Essanay Film Manufacturing Company. 1,000 feet. Cast: Francis X. Bushman (Jim Drake), Frank Dayton, Baby Lynch, Martha Russell (Mrs. Drake), Bryant Washburn.

Two tramps learn about a bullion train arriving from Goldfield and plan to steal the gold cargo. The tramps hold railroad station agent Jim Drake (Bushman) at gunpoint and change the train signal to red to stop the train. Jim's young daughter Mary goes to the train station and changes the signal lights, giving the gold train a clear track. Mary is revered as a hero for unknowingly saving the bullion.

The Understudy

Release Date: July 20, 1912. Essanay Film Manufacturing Company. 1,000 feet. Cast: Beverly Bayne (Mary), Francis X. Bushman (Bradley), Martha Russell (Pauline Ray).

Actress Pauline Ray (Russell) befriends Mary (Bayne), the daughter of the owner of the country inn where she is staying. She teaches Mary her part in an upcoming Broadway play while Mary's prompting helps Pauline prepare for the role. On the way back to the city, Pauline is injured in a car accident. Theater manager Bradley (Bushman) arrives to assess Pauline's condition. He realizes she will not be able to make her scheduled performance. Mary steps in as Pauline's understudy and saves the show.

Her Hour of Triumph

Release Date: July 27, 1912. Essanay Film Manufacturing Company. 1,000 feet. From the short story "A String of Pearls" by Guy de Maupassant. Cast: Lily Branscombe (The Friend), Francis X. Bushman (Frederick Barton), Martha Russell (Mrs. Barton).

A society drama involving a young broker, Frederick Barton (Bushman), and his wife (Russell). The wife borrows a string of pearls from a friend (Branscombe) to wear at a fashionable ball. She is a hit at the ball, but loses the pearls. In order to make amends to their friend, the couple sells everything they possess. Years later, the now-widowed Mrs. Barton pays off her last creditor. She also confesses to her friend the truth about the lost string of pearls and how she and her husband replaced it. Her friend then reveals that the "precious" string of pearls was a cheap imitation. Mrs. Barton breaks down in agony.

Essanay ads praised Martha Russell as "Essanay's popular leading lady, in one of the greatest emotional subjects since *The Adventuress*, which won her world fame. A startling drama, richly mounted, wonderfully portrayed. A distinct feature production."

Russell received popular acclaim for her emotional portrayal of Mrs. Barton. *The Moving Picture World* reported, "Miss Russell's portrayal of the wife is a masterpiece of character conception and forceful interpretation."

The New Church Organ

Release Date: August 3, 1912. Essanay Film Manufacturing Company. 1,000 feet. Cast: Beverly Bayne (Beverly Barlow), Francis X. Bushman (Austin Strong), Eva Prout (Snobbish Church Girl).

Austin Strong (Bushman), an organ salesman, falls deeply in love with the minister's daughter, Beverly Barlow (Bayne). Ashamed of her sparse clothing, Beverly avoids going to the church festival and instead works in the kitchen. An explosion severely burns Beverly's eyes. Austin takes her to her bedroom to recover and then has to leave on business. Months later, he returns to hear her playing the new church organ. He rushes to Beverly, finding her completely healed. He confesses his love and they embrace.

Essanay described *The New Church Organ* as "a fine subject replete with the deepest heart-interest. The passing of two young lovers through the fires of misfortune and bitter agony before being reunited in the wonderful light of happy years to come. Beverly Bayne and Francis X. Bushman featured in exquisite roles."

The Old Wedding Dress

Release Date: August 3, 1912. Essanay Film Manufacturing Company. 1,000 feet. Cast: Beverly Bayne (Jennie), Lily Branscombe (Aunt Betsy), Francis X. Bushman (Bridegroom).

Jennie (Bayne), about to be married, will wear the dress her old spinster aunt Betsy (Branscombe) had planned to be married in years earlier. The aunt reflects on her memories of the dress and events in her life which prevented her from marrying. A flashback shows the tragic railroad accident killing her betrothed. The film ends with a return to the country church wedding of the young niece and her bridegroom (Bushman).

Essanay advertised *The Old Wedding Dress* as "the tragic story of a sweet old lady whose life has been blighted by a bitter prank of Fate. Redolent with beautiful pathos and fragrant with the tender memories of 'the old wedding dress.'" *The Moving Picture World* commented, "A good and very emotional situation makes the latter two-thirds of this picture a real interpretation of human life.... The early scenes ... were pitiably weak...." They summed it up with, "It makes a very good offering."

An Adamless Eden

Release Date: August 10, 1912. Essanay Film Manufacturing Company. 1,000 feet. Cast: Francis X. Bushman (Adam Boob).

A comical case of misidentification as a bedraggled young man is mistaken for visiting royalty, Prince Augustus Busch. Eva Dixon falls in love with the young man only to find out he is Adam Boob (Bushman), an escapee from an insane asylum.

Essanay advertised *An Adamless Eden* as "a rollicking comedy subject of the funniest sort." *The Moving Picture World* took exception, finding little to like about the film: "Not good acting even of the Essanay players, nor extremely fine scenes, nor perfect photography, nor a good producer ... can make an acceptable artistic offering with a crazy man for its hero.... This release falls as flat as a heavy and watery pancake."

The Magic Wand

> Release Date: August 10, 1912. Essanay Film Manufacturing Company. 1,000 feet. Director: Theodore Wharton. Screenplay: Louella O. Parsons. Cast: Beverly Bayne, Francis X. Bushman, Helen Dunbar, Baby Harriet Parsons (Harriet).

A young child, Harriet (Baby Harriet Parsons), steals a "magic wand" from the school play in order to improve the lot of her destitute mother. Essanay advertised *The Magic Wand* as "a modern fairy story with an undercurrent of pathos that strikes deep and true. The magic wand of a poor little waif of the stage is made to work wonders when she pathetically tries to transform her sick mother's hovel into a beautiful palace."

The Moving Picture World was less enthusiastic, calling the production "almost without atmosphere" and criticizing the performance of Baby Harriet Parsons as "quite wooden throughout ... and the major problem with the film."

The Hermit (of Lonely Gulch)

> Release Date: August 24, 1912. Essanay Film Manufacturing Company. 1,000 feet. Cast: Beverly Bayne (Diana Trevor), Francis X. Bushman (Bob Wayne/The Hermit), Billy Mason.

College boy Bob Wayne (Bushman) and his sweetheart Diana Trevor (Bayne) have a falling out. Bob writes that he is going to become a hermit and goes off to camp in the woods. Diana joins some girlfriends on a camping outing and learns of a young hermit living near their campsite. Cooking up a scheme to harass the hermit, the girls approach his place dressed as ghosts. The hermit chases them away but Diana falls as she retreats. The hermit picks her up and her sheet falls away. The lovers rediscover each other.

Essanay advertised *The Hermit* as "a captivating comedy-drama redolent with the breath of the pine forests in the good old summertime."

Twilight

Release Date: August 31, 1912. Essanay Film Manufacturing Company. 1,000 feet. Cast: Francis X. Bushman (Silas Grant), Harry Mainhall (Harry), Martha Russell (Mrs. Grant), Ruth Stonehouse (Ruth).

An older couple, Silas (Bushman) and Mrs. Grant (Russell), flashback to their own young romance as they observe their granddaughter Ruth (Stonehouse) and her sweetheart Harry (Mainhall).

Essanay advertised *Twilight* as "a masterly dramatization of one of the sweetest songs ever written. ... A wonderful story told amid the enchantment of the twilight."

The Fall of Montezuma

Release Date: September 15, 1912. Essanay Film Manufacturing Company. Three reels. Director: Henry McRae Webster. Cast: William Bailey, Francis X. Bushman (Cortez), Harry Cashman, William Walters.

A tale of Mexico's conquest featuring Bushman as the conquering Cortez during the overthrow of Montezuma. Essanay continuously advertised the film from June 1912 through October 1912 and yet no reviews of the film were located. Essanay ads proclaimed *The Fall of Montezuma* "a three-reel Wonderfully Attractive Special Feature Historical Pageant," "Unquestionably a Film-Triumph," "Masterpiece of Film Craft" and "A Magnificent Tale of Cortez' Conquest of Mexico." From a lot of indications, it seems to have been everything but released.

Neptune's Daughter

Release Date: September 21, 1912. Essanay Film Manufacturing Company. 1,000 feet. Director and Screenplay: W. Christy Cabanne. From the fairy tale *Undine* by Friedrich de la Motte Fouque. Cast: Francis X. Bushman (Charles Fleming), Harry Cashman, Martha Russell (Undine), Ruth Stonehouse, William Walters.

Charles Fleming (Bushman), a young artist, catches a glimpse of Neptune's daughter, Undine (Russell), near the shore. He returns the next day, determined to meet her. Neptune warns Undine that if she takes human form, she can never again return to the sea. She ignores his admonition and meets Fleming. They fall in love and marry. After an argument, Undine leaves Fleming and begs forgiveness from Father Neptune. The artist regrets their fight and rushes to the sea to make amends with Undine only to find her dead body. At this shock, Fleming awakens from his dream.

The Moving Picture World rated *Neptune's Daughter* a fair offering but gave Martha Russell praise: "Miss Russell gives character to the picture by her interpretation of the sea-maiden turned human and out of water."

The Voice of Conscience

Release Date: September 21, 1912. Essanay Film Manufacturing Company. 1,000 feet. Director: Theodore Wharton. Screenplay: Harry Mainhall. Cast: Francis X. Bushman (William Sherman), Harry Cashman (Sheriff), Helen Dunbar (Mother), Harry Mainhall (Tenny), Martha Russell (Sweetheart), William Walters (Craig), Bryant Washburn (Morgan).

An accidental death on a hunting trip results in an innocent man being accused of murder. Young Sherman (Bushman) is discovered by the sheriff (Cashman) over the dead man's body and arrested. As Sherman is convicted in court, the man involved in the accidental death bursts into the courtroom, and dies in the arms of the sheriff.

The End of the Feud

Release Date: October 5, 1912. Essanay Film Manufacturing Company. 1,000 feet. Cast: Francis X. Bushman (Jim Parker), Harry Cashman (Rose's Father), Helen Dunbar, Harry Mainhall, Martha Russell (Rose Simpson), Ruth Stonehouse, William Walters, Bryant Washburn (Dave Simpson), Fred Wulf.

A Hatfield and McCoy romance where a young mountaineer, Jim Parker (Bushman), returns home from college, meets Rose Simpson (Russell) and falls in love. The families oppose the relationship but the two prevail and get married. Years later, the two clans are battling each other when the young daughter of Jim and Rose walks into the midst of the battle. Rather than shed the blood of their youngest kin, both sides agree to put an end to the feud.

The Warning Hand

Release Date: October 12, 1912. Essanay Film Manufacturing Company. 1,000 feet. Cast: Lily Branscombe, Francis X. Bushman (Jack Wayne), Harry Cashman, Frank Dayton, Helen Dunbar, Harry Mainhall, William Walters.

Jack Wayne (Bushman) discovers his father on his death bed. The old man warns Jack about a family painting of an evil bejeweled hand holding a sword by a chain. Later, as Jack is about to plunder his mother's safe in order to pay gambling debts, the hand points at him, warning Jack that he is about to do wrong. The son relents.

Essanay called *The Warning Hand* "a wonderful and startling dramatic subject, enthralling in plot-strength and portrayed with gripping intensity. The salvation of a dissolute son through the medium of an old family painting. Francis X. Bushman featured in a great study!"

Chains

Release Date: November 2, 1912. Essanay Film Manufacturing Company. 1,000 feet. Screenplay: Louella O. Parsons. Cast: Francis X. Bushman (Robert King), Ruth Stonehouse (Ruth Keene), Bryant Washburn (Harry Madden).

Ruth Keene (Stonehouse) falls in love with Harry Madden (Washburn), who is sentenced to 15 years in jail after killing a man in a card game dispute. Over the protests of her friends, Ruth marries Harry in prison. In order to support herself, she goes to work for Robert King (Bushman), a wealthy young lawyer. Ruth falls in love with her employer and asks for a divorce, which Harry will not give her. She remains forever "chained" to her degenerate convict husband.

The Moving Picture World called Bushman's work "just the character we always expect from him ... the best ... *Chains* is a story that will stir the heart."

When Wealth Torments

Release Date: November 2, 1912. Essanay Film Manufacturing Company. 1,000 feet. Cast: Francis X. Bushman (Jim O'Brien), Helen Dunbar (Mrs. Mahoney), Mildred Weston (Maggie).

Mrs. Mahoney (Dunbar) wants her beautiful daughter Maggie (Weston) to marry well. Jim O'Brien (Bushman) disguises himself as a French count and a German baron in efforts to gain Mrs. Mahoney's approval as a worthy mate for Maggie. As both the count and baron, Jim acts disgustingly, succeeding in getting Mrs. Mahoney to pine for the decent young man she drove away from her daughter. Re-enter Jim as himself to the joy of all.

The Moving Picture World praised Bushman for his adeptness at playing several roles in quick succession; "the cleverness with which he (Bushman) does it is the best thing in the offering."

House of Pride

Release Date: November 9, 1912. Essanay Film Manufacturing Company. 1,000 feet. Director: Jack Conway. Cast: Beverly Bayne (Mrs. Williams),

Francis X. Bushman (James Williams), E. H. Calvert, John Steppling. Director Jack Conway married Virginia Bushman, a daughter of Francis X. and Josephine Bushman. In later years, Conway directed a number of films featuring Francis X. Bushman, Lenore Bushman and Francis X. (Ralph) Bushman, Jr. D.W. Griffith also had a hand in the production of this film.

James Williams (Bushman), an honest city purchasing agent, struggles against political corruption. He is being pressured to award a contract to the Acme Paving Material Company with a bribe from Flannery, a corrupt politician. Williams rejects the bribe and orders Flannery out of his office. Later, Williams argues with his wife (Bayne) over her extravagant spending. She demands that he support her like other husbands do their wives. He reluctantly agrees to accept the bribe. During a reception at Williams' home, Frank Holt, the owner of the Acme Paving Material Company, makes a play for Mrs. Williams. James Williams finds out and threatens to expose the bribe and send the crooked men to jail.

The Penitent

Release Date: November 16, 1912. Essanay Film Manufacturing Company. 1,000 feet. Cast: William Bailey (Hugh Thompson), Beverly Bayne (Alice Danville), Francis X. Bushman (Bob Arling), Helen Dunbar (Mrs. Danville), Howard Messimer (Prof. Danville), William Walters (Dr. Hardcastle), Mildred Weston (Dorothy Haddon).

Bob Arling (Bushman) and Hugh Thompson (Bailey) vie for the love of Alice Danville (Bayne). Hugh wins the love match but Alice is blinded in an explosion in her father's laboratory. Hugh loses interest in Alice and makes a play for her cousin, Dorothy Haddon (Weston). Dr. Hardcastle (Walters) restores Alice's sight via an operation. Alice catches her fiancé and cousin together and realizes that he does not love her. Bob once again proposes to Alice and this time she accepts.

Essanay called *The Penitent* "a splendid romantic study, involving the happiness of four young lovers. A photoplay with 'punch.'"

The Iron Heel

Release Date: November 23, 1912. Essanay Film Manufacturing Company. 1,000 feet. Cast: Beverly Bayne, Francis X. Bushman (Robert Gregg), Harry Cashman, Helen Dunbar, Norman McDonald (Old Abner Wiley), Mildred Weston.

Old Abner Wiley (McDonald) plots to have his enemy's son Robert Gregg (Bushman) convicted of his (Wiley's) murder. The old man leaves a will making Gregg his heir, thus giving Gregg motive. Wiley then bloodies Gregg's walking stick, creates a scene indicating a struggle and then sets his own cottage on fire. Wiley hides in seclusion to watch the events unfold. The police arrest Gregg for murdering Wiley and burning the body to destroy the evidence. A savvy detective uncovers the plot, saving Gregg from execution. Wiley dies of heart failure when discovered in hiding.

Essanay advertised *The Iron Heel* as "one of the month's greatest dramatic productions. A plot of circumstantial evidence entwined about an innocent victim that is fiendish in its unyielding clutch until fathomed in the nick of time."

The Virtue of Rags

Release Date: December 14, 1912. Essanay Film Manufacturing Company. 1,000 feet. Director and Screenplay: Theodore Wharton. Cast: Francis X. Bushman (Grouch), Dolores Cassinelli, Helen Dunbar (Widow), Howard Messimer, Margaret Steppling, Ruth Stonehouse, Bryant Washburn (Rent Collector).

A kind-hearted rent collector (Washburn) is discharged for failing to collect rent from an impoverished widow (Dunbar). Grouch (Bushman), the landlord, evicts the widow himself. Upon returning to his club, he is given a sleeping powder, clothed in rags and left on a park bench. His sordid experiences as a destitute man change his heart. When he awakens, he returns the widow to her room, purchases furniture for her and gives her money.

When Soul Meets Soul

Release Date: December 28, 1912. Essanay Film Manufacturing Company. 1,000 feet. Director: Mr. MacDonald. Cast: Francis X. Bushman (Arames), Dolores Cassinelli (Princess Charazel), Fred Wulf (Prof. Delaface).

Prof. Delaface (Wulf) receives a well-preserved mummy. Inside the wrapping he discovers an ancient parchment telling of Princess Charazel (Cassinelli) and her search for her lost lover, Arames (Bushman). A flashback transports the audience to ancient Egypt to see Princess Charazel take her own life because Arames is found showering his affections on a young slave girl. In the end, Prof. Delaface awakens to discover he is the reincarnation of Arames.

Daydream of a Photoplay Artist

Release Date: Circa 1912. Essanay Film Manufacturing Company. This may never have been released, or perhaps it was released under a different title. Essanay used an innovative series of double exposures to enable

Bushman to play two separate characters appearing in the room at the same time. A photo of Bushman in the same room with himself appeared in *The Moving Picture World*.

The Romance of the Dells

Release Date: unknown. Essanay Film Manufacturing Company. Publications of the period cover the filming of *The Romance of the Dells* but no release date or review could be found. The 1912 production may have been suspended before completion or released under a different title.

The Trade Gun Bullet

Release Date: 1912. Selig.

Francis X. Bushman is credited in the *National Film Institute Catalog* as an actor in this 1912 Selig production. This is doubtful but not impossible. No other substantiating evidence was found but the authors have included the citation here in the event it holds true.

An Apache receives a trade-gun from an Englishman. The gun is involved in the murder of the Englishman's rival for the love of Bertha. The truth is discovered before Jim is executed and the Apache is shot trying to flee.

1913

The Farmer's Daughter

Release Date: January 18, 1913. Essanay Film Manufacturing Company. 1,000 feet. Beverly Bayne (Nellie Allen), Francis X. Bushman (Reginald Hoops, Jr.), Harry Cashman (Reginald Hoops Sr.). Cashman died before the release of this film.

An automobile accident causes Reginald Hoops, Jr. (Bushman), to be treated for his injuries at John Allen's farm. Young Hoops and the farmer's daughter, Nellie Allen (Bayne), fall in love and elope to the city. Things get complicated when Reginald's prior engagement to a young debutante, Alice St. John, threatens to stand in the way. Reginald Hoops, Sr., tears up the engagement papers to Alice St. John when she admits she would not marry young Hoops if he were poor.

The Moving Picture World commented, "[Beverly Bayne] distinguishes herself admirably as Nellie Allen. Francis X. Bushman plays the part of Reginald Hoops, Jr., well."

The Thirteenth Man

Release Date: January 18, 1913. Essanay Film Manufacturing Company. 1,000 feet. Cast: Francis X. Bushman, Ruth Stonehouse, William Walters, Bryant Washburn, Raymond Whitney.

The senior class of 1912 is comprised of 13 young men who vow to return as "The Thirteen Club" for an annual banquet. Over the years, Jack Hanney does not return for the event because he feels he has failed to reach the proper social status. His wife convinces him to attend this year's banquet. Jack rents a suit from a pawn shop and attends the event. During the evening, a precious jewel disappears and Jack refuses to be searched because he has pocketed food for his family. The other members find out about Jack's unfortunate situation and offer him a good position.

The Moving Picture World remarked, "It is not a very strong picture.... The photography is good."

The Discovery

Release Date: March 1, 1913. Essanay Film Manufacturing Company. 1,000 feet. Cast: Francis X. Bushman (Young Monion), Howard Messimer (Mr. Monion), Mildred Weston (Maud Mueller).

Father (Messimer) and son (Bushman) profess love for the same girl, stenographer Maud Mueller (Weston). She accepts the younger man's proposal of marriage. An automobile accident necessitates that Maud be treated by a doctor who recognizes her. She returns to her employer's office where both father and son produce engagement rings. She then informs them that she is their long-lost daughter and sister, respectively.

A Mistaken Accusation

Release Date: March 1, 1913. Essanay Film Manufacturing Company. 1,000 feet. Cast: Francis X. Bushman (Pietro).

Bushman plays the role of an Italian laborer, Pietro, seeking employment. He visits the home of a contractor looking for work, only to find the contractor's little son playing in the yard. Before leaving, Pietro helps the child build a mud castle. After the laborer leaves, the child wanders off into the woods. The mother returns and finds the Italian's handkerchief and believes her child has been kidnapped. A chase ensues and Pietro accidentally finds the child in the woods and returns him to the parents. The child explains what happened and Pietro is rewarded with a good job.

The Moving Picture World commented, "Bushman gives the picture what virility it possesses."

The Pathway of Years

Release Date: March 15, 1913. Essanay Film Manufacturing Company. 1,000 feet. Cast: Francis X. Bushman (John Mason), Ruth Hennessey (Flower Girl/Adopted Daughter), Ruth Stonehouse.

Bushman plays another dual role of both the young and older John Mason. The elder Mason reflects on the past triggered by seeing a piece of jewelry.

The Moving Picture World commented, "It was no easy task to put over. It is a story that will please adults, thoughtful ones especially. Splendid aid is given in the making of the picture by Ruth Hennessey...."

Spy's Defeat

Release Date: March 29, 1913. Essanay Film Manufacturing Company. Two reels. Director and Screenplay: Henry McRae Webster. Cast: Francis X. Bushman (Carl Heinrich), Frank Dayton, Lillian Drew, Ruth Stonehouse, William Walters.

During the Franco-German War, a Russian spy hypnotizes Fredericka, the daughter of the German prime minister of war, and secures her father's secret papers and fortification plans. Carl Heinrich (Bushman) captures the spy, saves the day and gains Fredericka's hand.

Essanay boasted, "The greatest spectacular historical photoplay ever produced. ... A revelation in the art of photoplay, and above all, a masterpiece."

Let No Man Put Asunder

Release Date: May 31, 1913. Essanay Film Manufacturing Company. Joseph Allen, Francis X. Bushman, John Steppling, Ruth Stonehouse, Bryant Washburn.

A couple splits up because the husband cannot control his temper. The man leaves town and finds employment at a mine. Through an inheritance, the mine becomes the property of his former wife. The man has to control his temper upon seeing the mine foreman make love to his estranged wife.

A Brother's Loyalty

Release Date: June 21, 1913. Essanay Film Manufacturing Company. Two reels. Director: Theodore Wharton. Cast: Beverly Bayne (Hal's Wife),

Francis X. Bushman (Paul and Hal), E.H. Calvert (Detective), Norman Fowler (Counterfeiter), Margaret Steppling (Hal's Child), Minor S. Watson.

Bushman plays two brothers. One sets out to prove the other's innocence of counterfeiting. The real counterfeitors are apprehended and the brothers united.

Essanay ads called *A Brother's Loyalty* a "red-blooded drama that grips the heart and holds the interest.... Sounds the depths of human emotions.... One feeling follows another in such rapid panorama that the audience is fairly 'swept off its feet' by the steady torrent of climactic events that crowd every scene of this heart-gripping play."

The Moving Picture World commended Bushman on his portrayal of the dual role of Paul and Hal: "[He] succeeds in accomplishing this and pulls the story through very creditably, some interesting examples of double exposure being recorded."

The Power of Conscience

Release Date: August 16, 1913. Essanay Film Manufacturing Company. Two reels. Director: Theodore Wharton. Screenplay: Henry McRae Webster. Cast: Beverly Bayne, Francis X. Bushman (Rev. Stanley Waters), E.H. Calvert (Edward Hale), Frank Dayton (Farmer Gordon), Helen Dunbar (Mrs. Waters), Dorothy Phillips (Dora Gordon), Bryant Washburn (Byron Waters). Many Beverly Bayne filmographies list this film among her credits; however, her name is absent from the cast of characters listed in the August 23, 1913, issue of *Motography* and the August 23, 1913 review in *The Moving Picture World*.

A mine explosion traps Edward Hale (Calvert), a miner guilty of mortally wounding the mine's owner Byron Waters (Washburn) because they both were in love with Dora Gordon (Phillips). Rev. Stanley Waters (Bushman) arrives at the explosion scene and goes into the mine to rescue any survivors. He comes upon Hale and brings him safely to the surface. Days later, on his death bed, Hale confesses to the murder.

Motography commented, "Mr. Bushman's art alone would make this picture one long to be remembered, but a well-managed scene of an explosion in a coal mine serves still further to make this two-reel subject a real feature." *The Moving Picture World* praised it highly, calling *The Power of Conscience* a production that "will commend itself not only to the great public of the moving picture theater world, but to people of finer critical tastes, who are zealous for the future of the photodrama and of photo-dramatic art.... The cast is particularly well assigned. Though Francis X. Bushman clearly, in the role of Reverend Stanley Waters, dominates the scenes in which he appears one does not lose sight of the merits of his co-workers.... Mr. Bushman's characterization of the minister will always remain a model of its kind."

The Whip Hand

Release Date: August 16, 1913. Essanay Film Manufacturing Company. 1,000 feet. Director: Arthur McMackin. Cast: Francis X. Bushman (Suitor), Frank Dayton (Husband), Juanita Dalmorez (Wife).

Another Bushman film with a mining setting. A wife (Dalmorez) unwittingly sets off a dynamite blast, killing her husband (Dayton). Bushman brandishes a whip in this movie.

Sunlight

Release Date: September 6, 1913. Essanay Film Manufacturing Company. 1,000 feet. Cast: Beverly Bayne (Young Woman), Francis X. Bushman (Young Man), Frank Dayton (Farm Husband), Helen Dunbar (Farm Wife).

A young man (Bushman) leaves the farm to find fame and fortune in the big city. He meets a young woman (Bayne) living in the slum. The girl is caught stealing coal and sent to the country. Later, the two are reunited when the young man returns to the farm he had abandoned in search of glory.

The Moving Picture World: "A good release ... full of poetry and sunlight, with interesting and suggestive contrasts between slum scenes and farm scenes.... Francis X. Bushman ... seems at his best in this lad of about 18 coming back to the country he had forsaken.... Beverly Bayne, as the girl grown up, is also good...."

The Right of Way

Release Date: September 13, 1913. Essanay Film Manufacturing Company. Two reels. Director: Arthur McMackin. Cast: Beverly Bayne (Rosemary), William Bayley, Francis X. Bushman (Robertson), Frank Dayton.

Robertson (Bushman), a railroad engineer, is torn between work and love for the beautiful Rosemary (Bayne), whose family burial ground lies in the path of the proposed new railroad. Robertson has an automobile accident and Rosemary nurses him back to health before she knows he works for the railroad. To stop the railroad workers from desecrating the burial grounds, Rosemary plants dynamite on the work site. Robertson is impressed by the family's determination and wires the railroad home office, recommending a detour. Robertson and Rosemary fall in love.

Essanay described *The Right of Way* as "one of the most thrilling and sensational railroad stories ever projected on the screen. A play that can easily be called 'The Dynamo of Magnetism.' It grips your audiences and will hold them from the first to the last stirring scene...."

For Old Time's Sake

Release Date: September 20, 1913. Essanay Film Manufacturing Company. 1,000 feet. Director: Theodore Wharton. Cast: William Bailey (Burglar/Former Boyfriend), Francis X. Bushman (Husband), Juanita Dalmorez (Wife).

A woman (Dalmorez) protects a burglar (Bailey) from her husband (Bushman) "for old time's sake," when she recognizes him as an old boyfriend.

Tony (Antoine) the Fiddler

Release Date: September 27, 1913. Essanay Film Manufacturing Company. Two reels. Director: Theodore Wharton. Cast: William Bailey (Big Bill/William Carson), Otto Breslin (Stage Driver), Francis X. Bushman (Tony, the Fiddler), Harry Carr (Deputy Joe Hall), Frank Dayton (Sheriff Bud Mercer), Juanita Dalmorez (Sue), Robert H. Townley (Deputy Jack Townsend).

Bandit Big Bill (Bailey) holds up the stage that Italian fiddler Tony (Bushman) is traveling on and relieves the driver of the silver shipment. Big Bill notices the fiddler and orders him to entertain him. Later, Tony meets and falls in love with Sheriff Mercer's (Dayton) daughter Sue (Dalmorez). Tony locates Big Bill's hideaway, lulls the bandit to sleep with his music and claims the reward. However, Sue gets engaged to another.

Motography said, "Never did Francis X. Bushman appear to better advantage...."

Dear Old Girl

Release Date: October 4, 1913. Essanay Film Manufacturing Company. Two reels. Director: Theodore Wharton. Cast: William Bailey, Beverly Bayne (Dora Allen), Eleanor Blanchard, Francis X. Bushman (Ted Warren), Frank Dayton (John Allen), Helen Dunbar (Mrs. Allen), Robert Walker. Filmed at Cornell University. Bushman once said he saw the film over 50 times and each time the whole audience was crying. Bushman also released sheet music of the song *Dear Old Girl*.

Dora Allen (Bayne) and Ted Warren (Bushman) are in love and due to be married upon Ted's graduation from Cornell. On the way to the train station to pick up his girlfriend, Ted hears the university chimes ring out the tune of "Dear Old Girl." Tragically, his fiancée is killed in a train accident. Ted loses his mind in his grief. Every day when he hears the chimes play "Dear Old Girl," he insists he is getting married that day and wants to go down to the train station to meet his bride-to-be. One day he eludes his caretaker and races to the train station. He is hit by the train and, dying, sees his bride coming to greet him.

Essanay promised that *Dear Old Girl* will bring tears to the eyes of the most hardened women: "A drama of heart interest ... a drama of appeal that will carry and hold the audience."

The Moving Picture World declared *Dear Old Girl* a rare picture and admonished viewers not to miss it. "Frank Bushman never had a better medium for showing what he can do; and he never had better support or better direction."

The Way Perilous

Release Date: October 18, 1913. Essanay Film Manufacturing Company. 1,000 feet. Cast: Beverly Bayne (Girlfriend), Francis X. Bushman (Young Man), Frank Dayton (Father).

A young man (Bushman) leaves his Southern home to make a name for himself, leaving behind his father (Dayton) and girlfriend (Bayne). He falls into bad company and ends up heavily in debt. He attempts to pay off his debts by conning his father out of a check.

Essanay described *The Way Perilous* as "a beautiful and absorbing love story...." Finding less favor with the production, *The Moving Picture World* review stated, "There is little real substance to the story as such at this stage of the game, but it has been so produced as to keep the artificial parts in the background and to accent what there is of human truth in it...."

The Toll of the Marshes

Release Date: October 25, 1913. Essanay Film Manufacturing Company. Two reels. Cast: Beverly Bayne, Francis X. Bushman (John Hammond), Frank Dayton, Helen Dunbar.

John Hammond (Bushman) and his mother are victimized by crooked land agents selling them worthless land as farm acreage. The young man saves the young daughter of the land company president after she wanders off into the marshes. In gratitude, Rogers returns the money paid for the poor land to the Hammonds.

The Motion Picture News commented, "[*The Toll of the Marshes*] hits a human strain and makes an interesting story...." *The Moving Picture World* remarked,

"The picture ... will no doubt accomplish good work in teaching people to avoid buying land in remote sections—sight unseen...."

The Woman Scorned

Release Date: November 5, 1913. Essanay Film Manufacturing Company. 1,000 feet. Cast: Francis X. Bushman, Josephine Duval (Josephine). Actress "Josephine Duval" was one of Francis X. Bushman's young daughters. Josephine was his wife's first name and Duval was a family name on his wife's side.

Josephine, a young child, is a "woman scorned" when her anonymous love letters to a man she admires are misconstrued. The man believes the love messages are from Josephine's older sister, whom he proceeds to court. All is reconciled in the end and the older sister and her suitor wed.

The Little Substitute

Release Date: November 22, 1913. Essanay Film Manufacturing Company. 1,000 feet. Cast: Beverly Bayne (Child's Mother), Francis X. Bushman (Father), Helen Dunbar (Aunt).

While a man (Bushman) is in Europe on business, his young child dies. The aunt (Dunbar), in whose care the child had been left, substitutes a deserted baby to try to hide the fact the father's child has died. The deserted child's mother (Bayne) becomes a nurse and tries to reclaim her child but the aunt tells her the baby died. When the child subsequently becomes ill, a nurse is sent for and the child's real mother arrives. The aunt confesses all. Both "parents" realize they love the child and marry.

Essanay called *The Little Substitute* a beautiful drama of love, affection and sacrifice. *The Moving Picture World* found the production less than convincing. "It looked like a retake being tangled.... Mr. Bushman and Miss Dunbar make the most of their parts."

The Stigma

Release Date: December 13, 1913. Essanay Film Manufacturing Company. Two reels. Cast: Beverly Bayne (Alice Madden), Betty Brown (Sweetheart Jane), Francis X. Bushman (Clifford Harvey), Thomas Commerford, (Mr. Harvey), Clara Smith (Mrs. Harvey).

A young woman, Alice Madden (Bayne), is washed ashore after a shipwreck and taken into the home of a man and woman for care. Their son Clifford (Bushman) falls in love with her. Unfortunately, she is afflicted with leprosy. Despite her dreadful disease, the young man leaves home to be with her. She cannot bear the thought of his suffering with her and jumps off a cliff to her death. He sees her do this and follows.

The Motion Picture News proclaimed *The Stigma* as "an exceptionally strong story.... Its author is to congratulated.... Francis X. Bushman and Beverly Bayne in the leading roles give the characters they visualize an individuality and personality that can come only from artists of their caliber. Mr. Bushman, as the lover, plays his part comprehendingly. He plays it as one would wish to see it played...."

The Moving Picture World criticized the author for "trying harder to make a picture than he was to create entertainment. Entertainment it is not.... Good acting and fine natural backgrounds are present.... Francis Bushman has the lead, but even he cannot overcome the handicap imposed upon him...."

1914

Hearts and Flowers

Release Date: January 13, 1914. Essanay Film Manufacturing Company. 1,000 feet. Cast: Francis X. Bushman (Mr. Swift), Ruth Stonehouse (Mrs. Russell), Eleanor Kahn.

Mrs. Russell's (Stonehouse) health deteriorates due to the pressures of a failed marriage. She is hospitalized and her young daughter Ruth visits often. In the hospital halls, Ruth meets Mr. Swift (Bushman), a wealthy clubman who is convalescing, and they become friends. The man gives the young girl money which she uses to purchase flowers for her mother. After leaving the hospital, Swift finds the little girl crying because she has no more money for flowers. He purchases a bouquet and brings the flowers to the lady's room only to discover she is his lost sweetheart from years ago.

Hearts and Flowers drew a rave review from *The Moving Picture World*: "This is a beautiful picture. The leading characters give a fine performance, sympathetic, tender. There is a steady pull throughout the whole reel. The acting and staging are of the best. There is an unusually pretty and effective finish."

The Hour and the Man

Release Date: January 13, 1914. Essanay Film Manufacturing Company. Two reels. Screenplay: Mr. Roach. Cast: William Bailey, Francis X. Bushman (Frank Maxwell), Clara Smith, Ruth Stonehouse.

Lawyer Frank Maxwell (Bushman) defends a woman accused of murdering her husband without knowing that the murdered man is his own brother. After he obtains her acquittal, she tells him the true identity of the dead man. Understanding that justice has been served, the lawyer forgives her.

Essanay's advertisements for *The Hour and the Man* called the production "an unusual drama founded on circumstantial evidence. It is a story with heart throbs and situations unparalleled."

According to *The Motion Picture News*, the film's audience applauded upon its completion during its New York showing. It called the production "a strong story which cannot but appeal to all.... Mr. Roach, of the Essanay scenario staff, has written another splendid play. It is psychological. It is strong and it brings forth a big lesson. Francis X. Bushman as the young lawyer plays the role convincingly."

Through the Storm

Release Date: January 17, 1914. Essanay Film Manufacturing Company. Two reels. Cast: Beverly Bayne (Susan Burton), Francis X. Bushman (Andy Burton), Baby Garity (Baby Burton).

Railroad telegrapher Andy Burton (Bushman) saves the mail train from being blown up by a gang of tramps. He is rewarded and his wife Susan (Bayne) earns the job as a telegrapher that she wanted.

Essanay advertisements read, "Mr. Exhibitor: If your audiences care for photoplays that are exciting and thrilling throughout, book *Through the Storm*, for it has the desired punch and entertaining features so often looked for."

The Moving Picture World called *Through the Storm* "one of the best two-reel railroad stories shown in a long time" while *The Motion Picture News* commented, "Both Mr. Bushman and Miss Bayne are up to their regular standard in their acting in this picture."

The Girl at the Curtain

Release Date: January 24, 1914. Essanay Film Manufacturing Company. Two reels. Cast: Beverly Bayne (Mary Burns), Francis X. Bushman (Warren Bradley).

Warren Bradley (Bushman) stands to inherit a large fortune from his uncle, but only under the condition that he marry a distant relative whom he has never met. Bradley is willing to marry anyone to get at his uncle's money, but the girl, Mary Burns (Bayne), has other thoughts and refuses to see him. In desperation, he writes to her asking if she would marry him without seeing him. In order to save her uncle's home, she agrees, and the two are married by proxy, a curtain separating them. Years later, she applies for an office position only to discover that her employer is her husband. She overhears him tell a young lady over the telephone that he will marry her as soon as he obtains a divorce. After Mary leaves the office, he discovers in her desk the proposal letter he sent her years ago. Warren dashes after Mary and claims her as his rightful wife.

Essanay called *The Girl at the Curtain* "a good, clean, wholesome comedy-drama that will make excellent entertainment for the most critical audience." *The Motion Picture News* commented that, "There is something unusual about this picture and the comedy and drama are intermingled in a most effective manner...." *The Moving Picture World* found favor with the actors' performances: "[Bushman and Bayne] do splendid work in a drama replete with strong situations.... The story has unusual appeal and stirring quality. It should be a real hit...."

Dawn and Twilight

Release Date: January 31, 1914. Essanay Film Manufacturing Company. 1,000 feet. Cast: Francis X. Bushman (Pietro Delani).

Blind violinist Pietro Delani's (Bushman) sight is restored by an operation paid for by a young woman, Mary Waters, who admires him. However, he is displeased with her appearance and abandons her for another woman, Edna Ainsworth. Fate intervenes and again strikes him with blindness. Edna leaves him and he seeks out Mary, only to discover she has died of a broken heart.

The Other Girl

Release Date: February 14, 1914. Essanay Film Manufacturing Company. Two reels. Director: E.H. Calvert. Cast: Francis X. Bushman (Frank Dixon), Ruth Stonehouse (Ruth Thomas).

Frank Dixon (Bushman) vies for the hand of a beautiful, young but poor girl, Ruth Thomas (Stonehouse). His mother favors a rich girl, Alice Williams, and tries to match him and Alice. Frank's mother intercepts a note from Ruth arranging a meeting to discuss marriage. When Frank fails to arrive for the meeting, Ruth joins the Salvation Army. While sorting donated clothes, Ruth finds her note to Frank and realizes it was never delivered. They reunite before Frank marries Alice.

Essanay promoted *The Other Girl* as "a unique drama of love, jealousy and ambition ... a worthy feature...." *The Moving Picture World* called the production "a good story of an interrupted love affair, with a happy ending." Bushman and Stonehouse received praise from *The Motion Picture News* for their portrayals: "Their individual personalities stand out in the productions in which they appear and register them as capable interpreters of the roles entrusted to them."

Shadows

Release Date: March 14, 1914. Essanay Film Manufacturing Company. Two reels. Director: R.E. Baker. Cast: Francis X. Bushman (Grayson), E. H. Calvert, Lillian Drew, Rapley Holmes, Irene Warfield, Bryant Washburn.

Secret Service agent Grayson (Bushman) pursues a gang of counterfeiters led by Damarest. Girl reporter Fanny Turner, assigned to get the story on Damarest, is kidnapped by the gang. Grayson rescues Fanny and captures the crooks.

Essanay promised exhibitors that *Shadows* was "positively one of the most sensational melodramas ever produced for the screen.... It is thrilling in the extreme...."

Motion Picture Story Magazine reported that friends of Bushman were saying that he had done his very best work in *Shadows*.

The Three Scratch Clue

Release Date: March 21, 1914. Essanay Film Manufacturing Company. Two reels. Cast: Francis X. Bushman (Norman Arnold), Thomas Commerford (Dr. Strong), Irene Warfield (Helen Strong), Bryant Washburn (Lynch).

Lynch (Washburn) steals art treasures and plots to pilfer Dr. Strong's (Commerford) new acquisition, a rare book purchased for $50,000. Dr. Strong's secretary, Norman Arnold (Bushman), is in love with the doctor's daughter Helen (Warfield). Norman and Helen foil the robbery and pursue Lynch, who crashes his automobile. Lynch is arrested and Helen falls in love with Norman.

Reviewer C.J. Verhalen of *The Motion Picture News* commented, "*The Three Scratch Clue* ... is a clean-cut play that does not reek of the cheap dime-novel effect.... Essanay has been building these kinds of photoplays (detective) with a considerable degree of success...."

In the Moon's Ray

Release Date: April 4, 1914. Essanay Film Manufacturing Company. Two reels. Cast: Francis X. Bushman (Richard Neal), E.H. Calvert (Meredith Blake), Charles Hitchcock (Squint), Gerda Holmes (Judith), Rapley Holmes (Robert Hamilton), Bryant Washburn (Spider). Another Richard Neal detective drama. See also *Finger Prints* (1914).

The reviews found for *In the Moon's Ray* reveal that its storyline is virtually identical to *Finger Prints*, also released in 1914. This time, the scarab is stolen when the thief slips into Mr. Hamilton's room "in the moon's ray." Also slightly different are the means used to capture the crook and save Judith. *The Moving Picture World* blasted *In the Moon's Ray*: "is filled with occurrences that are not entertaining or satisfying. To the spectator who sits through it, it is disgusting...." But C.J. Verhalen's *The Motion Picture News* review praised the film: "One event follows another in this thrilling detective picture.... The scenes are well laid and the unfolding of the plot makes one wonder what the next move will be...."

A Man for A'That

Release Date: April 18, 1914. Essanay Film Manufacturing Company. Two reels. Cast: Francis X. Bushman (Frank Willard), Annie Edney (Mrs. Davis), Thomas Harper (Dick Davis), Ruth Stonehouse (Ruth Davis), Irene Warfield (Grace Meredith), Bryant Washburn (Count Ver Sailles).

Frank Willard (Bushman) is a wealthy clubman who becomes disenchanted with the life of the idle rich and takes up work among the poor. He falls in love with Ruth (Stonehouse), but his prior engagement to socialite Grace Meredith (Warfield) creates complications. When Ruth and Frank go to see Grace to straighten things out, they discover she has eloped with Count Ver Sailles (Washburn), leaving them free to marry.

The Motion Picture News said "interesting." *The Moving Picture World* wrote that Willard's "adventures make an interesting story that is clean and enjoyable."

The Spirit of the Madonna

Release Date: April 18, 1914. Essanay Film Manufacturing Company. 1,000 feet. Cast: Francis X. Bushman.

Employer James Thompson shows little consideration for one of his workers, Fred Martin, who lost his arm on the job, and refuses Mrs. Martin's request for aid. Thompson purchases a painting of the Madonna. At night, he imagines that the Madonna visits and pleads with him to help his employees.

The Moving Picture World called the production "a superior picture, especially in photography and lighting."

The Mystery of Room 643

Release Date: May 2, 1914. Essanay Film Manufacturing Company. Two reels. Cast: Francis X. Bushman (Richard Neal), John Cossar (Blackburn) Gerda Holmes (Judith Hamilton), Rapley Holmes (Robert Hamilton), Bryant Washburn (Milton Wade). This ongoing detective storyline picks up from where *In the Moon's Ray* left off.

Richard Neal (Bushman) is called upon to locate some valuable missing papers which were last seen in Mr. Hamilton's (Holmes) safe. The trail leads to Milton Wade (Washburn), a suitor of Hamilton's daughter Judith (Gerda Holmes). The final bit of evidence linking Wade to the crime is a letter typed on a typewriter with clogged "e's."

The Motion Picture World commented, "Francis X. Bushman, in these Richard Neal stories, is well cast as the polished gentleman...."

Ashes of Hope

Release Date: May 9, 1914. Essanay Film Manufacturing Company. Two reels. Cast: Francis X. Bushman (Fred Willard), E.H. Calvert (Charles Donald), Ruth Stonehouse (Zalata), Bryant Washburn.

Theatrical manager Fred Willard (Bushman) played a big role in the success of dancer Zalata (Stonehouse). Attorney Charles Donald (Calvert) becomes infatuated with Zalata. He makes unwanted advances towards her. Zalata slaps the attorney's face. She quits dancing to become a teacher. When one of her students dies in her care, she is accused of murder. In spite, prosecuting attorney Charles Donald demands a conviction and jail for Zalata despite evidence that the young boy died from a heart ailment. The jury acquits her.

The Motion Picture News stated, "With such a cast as Francis X. Bushman, Ruth Stonehouse, E.H. Calvert and Bryant Washburn ... this picture can hardly help but 'get across.' Mr. Bushman again displays his great versatility.... The court scene that appears in the second reel is unusually good...."

Mongrel and Master

Release Date: May 16, 1914. Essanay Film Manufacturing Company. Three reels. Francis X. Bushman (Frank Mitchell), Rapley Holmes (Big Bill Denton, the Mongrel), Ruth Stonehouse (Ruth Stone).

Big Bill Denton and his cohort Frank Mitchell (Bushman) are set to burglarize a house when a small girl, Ruth Stone (Stonehouse), gives Frank a rose. Ironically, the house they burglarize belongs to the girl's parents. Realizing this, Frank vows to give up his life of crime. Big Bill continues his low life and becomes a political boss. Ruth's father enters politics and is elected mayor. Frank becomes his personal secretary and falls in love with Ruth. Big Bill also takes a fancy to Ruth, but when she refuses his advances, he vows to ruin her father's political career. Frank learns of a crime committed by Big Bill and his gang and informs the police, who arrest them. In revenge, Big Bill tells the mayor about Frank's criminal past and that he participated in robbing Mr. Stone's house years ago. Instead of being angry, the mayor applauds Frank for turning his life around.

The May 30, 1914, *Photoplay* carried a 16-page synopsis of *The Mongrel and the Master*, complete with photo illustrations. *The Motion Picture News* praised Bushman's tackling of a difficult role: "Mr. Bushman has a part here that most actors would fall down on, for the character depends on the actor, not the actor on the character, as is very often the case. Of course he handles this part well as he does any part he takes."

Variety sniped, "It's an ordinary sort of a crook-politician story, improbable in the frankness displayed by the crooks and the politicians, but still those who like Mr. Bushman in romantic roles (as no doubt he nearly always plays) will be satisfied with this feature, because Francis is in it...."

The Voice in the Wilderness

Release Date: May 23, 1914. Essanay Film Manufacturing Company. Two reels. Cast: Francis X. Bushman (The Author), Gerda Holmes (The Wife), Irene Warfield (The Sculptress). Reissued by Essanay in 1916.

An author (Bushman) falls into a precipice and a sculptress (Warfield) nurses him back to health. When he returns home, he finds his wife (Holmes) marrying another man. He returns to the sculptress.

Variety took exception with Bushman's tendency to pose: "Mr. Bushman goes about his business of picture play acting in a good direct way at times, but again he seems to believe the acme of the art is to become expressive before the camera, when repression instead of expression would be vastly more value to him.... Mr. Bushman may note how much better the actor he is when divested of all staginess...."

Blood Will Tell

Release Date: May 30, 1914. Essanay Film Manufacturing Company. Three reels. Director: Theodore Wharton. Screenplay: Henry McRae Webster. Cast: Robert Bolder, Francis X. Bushman, E.H. Calvert, Ruth Hennessey, Ruth Stonehouse, Irene Warfield, Bryant Washburn. Bushman and others played dual roles in this film.

An illicit love affair leads to the married woman and her lover being pursued by the estranged husband. The lover kills the husband in a duel and is subsequently denounced by the wife. He leaves for Colonial America and marries. The plot is complicated by a letter he wrote to the woman, lamenting that he only has memories while she has their child. A century later, the letter is discovered by the great granddaughter, who is about to be married to a descendant of the woman's lover. Learning the story, the young woman calls off the wedding. Her fiancé drives away angry, only to be killed in an automobile accident.

Variety concluded, "[*Blood Will Tell*] will be fairly well liked by women and girls, leaving no impression on the males."

The Elder Brother

Release Date: May 30, 1914. Essanay Film Manufacturing Company. Two reels. Cast: Francis X. Bushman (Dr. Phillip Caldwell), John Cossar, Gerda Holmes (Cabaret Dancer), Bryant Washburn (Irving Caldwell).

Dr. Phillip Caldwell (Bushman) and his brother Irving (Washburn) find themselves in love with the same woman, a cabaret dancer (Holmes). When Phillip finds out his love is also his brother's girlfriend, he casts her off. In revenge, she plans to dope Irving. When the cocaine takes a terrible toll on Irving, the dancer takes pity on him and nurses him back to health. Phillip forgives her for her rash act.

Essanay advertised *The Elder Brother* as "an impressive heart interest dramatic story...." *The Motion Picture News* commented, "Bushman played his part well.... As the younger brother, Bryant Washburn is seen in one of his best-acted parts. Gerda Holmes, who has been with the company only a short time, is well cast, and convincingly portrays the part of the dancer. Miss Holmes, besides possessing good looks, is a capable actress...."

Likewise, *The Moving Picture World* gave ample praise: "The heart of the picture is fine and the real story is made effective by the human acting...."

The Countess

Release Date: June 20, 1914. Essanay Film Manufacturing Company. Two reels. Cast: Beverly Bayne (Countess Ysioff), Francis X. Bushman (Richard Hasbrook).

Morning Globe reporter Richard Hasbrook (Bushman) takes a job as Countess Ysioff's (Bayne) butler in order to get a story. She also makes him her personal representative and bodyguard because she anticipates trouble from a European gang. He successfully protects her from harm and the film concludes with the *Morning Globe* carrying his scoop ... their impending marriage.

The Motion Picture World: "This highly colored melodrama is not very convincing, but will find plenty of admirers."

Finger Prints

Release Date: June 23, 1914. Essanay Film Manufacturing Company. Two reels. Cast: Francis X. Bushman (Richard Neal), Gerda Holmes (Judith), Rapley Holmes. See *In the Moon's Ray*, also released in 1914.

The third and last adventure of Richard Neal, private investigator. A gang of crooks headed by Meredith Blake plots to steal a valuable scarab from Robert Hamilton. Detective Richard Neal (Bushman) is enlisted to find the crooks and the stolen scarab by Hamilton, the father of Neal's girlfriend Judith (Holmes). Neal discovers some fingerprints at the scene of the crime. Judith is kidnapped and taken to an underground hideout. She escapes through a trap door leading to a manhole. After a series of fights, the crooks are captured and the scarab returned to Mr. Hamilton.

Trinkets of Tragedy

Release Date: June 27, 1914. Essanay Film Manufacturing Company. Two reels. Cast: Francis X. Bushman (Harrison Hyde), E.H. Calvert, Rapley Holmes, Ruth Stonehouse (Miriam), M.C. Von Betz.

In this thrilling mystery, rich art collector Frederic de Peyton-Reuter falls in love with Miriam (Stonehouse), the niece of curio shop proprietor Fangbone. Fangbone's enemy Iriski leaves a black hand insignia on an ivory fan, signifying death. Fangbone is murdered and his niece is blamed for the crime. Detective Harrison Hyde (Bushman) is called in on the case and captures the real murderer.

A Night with a Million

Release Date: July 4, 1914. Essanay Film Manufacturing Company. Cast: Francis X. Bushman (Jack Wilton).

Jack Wilton (Bushman), a clerk in a broker's office, is left in charge when his employer, Judson Clarke, leaves to visit Mr. Dwight. A stranger mistakes Wilton for Clarke and leaves a million dollars in railroad bonds in his care. Wilton undergoes a number of misfortunes, including being arrested for theft, while trying to deliver the bonds to Clarke. In the end, Wilton discovers the bonds are worthless (the railroad went bankrupt years ago) but for his efforts he is rewarded with a new position as private secretary.

The Moving Picture World found the film both tragic and amusing, adding, "This is a very good picture."

His Stolen Fortune

Release Date: July 11, 1914. Essanay Film Manufacturing Company. Two reels. Cast: Beverly Bayne (Lola), Francis X. Bushman (Frank Wentworth), John Cossar (Hotel Clerk), Helen Dunbar (Mrs. Holcombe), Charles Hitchcock (Hotel Clark), Rapley Holmes (Attorney).

Frank Wentworth (Bushman) discovers a letter that explains that the vast fortune left to him by his uncle was stolen from a poor inventor, Max Illuski. Frank sets out to right the wrong and advertises to find Max or his relatives. He is beset by multitudes of people falsely claiming to be rightful heirs to the fortune. Finally, the family attorney (Holmes) explains that the letter is a fake designed to test Frank's honesty. Frank rejoices and marries his sweetheart (Bayne).

The Motion Picture News said *His Stolen Fortune* featured "a cleverly conceived plot which affords Francis X. Bushman a chance to reveal his abilities as an actor and incidentally to appear as his best as a matinee idol...."

Night Hawks

Release Date: July 14, 1914. Essanay Film Manufacturing Company. Two reels. Cast: Francis X. Bushman (Humphrey), John Cossar (District Attorney), Royal Douglas (Murphy, Ward Heeler), Lillian Drew (The Woman), Ed Dunkinson (Kerns), Charles Hitchcock (Stone), Rapley Holmes (Wardell), Ruth Stonehouse (Mildred Varing), M.C. Von Betz (Nichols, Ward Heeler).

Another story of political corruption. Humphrey (Bushman) rescues Mildred Varing (Stonehouse) from the clutches of political boss Wardell's (Holmes) henchmen. Humphrey also gathers evidence to help the District Attorney (Cossar) implicate the political gang in murder.

The July 1, 1914, *Essanay News* advertised *Night Hawks* as a "melodrama filled with thrills and sensationalism." *The Moving Picture World* called the production "a superlative feature."

One Wonderful Night

Release Date: July 18, 1914. Essanay Film Manufacturing Company. Four reels. Director: E.H. Calvert. Adapted from a story by Louis Tracy. Cast: Edward Babille (Antoine Lamotte), Beverly Bayne (Lady Hermoine), Robert Bolder (Otto Schmidt), Francis X. Bushman (John Delancey Curtis), E.H. Calvert (Chief Detective Steingall), Thomas Commerford (The Earl of Valletort), John Cossar (Horace P. Curtis), Lillian Drew (Marcelle), Helen Dunbar (Mrs. Horace P. Curtis), Charles Hitchcock (Gregory Martiny), Rapley Holmes (Count Vassilan), Harry Mainhall (Clancy), M.C. Von Betz (Ferdinand Rossi), Howard Watrous (Henry R. Hunter), Bryant Washburn (Howard Devar), Leo White (Jean de Curtois).

Bushman earned the leading role in *One Wonderful Night* by winning *The Ladies' World* "Hero Contest." He received critical praise for his portrayal, "one of the best acting roles in the history of motion picture plays," from newspapers across the country. Bushman was also featured on the cover of the sheet music for *One Wonderful Night*.

One Wonderful Night is a tale of romance and intrigue. Lady Hermoine (Bayne) flees to New York to escape her upcoming ill-conceived marriage to Count Vassilan, arranged by her father, the ne'er-do-well Earl of Vallefort. In an effort to rid herself of the Count, she agrees to marry Frenchman Jean de Curtois (White). American railroad builder John D. Curtis (Bushman) intervenes and falls in love with Lady Hermoine. Alleged murder and a series of misadventures complicate their lives, but at least all is well and they can begin their married life.

Essanay took out a full page ad proclaiming, "10,000,000 people are waiting to see the Photoplay Masterpiece *One Wonderful Night* written by Louis Tracy.... Francis X. Bushman, the winner of *The Ladies' World* Hero Contest, will play the leading role—your audience elected him to play it...." The cover of the July 18, 1914, *The Moving Picture World* featured a photo of a scene from *One Wonderful Night*.

The Motion Picture News also gave the film good press with several articles and photos. "Not only has the Essanay Company built a credible picture from the novel ... but they have built a photoplay that will stand out as something extraordinary in the staging of picture productions.... While [Bushman's] acting has always been notable, it stands out even stronger in this four-reel production. It shows him practically at his best."

Variety described *One Wonderful Night* as "well staged, well photoplayed.... The leads are capably taken and Bushman does some capital work throughout...." The July 25, 1914, *Motography* enthused. "The choice of Francis X. Bushman, by the readers of *The Ladies' World*, to play the role ... was a happy one, for never before during his successful career in the photo-drama has the popular star been seen to better advantage than in this picture.... Mr. Bushman's delineation of the leading character ... can be described by only one word which will cover it adequately—Great. The role fits him perfectly and had the story been written to play up the numerous strong points in his expressions and actions, it could not have presented him to any better advantage...."

The Motor Buccaneers

Release Date: August 1, 1914. Essanay Film Manufacturing Company. Two reels. Adapted from a *Munsey Magazine* story by Edward Franklin. Cast: Francis X. Bushman, Thomas Commerford, John Cossar, Rapley Holmes, William Robinson, Arthur Steinguard, Ruth Stonehouse, M.C. Von Betz.

A young lawyer (Bushman) breaks up a conspiracy and wins fame and the affections of his sweetheart. A notorious crook murders an older lawyer, framing the young lawyer in the process. He proves his innocence and the crook is rounded up.

Essanay advertised *The Motor Buccaneers* as "a gripping photoplay of adventure that cannot help but hold the interest of any audience...." *The Moving Picture World* pointed out quite a number of thrills featuring motor chases and fights, summing up, "This is a favorable offering."

Ambushed

Release Date: August 15, 1914. Essanay Film Manufacturing Company. Three reels. Cast: Francis X. Bushman.

Listed as a western in *A Guide to Silent Westerns*.

The Masked Wrestler

Release Date: August 15, 1914. Essanay Film Manufacturing Company. Two reels. Director: E.H. Calvert. Cast: Beverly Bayne (Margery Winters), Francis X. Bushman (Louis De Luzon), Rapley Holmes (Her Father), Paul Raas (The Lion), Bryant Washburn (M. Lefevre).

Margery Winters (Bayne), a young American girl, and her father (Holmes) attend a wrestling match in Paris. She throws a bouquet of flowers to the victorious "Masked Wrestler" (Bushman). When he kisses her hand in return, it is love at first sight. Later she asks Louis De Luzon (Bushman), a suitor, to arrange a meeting with the Masked Wrestler. Villain M. Lefevre (Washburn) bribes "The Lion" to unmask the Masked Wrestler in an upcoming match. The Masked Wrester wins the championship match and then unmasks himself, letting everyone see he is Louis De Luzon. Although Winters fell in love with the Masked Wrestler, she realizes she can only love Louis and cancels her return trip to America.

Motography called the acting in *The Masked Wrestler* "splendid with Francis X. Bushman outdoing himself in a sort of double role, which dissolves into one character in the denouement. He incidentally proves himself to be a mat artist of no mean ability and the disclosure of his splendid physique will be a delight to his countless admirers. Miss Beverly Bayne, playing opposite him, carries her part with equal success and gives a real French touch to her expressions."

The Motion Picture News commented, "Bushman is handsome both in his evening clothes and in his wrestling togs. The bouts are realistic."

Under Royal Patronage

Release Date: August 29, 1914. Essanay Film Manufacturing Company. Two reels. Director: E.H. Calvert. Cast: Beverly Bayne (Helen Churchill),

Francis X. Bushman (Richard Savage), E.H. Calvert (Count Karl von Blumen), Thomas Commerford H.R.H. Francis of Hofgarten, Lester Cuneo (Baron Spitzhausen), Harry Dunkinson (Humphrey the Spy), Charles Hitchcock (Frederick of Strelitzburg), Jane Paddock (Princess Stella), Betty Scott (Baroness Karm), Bryant Washburn (Prince Phillip). Essanay reissued *Under Royal Patronage* in 1916. The scenario was adapted from a story that appeared in *Munsey Magazine*. The movie was filmed in a Chicago millionaire's mansion in order to capture the elegance of the story's Hofgarten Palace.

To avoid marrying, Prince Phillip (Commerford) of Hofgarten and Princess Stella (Paddock) of Strelitzburg separately prevail upon two American friends, Richard Savage (Bushman) and Helen Churchill (Bayne), to pass themselves off as the prince and princess. Neither Richard nor Helen knows about the dual deception; each assumes the other is genuine royalty. Naturally, these two attractive Americans fall in love with one another—and, in a twist of fate, so do the real Prince of Hofgarten and Princess of Strelitzburg.

Reviewer James S. McQuade of *The Moving Picture World* praised the cast and storyline: "In appearance, and physique and action, Mr. Bushman is especially fitted for romantic roles. He is an athlete of no mean prowess and an adept swordsman. In his clash ... with three men of stalwart build and determined onslaught, he puts up a fight of such lively interest that one unconsciously cries, 'Bravo!' In the love scenes with supposed Princess (Bayne), he will convince the coldest spectator of the opposite sex that he is an apt master of affairs of the heart...."

The Motion Picture News commented, "Two big powerful acts with just the right amount of snap and mystery to it, plenty of good acting and a corking good story make this production stand out as something different and stamp it a splendid photoplay...."

Sparks of Fate

Release Date: September 12, 1914. Essanay Film Manufacturing Company. Two reels. Cast: Francis X. Bushman (Frank Graham), Ruth Stonehouse (Ruth), Bryant Washburn (Wilbur Hayes).

Two wireless operators are in love with the same girl, Ruth (Stonehouse). An explosion aboard ship causes the sinking of the *Melba* with Frank Graham (Bushman) thrown overboard, but the rival wireless operator on shore, Wilbur Hayes (Washburn), does not spread the alarm in order to have Ruth to himself. A dramatic rescue ensues and Frank arrives in town just in time to prevent Ruth's marriage to Wilbur.

"A drama of absorbing interest and intensity," said *The Moving Picture World* approvingly.

The Plum Tree

Release Date: September 19, 1914. Essanay Film Manufacturing Company. Released through General Film Company. Three reels. Director: E.H. Calvert. Cast: Beverly Bayne (Alice Graham), Wallace Beery, Francis X. Bushman (Craig Ewell), Lester Cuneo (Norris Griggs), Frank Dayton (John Graham), Helen Dunbar (Mrs. Ewell), Harry Dunkinson ("Dug" Taylor). Adapted from a story in *The Ladies' World*.

Craig Ewell (Bushman) loves Alice Graham (Bayne) but banker Norris Griggs (Cuneo) intervenes with due notes issued by Alice's father, John Graham (Dayton). Graham cannot repay the notes and suggests a marriage between Griggs and his daughter to settle the debt. However, Alice professes her love for Craig. Griggs plots with "Dug" Taylor (Dunkinson) to trick Craig into a meeting at Lone Man's Cove. When Craig arrives, he find's "Dug" dead with a strongbox next to him. Craig is arrested by railmen in search of the desperadoes who robbed the express. He is tried, found guilty and sentenced to ten years in the state penitentiary. While in prison, he learns that Alice has been forced into marriage with Griggs. Released from jail after serving his term, Craig finds himself captured by roustabouts and forced to load contraband arms aboard a ship for delivery to Mexican revolutionists. Griggs is a leader of the revolutionaries. Craig escapes and warns the federal garrison of the impending invasion. Spectacular battle scenes show the federal forces vanquishing the revolutionaries. Craig and Griggs engage in hand-to-hand combat with Griggs receiving a mortal wound. On his death bed, Griggs confesses to his robbery of the express train and the killing of "Dug" Taylor. Craig and Alice are reunited under "The Plum Tree."

Motography praised *The Plum Tree* in its review: "Acting of a really superior sort, stage settings that show care and detail, photography that is above criticism and several spectacular battle scenes ... all tend to make Essanay's three-reel offering ... one of the best that has recently come from the Essanay studios.... Francis X. Bushman has the male lead and does splendid work...."

A Splendid Dishonor

Release Date: September 19, 1914. Essanay Film Manufacturing Company. Two reels. Cast: Francis X. Bushman (Frank Sergeant), E.H. Calvert (Attorney Van Epworth), John H. Cossar (Detective Havers), Thomas Commerford (Brewster), Charles Hitchcock (Kerns), Lester Cuneo (Dr. Appledane), Ruth Stonehouse (Julia), Bryant Washburn (Hugh Annersley).

A physician informs his patient, Sergeant (Bushman), that he only has a short time to live. Unknown to the authorities, the patient exchanges places with a young man sentenced to die for his crimes. The patient then learns the doctor's fatal diagnosis was in error.

In the Glare of the Lights

Release Date: October 10, 1914. Essanay Film Manufacturing Company. Three reels. Director: E.H. Calvert. Cast: Beverly Bayne (Martha Stedman), Francis X. Bushman (Glen Duval), Lester Cuneo (Joe Brandigan), Lillian Drew (Wanda Dawson). Adapted from a story in *The Ladies' World*. Bushman again used the character name Duval from his wife's side of the family.

Steel mill worker Glen Duval (Bushman) aspires to be an actor. He finds Wanda Dawson (Drew), a leading lady in a traveling opera troupe, alongside the railroad embankment where she has been accidentally stranded. In gratitude for rescuing her, Wanda gets Glen an engagement with her manager. Over time he rises to star status. He has fallen in love with Wanda but she is in love with another leading man. Heartbroken, Glen returns home to resume work in the steel mill. Foreman Joe Brandigan (Cuneo) despises Glen because his wife Martha Brandigan (Bayne) once had a crush on Glen. Brandigan pushes Glen hard until he will take no more. The two men face off in front of a blazing blast furnace and Glen is about to throw his opponent into the molten steel when the foreman's young son appears. He gently lays down the body of the foreman and sees Wanda, who has followed him back to the steel town, realizing she loves him.

Essanay made up joint ads for *In the Glare of the Lights* and *The Plum Tree* featuring Bushman. "The man who was voted the world's most popular photoplayer is at his best in these two tremendous dramas, the first of Essanay's prize mystery dramas...."

According to the October 10, 1914, *Motography* review, "Powerful acting, spectacular settings, splendid tinting and photography of the deluxe sort, all tend to make [this] three-reel production a most welcome offering...."

The Other Man

Release Date: October 10, 1914. Essanay Film Manufacturing Company. Two reels. Screenplay: Maibelle Heikes Justice. Cast: Francis X. Bushman (Harry Ross), Thomas Commerford (Bleeker, the Butler), John Cossar, Lester Cuneo, Lillian Drew (Mildred Braddon). Reissued in 1916.

A love triangle with an unusual twist. Harry Ross (Bushman) runs into his former wife, Mildred Braddon (Drew), who finds her love for him rekindled. He asks her to leave with him and she consents. Before she can leave, Bleeker the butler (Commerford) stands in her way with her daughter and beseeches her not to ruin her child's life by this action. She agrees and sends Bleeker to Ross with a letter and locket in remembrance.

The Moving Picture World's review found the film "fairly interesting, with an ending of anguish, that leaves in the mind of the spectator a feeling of pity for human weaknesses."

The Private Officer

Release Date: October 17, 1914. Essanay Film Manufacturing Company. Two reels. Cast: Beverly Bayne (Muriel March), Francis X. Bushman (Harry Lampton and Lt. Frothingham), Thomas Commerford (Col. Porter), Lester Cuneo (Capt. Osborne). Bushman plays another dual role. *The Private Officer* was reissued in 1916. Part of the filming took place at Ft. Sheridan and Bushman was cheered when he arrived at the fort for the initial showing of the film. The football game scene was shot at Northwestern University.

Bushman performs double duty in the roles of two men, Harry Lampton and Lt. Frothingham, who compete for the hand of Muriel March (Bayne).

The Moving Picture World called Bushman's acting "in every way worthy, and Miss Beverly Bayne as Muriel, the rich and beautiful heiress, is both fascinating and effective." An October 17, 1914, review in *Motography* commented, "It is always difficult for an actor to distinctly characterize two roles, but in this production Mr. Bushman has turned the trick admirably and, through his poise and manner of registering emotions, he stamps both Harry Lampton and Lt. Frothingham with personalities which do not in any way conflict with each other...."

An Unplanned Elopement

Release Date: October 24, 1914. Essanay Film Manufacturing Company. Director: E.H. Calvert. Screenplay: H. Tipton Steck. Cast: Francis X. Bushman (Frank Melbourne), E.H. Calvert, Ruth Stonehouse (Dorothy).

Frank Melbourne (Bushman) and his girlfriend Dorothy (Stonehouse) quarrel and separate. Melbourne accidentally injures his friend Courtland in a wrestling match. The newspapers mistakenly report that Courtland was killed. Frank's girlfriend, Amy, refuses to have anything more to do with him. He decides to go to Europe and Dorothy goes to the docks to see him off. She lingers too long on the boat and embarks on an unexpected voyage. Frank proposes and she accepts. When they return to America as husband and wife, they are greeted by Courtland.

The Prince Party

Release Date: November 7, 1914. Essanay Film Manufacturing Company. Two reels. Cast: Beverly Bayne (Betty Ogilvie), Francis X. Bushman (Prince Francis of Fournia), Lester Cuneo (James Atteridge), Helen Dunbar (Mrs. Ogilvie), Harry Dunkinson (Mr. Ogilvie). The November 21, 1914, *Essanay News* reported that during filming, Bushman tossed Lester Cuneo over a cliff and Cuneo found the experience a bit too real for comfort.

Prince Francis of Fournia (Bushman) masquerades as a vagabond in order to gain the love of a beautiful heiress, Betty Ogilvie (Bayne).

Scars of Possession

Release Date: November 21, 1914. Essanay Film Manufacturing Company. Two reels. Cast: Beverly Bayne (Louise Cartwright), Francis X. Bushman (Payne Forsythe), John Cossar (Dr. Gordon), Harry Dunkinson (Dr. Graham), Bryant Washburn (J. Dukes Cartwright). During the filming, Bushman received a jab from a surgeon's knife as reported the November 27, 1914, *Essanay News*. The screenplay was taken from a story appearing in *Munsey Magazine*.

The Forsythe fortune has evaporated. Young Payne Forsythe (Bushman) donates blood to save the life of a young woman. He does not know that the life he saved was that of Louise Cartwright (Bayne), a wealthy heiress. Payne accepts a position at a stock exchange firm and over two years' time accumulates a small fortune. Through business contacts, he meets J. Dukes Cartwright and subsequently falls in love with J. Dukes' sister Louise. However, she does not return his affections. Payne corners Louise and inquires why she cannot love him. She responds by showing her scars and stating that she belongs to an unknown young man who saved her life with his blood donation. The film ends with J. Dukes walking in on his friend and sister kissing.

The Motion Picture News remarked, "The part of Payne gives Francis X. Bushman a chance to display a lot of his ability, and Beverly Bayne will make a decided and perfectly deserved hit as Louise...." *The Moving Picture World* review called *Scars of Possession* an "original and touching love story.... The acting is delightful. All the details in this production deserve mention...."

Motography commented, "Splendid and lavish stage settings, odd lighting effects and capable acting by all the members of the cast, make ... *Scars of Possession* a decidedly worthwhile feature offering."

Every Inch a King

Release Date: December 5, 1914. Essanay Film Manufacturing Company. Two reels. Cast: Beverly Bayne (Elba Allen), Francis X. Bushman (King Liporie of Vidonia), Lester Cuneo (King Livian), Lillian Drew, Helen Dunbar, Bryant Washburn (Kevin, Court Spy)

During the filming of *Every Inch a King* in the woods near Niles Center, Illinois, Beverly Bayne was bitten by a copperhead snake. Fortunately, she was wearing riding boots and the snake's fangs did not penetrate all the way through the boot leather. *Motography* reported that Bushman and E.H. Calvert came to her rescue by killing the snake.

King Livian (Cuneo) plots to crush the neighboring kingdom of Vidonia headed by King Liporie (Bushman). He proposes a marriage between his daughter Princess Irmingarde and King Liporie. Although King Liporie loves American Elba Allen (Bayne), he agrees to the proposal in order to save his kingdom. After the marriage, Queen Irmingarde plots to overthrow her royal husband with Court Spy Kevin. King Liporie intercepts a note and divorces the Queen. In retaliation, Irmingarde sends Elba Allen a poisoned note which overcomes her with fumes. Irmingarde then has Elba locked in a dungeon. Elba is rescued and King Liporie goes off to battle King Livian's forces. King Liporie's army is losing the battle when the U.S. Marines come to the rescue, summoned by an American newspaper friend of Elba's. Elba marries King Liporie and becomes Queen of Vidonia.

The Moving Picture World review found Bushman "very impressive as the king.... This is a finely acted, well photographed, and pleasing production."

The Fable of the Bush League Lover Who Failed to Qualify

Release Date: December 5, 1914. Essanay Film Manufacturing Company. Director and Screenplay: George Ade. Cast: Beverly Bayne (Lucy Livingston), Wallace Beery (Homer Splivens), Rapley Holmes (Lucy's Father), Francis X. Bushman. Bushman makes a cameo appearance as a matinee idol.

Homer Splivens (Beery) copies the actions of Bushman in order to woo Lucy Livingston (Bayne) in this George Ade comedy.

The Battle of Love

Release Date: December 12, 1914. Essanay Film Manufacturing Company. Three reels. Released by General Film Company. Cast: Francis X. Bushman (Arthur Chandler), Thomas Commerford (Ezra Chandler), Lillian Drew (Vivian LaMar), Helen Dunbar (Mrs. Wells), Harry Dunkinson (Jack Sanford), Rapley Holmes (John Wells), Ruth Stonehouse (Bessie Wells), Leo White (Kirby).

Adapted from a *Ladies' World* story by Mrs. Wilson Wilson, this was one of four mystery plays made in conjunction with that magazine; the others were *The Tell-Tale Hand* with Broncho Billy Anderson, *In the Glare of the Lights* with Bayne and Bushman and *The Plum Tree* with Bushman.

An intricate series of exposures were used in this film as reported in the December 19, 1914, *The Motion Picture News*. Bushman sat in his office on one side of the screen while Ruth Stonehouse was seen at the other end of the phone at another location on the opposite side of the screen. The center of the picture showed a street with telephone wires running across it. The wires sent letters across the screen, spelling out a message.

In this comedy, Ezra Chandler (Commerford) and John Wells (Holmes) belong to a gentlemen's club. They plan the wedding of Ezra's son Arthur (Bushman) to John's daughter Bessie (Stonehouse), only to have it go awry when a showgirl, Vivian LaMar (Drew), showers affection on the young man. A plot is hatched to fake the murder of the showgirl with evidence pointing to the young man. The youth and his girlfriend flee to her father's yacht only to discover it was all a ruse. All ends happily with the young couple wed.

The December 19, 1914, *Motography* said, "The splendid acting of Francis X. Bushman and Ruth Stonehouse, and the delicious comedy touches which appear at every crisis, are the chief requisites ... of a most enjoyable subject...."

Any Woman's Choice

Release Date: December 19, 1914. Essanay Film Manufacturing Company. Two reels. Cast: Beverly Bayne (The Woman), Francis X. Bushman (The Mutual Friend), Helen Dunbar (The Other Woman), Bryant Washburn (The Man). Adapted from a story featured in *Munsey Magazine*.

The Mutual Friend (Bushman) had expressed a strong interest in the Woman (Bayne) before she married the Man (Washburn). The plot takes a twist when the Mutual Friend takes up residence in the home of his newly married friends. The plot is further complicated when he spends a large part of his time with the Other Woman (Dunbar).

James S. McQuade's *The Moving Picture World* review predicted instant approval and much praise from intelligent patrons of moving picture. "Miss Bayne is seen to fine advantage in the strong part of the Woman. The varying moods of this delightfully good and much-tried gentlewoman are expressed with refined art."

The Shanty at Trembling Hill

Release Date: December 26, 1914. Essanay Film Manufacturing Company. Two reels. Cast: Leona Anderson (Frances Warfield), Milton Bromley, Francis X. Bushman (Richard Scott), Lester Cuneo, Thomas Commerford (Father Lefevre), Nellie R. Craig (Gabrielle Boileau). Both Craig and Anderson made their Essanay debuts in this film.

Richard Scott (Bushman), a promising young Canadian politician, seeks outdoor life in the Northwest due to ill health. Before he leaves, he breaks his engagement to socialite Francis Warfield (Anderson). In the north woods, he meets a beautiful but unworldly young woman, Gabrielle Boileau (Craig). A series of complications arise before they are happily married.

Essanay advertised *The Shanty at Trembling Hill* as "a thrilling drama of love and strife in the north woods." *Motography* found that Bushman "has an ideal role and appears to splendid advantage...."

1915

The Gallantry of Jimmie Rodgers

Release Date: January 5, 1915. Essanay Film Manufacturing Company. Cast: Francis X. Bushman (Jimmy Rodgers), Lester Cuneo (Ralph Morrison), Lillian Drew (Sara Sanderson), Addison Madeiro, Jr. (Dick Greenbrough), Bryant Washburn (Gerald Livingston). Screenplay adapted from a story appearing in *Smart Set Magazine*.

Jimmie Rodgers (Bushman) is the victim of a joke. Sara Sanderson (Drew) confides to him that Ralph Morrison (Cuneo) possesses some indiscreet letters she wrote. Rodgers enlists Gerald Livingston (Washburn) to retrieve the letters from Morrison's room. They are caught and accused of theft in front of their friends. Rodgers confesses to shield Sara from embarrassment. Everybody breaks up laughing because the episode has been a ruse set up by Livingston and the rest.

The Moving Picture World called *The Gallantry of Jimmie Rodgers* a "fine little comedy ... well made and acted."

The Ambition of the Baron

Release Date: January 23, 1915. Essanay Film Manufacturing Company. Two reels. Cast: Beverly Bayne (Annetta), Francis X. Bushman (Count Jean De Lugnan), Thomas Commerford, Lester Cuneo. Screenplay adapted from a story appearing in *Smart Set Magazine*. Gloria Swanson played a pit part in this film.

Baron von Tollen plans to take over adjoining Leutala by installing his pawn, Count Jean de Lugnan (Bushman), as its king. To entice the Count into the plot, the Baron uses his daughter Annetta (Bayne). She pretends to be in distress and the Count "rescues" her, returning her "safely" to the Baron's castle. The Count falls in love with Annetta and asks for her hand. The Baron consents on condition that the Count join the revolution and assume kingship of Leutala after the plot succeeds. Capt. Tanner, in charge of the military operations to conquer Leutala, also asks for Annetta's hand. When refused, Tanner exposes the plot to Leutala authorities, who repay his action by executing him as a revolutionary. The Baron and his cohorts escape. Annetta confesses that she is in love with the Count.

Thirteen Down

Release Date: February 6, 1915. Essanay Film Manufacturing Company. Two reels. Director Lester Totten. Screenplay: Victor Eubank. Cast: Beverly Bayne (Jeanne Lamarde), Francis X. Bushman (Arnold Austin),

Thomas Commerford (Dr. Lamarde), John Cossar (Robyns, the Butler), Lester Cuneo (Baron Schoman), Harry Dunkinson (James Gordan), Addison Madeiro, Jr. (Baron's Secretary), Bryant Washburn (Robert Orson).

Foreign spies attempt to steal Dr. Lamarde's (Commerford) innovative gun design created for the U.S. Government. Dr. Lamarde picks out the thirteenth man in a bread line, presenting the vagabond with an opportunity to make something of himself by giving him a job as his secretary. The vagabond turns out to be secret agent Arnold Austin (Bushman), who foils the plot to steal the gun design and apprehends Baron Schoman (Cuneo) and his secretary (Madeiro). Dr. Lamarde's daughter Jeanne (Bayne) falls in love with Austin.

The Moving Picture World called Beverly Bayne "the only lady of prominence in the pictures."

The Accounting

Release Date: February 12, 1915. Essanay Film Manufacturing Company. Distributed by the General Film Company. Three reels. Screenplay: H. Tipton Steck. Cast: Beverly Bayne (Olga Petroff), Francis X. Bushman (Gordon Bannock), Lester Cuneo (Sargall). Adapted from a story presented in conjunction with *The Ladies' World*.

Olga Petroff (Bayne), the cleverest spy in Petrograd, strives to recover documents relating to a European alliance from Secret Service agent Gordon Bannock (Bushman). Olga gets Bannock to fall in love with her and they marry. She steals away with the papers to take them to Sargall (Cuneo) only to discover Bannock had replaced them with blank documents. Bannock realizes he still loves Olga, retrieves her from Sargall's clutches and returns with her to America.

Essanay advertised *The Accounting* as "a thrilling drama of love and international politics." Reviewer T.S. Mead of *The Motion Picture News* found great favor with the production: "It is a completely satisfying and realistic picturization of an intensely interesting story dealing with love and international intrigue. Surprise after surprise occurs throughout the three reels, that will keep the audience in suspense to the very end.... Mr. Bushman's impersonation of the secret service operator is excellent throughout.... Miss Bayne's emotional acting is of a fine quality, not in the least overdone, and she is most convincing as the irresistible enchantress—spy...."

Stars and Their Courses Change

Release Date: February 20, 1915. Essanay Film Manufacturing Company. Three reels. Screenplay: Edward T. Lowe, Jr. Cast: Francis X. Bushman (Robert Cameron), Edna Mayo (Olivia Staunton), Bryant Washburn.

Young Robert Cameron (Bushman), author of the successful book *The Lip You Press* accepts a challenge from Olivia Staunton (Edna Mayo) that he won't be able to conquer her but she will make him fall in love with her within three weeks. After a week, he proposes but she only laughs it off. He kisses her and warns that the memory of that kiss will bring her to him. His prophecy comes true but this time he is indifferent to her. Olivia announces her engagement to another. Cameron realizes he really does love Olivia and leaves for a cabin in the woods to forget her. She follows and, after many hardships, is reunited with Robert.

The Moving Picture World predicted, "Admirers of Mr. Bushman will find it a highly satisfactory picture presenting their hero in a favorable light...." *Variety* commented, "The story has some novel twists and the cast does very well."

The Great Silence

>Release Date: March 20, 1915. Essanay Film Manufacturing Company. Three reels. Adapted from a novel by H. Tipton Steck. Cast: Beverly Bayne (Loyal Channing), Chester Beery, Francis X. Bushman (John Landon), Frank Dayton (Nicholas Channing), Bryant Washburn (Arthur Channing). Released in conjunction with *The Ladies' World* as a prize mystery drama.

In an Alaska gold mining camp, John Landon (Bushman), president of the Nugget Gold Mine Corporation, marries Loyal Channing (Bayne), whose father sells Loyal's wedding gift (Nugget Gold Mine stock) from Landon. Confronted with the evidence, Nicholas Channing (Dayton) dies from a heart attack. Loyal blames John for her father's death. They reconcile after she learns the whole truth.

The Return of Richard Neal

>Release Date: April 10, 1915. Essanay Film Manufacturing Company. Three reels. Screenplay. Edward T. Lowe, Jr. Cast: Francis X. Bushman (Richard Neal), Nellie Craig (Doris Blake), Ernst Maupain (Count Nikola), Bryant Washburn (Gideon Hall).

A good hypnotist, Richard Neal (Bushman), attempts to break the hypnotic spell the evil, Count Nikola (Maupain) has cast over, Doris Blake (Craig) in order to get her to deliver a rare painting from her father's art gallery. Neal awakens Doris from the trance and exposes Count Nikola.

T.S. Mead's review commented, "The portrayal by Francis X. Bushman of the character of Richard Neal, a psychological specialist possessing hypnotic powers ... brings out some remarkable acting. The high standard he sets is, however, lived up to throughout the rest of the cast...."

The Moving Picture World found the picture "a high-class production throughout.... Nellie Craig is excellent as the hypnotist's victim...."

Thirty

Release Date: May 1, 1915. Essanay Film Manufacturing Company. Two reels. Screenplay: Victor Eubank. Cast: Beverly Bayne (Ellen March), Francis X. Bushman (Dick Thompson), Helen Dunbar (Mrs. March), Harry Dunkinson (Tubby).

Millionairess Ellen March (Bayne) detests the press. Reporter Dick Thompson (Bushman) of the *Clarion* is assigned to check out the rumor of her engagement to Count Dangloff. Thompson is caught sneaking into Miss March's estate and is told he will be jailed if he does not keep her name out of the newspapers. Smitten with Miss March, he agrees. He distracts the press from Miss March by concocting a story about anarchists and another millionaire. Ironically, real anarchists are discovered and apprehended as a result. Miss March not only marries Thompson, she is revealed as the owner of the *Clarion*. She makes her new husband the managing editor.

The Moving Picture World credited Bushman with "the requisite amount of dash, nerve and physical perfection demanded of the hero, and Beverly Bayne looks and acts every penny of the several millions she is supposed to possess."

An Essanay ad for *Thirty* described the film as "a newspaper story with a real newspaper atmosphere. BUSHMAN is your guarantee of a good story." Admission for the showing was ten cents for all seats, ten cents for a lady and one child, and five cents for an unaccompanied child.

Graustark

Release Date: May 8, 1915. Essanay Film Manufacturing Company. Six reels. Director: Fred E. Wright. Screenplay: H. Tipton Steck. Adapted from the novel *Graustark: A Story of Love Behind a Throne* by George Barr McCutcheon. Cast: Beverly Bayne (Princess Yestive), Francis X. Bushman (Grenfall Lorry), Thomas Commerford (Uncle Caspar), Lester Cuneo (Prince Gabriel), Helen Dunbar (Aunt Yvonne), Ernest Maupain (Prince Bolrez), Endo Mayo (Countess Dagmar), Albert Roscoe (Harry Anguish), Bryant Washburn (Prince Lorenz). A number of scenes were shot in New York City and Washington, D.C. *Graustark* was the first Essanay film to be released through the newly formed distribution network of V.L.S.E. (Vitagraph, Lubin, Selig & Essanay).

Grenfall Lorry (Bushman) encounters Princess Yestive (Bayne) traveling incognito on a train in the United States. He falls in love and follows her back to Graustark. Her kingdom is threatened and she is faced with marrying Prince Lorenz of Asphain (Washburn) in order to spare her country. In the end, Lorry weds the princess and receives Graustark's crown.

The *Essanay News* proclaimed *Graustark* "the most powerful and thrilling love romance ever screened. It holds the spectator tense with its gripping interest."

Reviewer Neil G. Caward of *Motography* agreed: "By long odds it is the best release ever made by the Essanay Film Manufacturing Company...."

The Motion Picture News review by Peter Milne found Bushman "just the type for the part—dashing, handsome and looking very much the hero.... No role is better suited to the personality of Bushman."

The Slim Princess

>Release Date: May 29, 1915. Essanay Film Manufacturing Company. Four reels. Director: E.H. Calvert. Screenplay: Edward T. Lowe from a story by George Ade. Cast: Wallace Beery (Popova), Terza Bey (Princess Jeneka), Francis X. Bushman (Alexander H. Pike), Lester Cuneo (The Only Koldo), Harry Dunkinson (Count Selim Malagaski), Ruth Stonehouse (Princess Kalora), Bryant Washburn (Rawley Plumston).

The comedy takes place in Morovenia, Turkey, where fat women are considered beautiful. Princess Kalora (Stonehouse) is slim and is therefore considered undesirable as a mate. Efforts to make her attractive to eligible Morovenians by stuffing pillows in her clothing are all in vain.

American businessman Alexander Pike (Bushman), visiting Morovenia, falls in love with Princess Kalora, but his suit is rejected by her father, Count Selim Malagaski (Dunkinson). Disappointed, Pike returns to America.

Later, Count Malagaski sees an ad for a clinic in America that boasts it can make thin persons fat. He sends his daughter to America to try the cure. Of course, she again meets millionaire Pike, and their courtship resumes. But when the miracle cure fails to put pounds on the princess, the Count orders her to return to Morovenia. Pike follows and introduces himself to the Count as the Grand Exalted Ruler of a fraternal order, a Knight Templar and King of the Hoo Hoos. Duly impressed with the lofty titles, County Malagaski grants Pike his daughter's hand.

The *Essanay News* promoted *The Slim Princess* as "one of the most delightful and pleasing comedy-dramas ever presented. Its humor is irresistible. Thousands are laughing with George Ade." According to Neil G. Caward's *Motography* review, "probably in all the realms of fiction there is no more gently humorous and refreshingly satirical comedy than George Ade's *The Slim Princess*.... Ruth Stonehouse is the outrageously impossible Princess Kalora ... it is Wallace Beery, however, to whom the great majority of the laughs fall...."

Variety also favored Beery's portrayal ("Beery, in a character part, did exceptionally well....") but took a stern view of Bushman's work: "Bushman gives a capable performance, but his persistency in monopolizing the spotlight was ever noticeable. Miss Stonehouse, as the slim princess, was up to expectations, but handicapped by Bushman's ambitiousness, her role being of secondary importance."

Providence and Mrs. Urmy

>Release Date: June 26, 1915. Essanay Film Manufacturing Company. Three reels. Beverly Bayne (Jeanette), Francis X. Bushman (Barton the

Chauffeur and Lord Chilminster), Louise Crolius, Helen Dunbar. This is the last picture Bayne and Bushman made together at Essanay.

A young American woman, Jeanette (Bayne), unknowingly marries an English nobleman when she proposes to her chauffeur (Bushman) in an attempt to get out of marrying Lord Chilminster (Bushman), whom her mother wants her to marry.

The Second in Command

Release Date: July 26, 1915. Quality Pictures Corporation. Distributed by Metro Pictures Corporation. Director: William J. Bowman. Screenplay: Eve Unsell. Based on the play *The Second in Command* by Robert Marshall. Camera: William F. Alder. Cast: Francis X. Bushman (Lt. Col. Miles Anstruther), Paul Byron (Hon. Bertie Carstairs), William Clifford (Major Christopher Bingham), Lester Cuneo (Lt. Sir Walter Mannering), Helen Dunbar (Lady Sarah Harbaugh), Evelyn Greeley (Lady Harburgh's Maid), Marcia Moore (Nora Vining), Marguerite Snow (Muriel Mannering).

The Second in Command is notable for some of the most extensive and sustained use of the mobile camera in the pre–1920s era. This film represented the beginning of the Quality/Metro relationship.

The story takes place during the Boer War with two fellow officers, Lt. Col. Miles Anstruther (Bushman) and Major Christopher Bingham (Clifford), in love with the same woman, Muriel Mannering (Marguerite Snow). Muriel refuses Bingham's marriage proposal but he tricks Anstruther into believing that she loves Bingham. Anstruther then writes her a letter releasing her from their engagement. She refuses Bingham's marriage proposal a second time. Both officers distinguish themselves with honor on the battlefield and Bingham admits his deceit. They return to England and Anstruther marries Muriel.

The July 31, 1915, *Moving Picture World* featured *The Second in Command* on its cover. *Variety* said, "Bushman's worth as a picture player is known, and from his first feature production he will score as easily in the long reelers as he has in the shorter, if given opportunities, with proper scenarios."

The Silent Voice

Release Date: September 25, 1915. Quality Pictures Corporation. Distributed by Metro Pictures Corporation. Six reels. Director: William Bowman and Fred Balshofer. Screenplay: William Bowman. Adapted from a play by Jules Eckert Goodman. Camera: William F. Adler. Cast: Frank Bacon (Spring), Francis X. Bushman (Franklyn Starr), William Clifford (Marjorie's Father), Lester Cuneo (Bobbie Delorme), Ann Drew (Mildred Hallan), Helen Dunbar (Starr's Mother), Miss C. Henry (Heloise Delorme), Marguerite Snow (Marjorie Blair).

After losing his hearing and his mother, violinist Franklyn Starr (Bushman) becomes despondent. He moves to the mountains where he is rescued by Marjorie Blair (Snow) from a landslide caused by a dynamite explosion. Starr and Blair fall in love and marry. Later, Starr's relative Bobbie Delorme (Cuneo) arrives and embraces Marjorie. Starr believes that his wife has been unfaithful. The misunderstanding is eventually cleared up and the couple reunited.

Variety reported that Bushman appeared in person at a private showing, discussing the film and answering questions. "His remarks were nicely worded.... Mr. Bushman said the picture was full of philosophy and other things, and though he didn't specifically mention the fact, it is fuller of Bushman than anything else. In this it may suffice, for a company owning a picture star of the Bushman magnitude can get away with one of these thin features once in a while, that is, where the star is over-exploited by continual presence before the camera."

In a hint of the future, *Variety* wondered if the women who adored him wanted to see him afflicted or married.

Harvey F. Thew's *The Motion Picture News* review called Bushman "the Matinee Idol of the films. Wide awake exhibitors do not have to be reminded of this.... His name is a great asset in any theater lobby: a conservative estimate is that there are 840,000 of the 'hometown girls' between Tenth Avenue in New York and Oakland, California, sighing over Mr. Bushman, and where the hometown girls go, the whole town goes...."

Pennington's Choice

Release Date: November 8, 1915. Quality Pictures Corporation. Distributed by Metro Pictures Corporation. Five reels. Producer: William J. Bowman. Director: O.A.C. Lund. Screenplay: John C. Culley. Camera: Don Short. Cast: Beverly Bayne (Eugenia Blondeau and Maria Blondeau), Francis X. Bushman (Robert Pennington), Lester Cuneo (Jean), Morris Cytron (Pierre), Helen Dunbar (Mrs. Allison), William Farris (Roland Blondeau), J.J. Jeffries [former heavyweight champion of the world] (Himself), H. O'Dell (Louis Blondeau), Wellington Playter (Jules Blondeau). Bushman purchased the story *Pennington's Choice* for $150 and set to work on the project immediately. He considered this film one of his greatest successes.

A light-hearted comedy set mainly in the Canadian Northwest. This time Beverly Bayne plays the dual roles, Eugenia Blondeau and her imaginary sister Maria. New Yorker Robert Pennington (Bushman), meets and falls in love with Eugenia. Before she accepts his offer of marriage, he must gain the approval of her backwoods family in the Canadian Northwest. Events take a comic turn when Pennington arrives in Canada only to meet Maria Blondeau (Eugenia pretending to be her own sister), who makes a play for Pennington. He resists the charm of the imagined sister. Eugenia's brothers Louis (O'Dell) and Roland (Farris) pose as local lumberjacks and give Pennington a thrashing. In retaliation, he searches out J.J. Jeffries, who is training nearby, learns the art of boxing and returns to teach the local yokels a lesson. Pennington's actions earn the respect of Eugenia's father Jules (Playter), and Pennington wins the hand of Eugenia. The film ends with Eugenia laying her head on Pennington's broad chest and whispering softly,

"Men of High North, fierce mountains love you; Proud rivers leap when you ride on their breast. See, the austere sky, pensive above you, Dons all her jewels to smile on your rest."

Metro Pictures Corporation and Quality Pictures Corporation heavily advertised *Pennington's Choice* with full-page and dual-page ads in the movie picture industry trade magazines. *Motion Picture Magazine* ran a 12-page synopsis of the production.

Variety's review summed up *Pennington's Choice* as "a good feature for any house—with class enough for the best, and not above the heads of the cheapest.... Mr. Bushman is an ideal type for the hero and Miss Bayne is equally competent."

The Man Without a Conscience

Release Date: Unknown. Mentioned in the December 25, 1915, *Motography*. No other information found. It could have been released under the title *A Man and His Soul* in 1916.

Pigeon Island

Release Date: Unknown. Mentioned in the October 30, 1915, *Moving Picture World*. No other information found.

Richard Carvell

Release Date: Unknown. Quality Pictures Corporation. Screenplay: I.K. Freeman and Eve Unsell. Based on the novel by Winston Churchill. Cast: Beverly Bayne, Francis X. Bushman. This film may never have been completed or released. It was mentioned in a *Motography* article in September 1915. The December 1915 *Photoplay* called *Richard Carvell* "an early Metro intention ... with Mr. Bushman in the title part. A more ideal selection for this role cannot be imagined. Miss Bayne will probably play the charming daughter of Marmaduke Manners."

To the End of the World

Release Date: Unknown. A photo of Bushman with the caption listing the film as *To the End of the World* was located. No other information was found.

The Yellow Dove

Release Date: Unknown. Mentioned in the October 16, 1915, *The Motion Picture News*. No other information found.

1916

Man and His Soul

Release Date: January 31, 1916. Quality Pictures Corporation. Distributed by Metro Pictures Corporation. Five reels. Director: John W. Noble. Camera: H.O. Carleton. Cast: Beverly Bayne (Mary Knowles), Edward Brennan (Rev. Edward Knowles), Francis X. Bushman (John Conscience/John Power), John Davidson (Stephen Might, Jr.), Helen Dunbar (Mrs. Conscience), Etta Mansfield, Charles H. Prince (Stephen Might, Sr.), Fred Sittenham, Grace Valentine (Eve).

John Conscience (Bushman) discovers that his girlfriend Mary Knowles (Bayne) plans to marry a rich man. He changes his name to John Power and leaves a college faculty position to become a ruthless businessman. Mary does not marry the rich man but instead finds employment in one of Power's factory offices. A fire engulfs the factory and Power saves Mary and regains his conscience.

Variety summed it all up with, "Bushman is there with the heroic thing, also the lovely stuff and they will like him. Miss Bayne may have a following also, since she is co-starred, but it's Bushman all the way.... Bushman and his play will put this feature over." Reviewer Peter Milne of *The Motion Picture News* also gave *Man and His Soul* a thumbs-up. He called the production "a most gratifying and worthwhile subject ... and if that is not enough of a recommendation, the presence of Francis X. Bushman in an ideal role should give it added multiplied weight."

The Wall Between

Release Date: March 27, 1916. Quality Pictures Corporation. Distributed by Metro Pictures Corporation. Five reels. Director: John Winthrop Noble. Screenplay adapted from a novel by Ralph D. Paine. Camera: H.O. Carleton. Cast: Beverly Bayne (Edith Ferris), Edward Brennan (Capt. Gildersleeve), Thomas Brooks (Mr. Barclay), Francis X. Bushman (Sgt. John Kendall), Robert Cummings (Col. Dickinson), Sidney Cushing (David Barclay), John Davidson (Lt. Burkett), Helen Dunbar (Mrs. Ferris), Alice Gordon (Mrs. Barclay), Charles Prince (Capt. Ramsey).

A real life skirmish along the Mexican–United States border provides good background for *The Wall Between*. Director John W. Noble served as an officer in the army and provided a good deal of realistic battle scenes.

Kendall (Bushman) joins the army after his father loses his fortune and dies. He rises to the rank of sergeant and falls in love with Edith Ferris (Bayne), the niece of Col. Dickinson (Cummings). However, Kendall falls out of favor with Lt. Burkett (Davidson), who disapproves of Kendall's relationship with Edith. Their regiment is ordered to Central America to quell an uprising. Burkett proves to be a coward and Sgt. Kendall becomes a hero. Upon his return to the States, Kendall is promoted to lieutenant and resumes his courtship of Edith.

The Motion Picture News reviewer Oscar Cooper commented, "*The Wall Between* provides Francis X. Bushman with one of those typical hero roles in which he shines.... This picture will serve to enhance Mr. Bushman's popularity.... Due opportunity is afforded Beverly Bayne to display her charms...."

A Million a Minute

Release Date: May 8, 1916. Quality Pictures Corporation. Distributed by Metro Pictures Corporation. Five reels. Director: John W. Noble. Screenplay: Howard Irving Young. Based on the novel *A Million a Minute: A Romance of Modern New York and Paris* by Robert Aiken. Cast: William Bailey (Mark Seager), Beverly Bayne (Dagmar Lorraine), Carl Brickert (Stephen Quaintance, Sr.), Francis X. Bushman (Stephen Quaintance, Jr./A. Nedman), Robert Cummings (Timothy O'Farrell), John Davidson (Duke de Reves), Helen Dunbar (Fanchette), Mary Moore (Ellen Sheridan/Mrs. Quaintance, Sr.), Charles Prince (Jules, the Valet), Mrs. Walker (Mrs. Smith), Jerome Wilson (Miles Quaintance).

Miles Quaintance (Wilson) promises to leave his fortune to Stephen Quaintance, Jr. (Bushman), but only if he marries Dagmar Lorraine (Bayne), a ward of Miles, by midnight on May 31. When Stephen refuses, others less scrupulous pursue Dagmar and the fortune. The plot includes murder and intrigue but in the end Stephen and Dagmar fall in love. Knowing it is nearly midnight on the 31st of May, they wait until June 1 to marry.

A Virginia Romance

Release Date: July 22, 1916. Quality Pictures Corporation. Distributed by Metro Pictures Corporation. Two reels. Director: Charles Belmore. Screenplay: Charles A. Taylor. Cast: Beverly Bayne (Georgia Daniels), Francis X. Bushman (Ralph Everly), Lester Cuneo (Harry Daniels), Helen Dunbar (Mrs. Daniels). In this film, Bushman plays the role of Ralph Everly. His firstborn son's name was Ralph Everly Bushman. Ralph first entered pictures under the name Ralph Bushman and later worked as Francis X. Bushman, Jr. (See Appendix II.)

A football adventure at the University of Virginia. Ralph Everly (Bushman) is in love with Georgia Daniels (Bayne), the sister of his fellow football team member Harry (Cuneo). Harry gets in deep with gambling debts and the mob forces him to agree to throw the upcoming game so they can make a killing. The game is close with Virginia leading 3-0 late in the game. Harry fumbles the ball and the opponents score, winning 7-3. Because of his love for Georgia, Ralph covers for Harry and accepts the blame for throwing the game. Georgia refuses to believe Ralph, but the rest of his class treat him with contempt. After college, Ralph becomes a lawyer and returns to prosecute a case against a man accused of embezzlement. The man turns out to be Harry Daniels, who still associates with gamblers. Ralph proves Harry guilty and he is sentenced to prison. After serving his time, Harry vows revenge. Georgia hears of Harry's plot and warns Ralph. She learns that Ralph took the heat for Harry's throwing the ball game. They resume their "Virginia Romance" and Harry vows to go straight.

Quality Pictures–Metro Pictures placed a full-page color advertisement for *A Virginia Romance* in the July 8, 1916, *The Moving Picture World*. The ad featured a photo of Bushman and Beverly Bayne dressed up in their riding outfits. The ad described *A Virginia Romance* as "a short length feature with the crowned king and queen of pictures ... a summer business boomer...."

In the Diplomatic Service

Release Date: October 16, 1916. Quality Pictures Corporation. Distributed by Metro Pictures Corporation. Five reels. Director: Francis X. Bushman. Screenplay: Francis X. Bushman. Camera: R.J. Berquist. Cast: Beverly Bayne (Beverly Ryerson), Henri Bergman (Dr. Montell), Harry D. Blakemore (Butler), Bella Bruce (Helen Wardlow), Francis X. Bushman (Dick Stansbury), William Davidson (Lynn Hardi), Helen Dunbar (Mrs. Ryerson), Edmond Elton (Major Blaine), Charles Fang (Valet), Mrs. La Roche (Mrs. Blaine), Liza Miller (Mammy). Bushman took the reins on this production, serving as writer, director and actor. Bushman also drives his famous Marmon in this picture.

Dick Stansbury (Bushman) poses as the inventor of a revolutionary new gun in order to capture Dr. Montell (Bergman), the mastermind of a ring of foreign spies stealing secrets from the U.S. government. Stansbury succeeds in capturing the spy leader and wins the hand of Beverly Ryerson (Bayne).

Romeo and Juliet

Release Date: October 19, 1916. Quality Pictures Corporation. Distributed by Metro Pictures Corporation. Eight reels. Director: John Winthrop Noble. Bushman served as one of several assistant directors. Screenplay: John Arthur, Rudolph de Cordova and John W. Noble. Based on the play by William Shakespeare. Camera: R.J. Berquist. Cast: Adele Barker (Nurse to Juliet), Beverly Bayne (Juliet), Edwin Boring (Balthasar), William H. Burton, Francis X. Bushman (Romeo), W. Lawson Butt (Tybalt), Robert Cummings (Friar Laurence), Joseph Dailey (Peter), John Davidson (Paris), Helen Dunbar (Lady Capulet), Edmund Elton (Capulet), Leonard Grover (Old Man), Alexandre Herbert (Friar John), Eric Hudson (Montague), Fritz Leiber (Mercutio), Ethel Mantell (Rosaline), Barry Maxwell, William Morris (Abraham), Genevieve Reynolds (Lady Montague), Olaf Skavlan (Benvolio), Horace Vinton (Escalus, Prince of Verona).

An early version of William Shakespeare's immortal play in which the star-crossed lovers meet their fates. Romeo comes to the tomb, discovering Juliet's motionless body. Assuming that she is dead, he commits suicide by drinking poison. Moments later, Juliet awakens to find her young lover dead and stabs herself to death. Bushman combined his physique and grace to portray Romeo while Beverly Bayne was hailed as the consummate Juliet.

Variety, often critical of Bushman's over-exuberance in films, praised the actor's portrayal of Romeo: "Francis X. Bushman makes a manly Romeo, playing simply. If anything he erred on the side of restraint, a fault that becomes a positive virtue before the camera.... Beverly Bayne's appealing brunette beauty was made to order for Juliet. In repose she realized the picture perfectly. But her admirers would have been satisfied to see in her acting a little more fire and spirit."

The Moving Picture World called the film "a great production, one that will rank with the best kinematographic efforts that have gone before.... To the making of the picture, director John W. Noble has contributed his best work for the screen." The review went on to call Bayne and Bushman the ideal combination for their roles: "Mr. Bushman, above all else, possesses the physique of a 'well-governed youth'.... He appears to unusual advantage in the scanted garb of the period—in the language of Juliet's nurse, 'His leg excels all men's.' He fits the part and he plays it. Miss Bayne is a rare Juliet. Kindly endowed by nature in figure and feature, she has entered the interpretation of the role of the heroine with marked sympathy and feeling."

The Quality Pictures–Metro Pictures production cost over $250,000. It was one of several Shakespearean films released in 1916 to coincide with the 300th anniversary of the playwright's death.

Boots and Saddles

Release Date: Unknown. Mentioned in the February 12, 1916, *Motion Picture News*. No other information found.

The Bribe

Release Date: Unknown. This production started to be advertised by Quality Pictures–Metro Pictures in early 1916 just as ads for *The Red Mouse* disappeared from listings of upcoming features. See *The Red Mouse*, also 1916.

The Red Mouse

Release Date: Unknown. Quality Pictures Corporation. Distributed by Metro Pictures Corporation. Five reels. Director: John W. Noble. Camera: H.O. Carleton. Cast: Beverly Bayne, Edward Brennan, Francis X. Bushman, J.W. Davidson, Etta Mansfield, Fred Sittenham. This film probably never went into production despite advance promotion in early 1916. A film titled *The Half Million Bribe* was released by Metro and based on the novel *The Red Mouse: A Mystery Romance* by William Howard Osborne. This film starred Hamilton Revelle and Marguerite Snow. At the same time that *The Red Mouse* disappeared from Quality Pictures–Metro Pictures advertisements, *The Bribe* showed up in the upcoming releases listings. However, that film also failed to materialize.

1917

The Great Secret

Release Dates: January 8, 1917 through May 7, 1917. Serial Producing Company for Metro Pictures Corporation. Distributed by Metro Pictures Corporation. Eighteen episodes. Two reels each except for episode one, which is three reels. Screenplay and Director: William Christy Cabanne. Story: Fred De Gressac. Camera: William Fildew. Cast: Sue Balfour, Beverly Bayne (Beverly), Thomas Blake, Belle Bruce, Matilda Brundage, Francis X. Bushman (William Strong), W.J. Butler, William Calhoun, Robert Carson, Marie de Chett, Edward Connelly, Helen Dunbar, Charles Fang, Dorothy Haydel, Ed Lawrence, John Leach, Arthur Ortega, Charles Ripley, Fred Roberts, Fred Stanton, Lillian Sullivan, Ivy Ward, Carl von Winther, Tammany Young. This serial represented Louis B. Mayer's first foray into motion picture production.

The 18-episode serial centers around the fortune inherited by a beautiful girl, Beverly (Bayne), and the efforts of a gang of villains, headed by the Great Master and Dr. Zulph, determined to steal it. A wealthy young athlete, William Strong (Bushman), comes to her aid.

Episodes:
1. Whirlpool of Destiny (1/8/17)
    The Secret Seven gang headed by the Great Master plots to get the money that dying gang member Thomas Clarke, has bequeathed to his niece Beverly. She is kidnapped but rescued by William Strong.
2. The Casket of Tainted Treasure (1/15/17)
    The gang pursues Beverly and William. Railroad shacks are blown up and Beverly is rescued from a speeding express train. Clarke entrusts a treasure-laden casket to Beverly and William. Dr. Zulph insists that Clarke change his will but the old man dies before he can sign the papers.
3. The Hidden Hand (1/22/17)
    The gang kidnaps William and steals the box containing the casket. Inside the box, they only find a note written in Chinese. William escapes and sets out to find Beverly.
4. From Sunshine to Shadows (1/29/17)
5. The Trap (2/5/17)
6. The Dragon's Den (2/12/17)
7. The Yellow Claw (2/19/17)
8. A Clue from the Klondike (2/26/17)
9. Cupid's Puzzle (3/5/17)
10. The Woman and the Game (3/12/17)
11. A Shot in the Dark (3/19/17)
12. Caught in the Web (3/26/17)
13. The Struggle (4/2/17)
14. The Escape (4/9/17)
15. The Test of Death (4/16/17)
16. The Crafty Hand (4/23/17)
17. The Missing Finger (4/30/17)
18. The Great Secret (5/7/17)

National Association's All-Star Picture

Release Date: August 1917. Assembled by the National Association of the Motion Picture Industry. Five reels. Comprised of individual scenes taken from a variety of motion pictures and grouped by themes such as love scenes. Cast: May Allison, Beverly Bayne, Carlyle Blackwell, Alice Brady, Francis X. Bushman, Donald Cameron, Charles Chaplin, Ethyl Clayton, Douglas Fairbanks, Franklin Farnum, Ella Hall, Rupert Julian, Harold Lockwood, Mary Miles Minter, Evart Emerson Overton, Olga Petrova, Mary Pickford, Anita Stewart, Edith Storey, Lillian Walker, Henry Walthall, Earle Williams, Clara Kimball Young.

George W. Graves, reviewer for *Motography*, found favor with *National Association's All-Star Picture*: "To the exhibitor looking for something novel and completely different from picture offerings that tread the beaten path, [this] all-star production should have a strong appeal.... The audiences, at least for a while, will be eager to accept the all-star pictures...."

Their Compact

Release Date: September 17, 1917. Metro Pictures Corporation. Distributed by Metro Pictures Corporation. Seven reels. Director: Edwin Carewe. Screenplay: Albert Shelby Levine. Adapted from a story by Charles A. Logue. Camera: R.J. Berquist. Cast: Mildred Adams (Verda Forrest), Beverly Bayne (Mollie Anderson), Francis X. Bushman (James Van Dyke Moore), Robert Chandler ("Pop" Anderson), Thomas Delmar ("Pay Dirt" Thompson), Henry Mortimer (Robert Forrest), Harry S. Northrup ("Ace High" Horton), John Smiley (Peters).

James Van Dyke Moore (Bushman) heads West to take over an inherited mine and flee a relationship turned sour. Town desperado "Ace High" Horton (Northrup), who is stealing ore from the mine, threatens Moore but he stands his ground, much to the admiration of Mollie Anderson (Bayne). The plot gets complicated when Robert Forrest (Mortimer) arrives in town with his bride Verda (Adams), Moore's former lover. "Ace High" makes a play for Verda but Verda tells her husband the culprit is Moore. Forrest discovers "Ace High" leaving with his wife and a shooting ensues. Moore is charged with killing Forrest but Mollie convinces the authorities he is innocent. Released, Moore tracks down "Ace High" and kills him. Verda is brought back to town where the angry townspeople drive her away. Moore proposes to Millie.

Motion Picture Magazine carried a nine-page synopsis of the storyline with numerous scenes from the picture. Edward Weitzel of *The Moving Picture World* called *Their Compact* well-produced: "Bushman is an excellent representative for the character of James Van Dyke Moore and lends it a touch of ever-present 'heroics' intended by the author...."

The Adopted Son

Release Date: October 29, 1917. Metro Pictures Corporation. Distributed by Metro Pictures Corporation. Six reels. Director: Charles J. Brabin. Screenplay: Albert Shelby De Vin. Based on the story by Max Brand. Camera: R.J. Berquist. Cast: Beverly Bayne (Marian Conover), Francis X. Bushman ("Two-Gun" Carter), J.W. Johnston (Henry McLane), Pat O'Malley (George Conover), Gertrude Norman (Mrs. Conover), John Smiley (Luke Conover), Leslie Stowe (Tom McLane).

A long-running mountain feud between the Conovers and McLanes comes to a climax with the killing of George Conover (O'Malley) by Henry McLane (Johnston). "Two-Gun" Carter (Bushman) carries the body of Conover to the family and accepts the grieving family's offer to adopt him. He falls in love with Marian Conover (Bayne), who is subsequently kidnapped by the McLane clan. Carter rescues Marion and works out a truce to end the feud when he discloses he was born a McLane and plans to marry a Conover.

The Voice of Conscience

Release Date: November 14, 1917. Metro Pictures Corporation. Distributed by Metro Pictures Corporation. Five reels. Director: Edwin Carewe. Screenplay: June Mathis. Camera: R.J. Berquist. Cast: Beverly Bayne (Allane Houston), Maggie Breyer (Mrs. Wallace Houston), Walter Broussard (Crazy Pete), Francis X. Bushman (William Potter and James Houston), Anthony Byrd (Uncle Mose), Pauline Dempsey (Aunt Jennie), Harry S. Northrup (Dick Liggett).

Bushman plays another dual role. William Potter (Bushman) is framed in a bank robbery and sent to prison where he meets his double, James Houston (Bushman). Just prior to Potter's release from jail, Houston convinces Potter to travel to Virginia and impersonate him so his mother's last days will be happy ones. Potter falls in love with Houston's sister Allane (Bayne) and confesses his deception. He also recognizes a family friend as the man who was behind his frame-up and prison time. The villain attempts to shoot Potter but mistakenly kills Houston, who recently obtained his release from prison. The police arrest Potter but a deathbed confession by the man who framed him clears Potter, who is then free to marry Allane.

Variety found *The Voice of Conscience* "all very satisfactorily filmed, and the whole thing makes for an important program feature...." Reviewer C.S. Sewell of *The Moving Picture World* commented, "Bushman gives a credible performance, and Beverly Bayne is particularly pleasing...."

Red, White and Blue Blood

Release Date: December 18, 1917. Metro Pictures Corporation. Distributed by Metro Pictures Corporation. Five reels. Director: Charles J. Brabin. Screenplay: June Mathis. Camera: R.J. Berquist. Cast: Adele Barker (Mrs. Molloy-Smythe), Beverly Bayne (Helen Molloy-Smythe), Francis X. Bushman (John Spaulding), Cecil Fletcher (Bob Molloy-Smythe), Arthur Houseman, C.R. McKinney (Charlie Jadwin), Duncan McRae (Count Jules Berratti), Jack Raymond (Light-Fingered Bertie), William H. Tooker (Patrick Spaulding). Bushman featured his Great Danes Gerda, Hamlet, Inga and Marcus in this movie.

John Spaulding (Bushman) rescues socialite Helen Molloy-Smythe (Bayne) and her mother (Barker) from a train robbery while they vacation out West. Spaulding falls in love with Helen and his efforts to cure her of social flirting create a bit of comedy before the two admit their love for each other.

The Moving Picture World reviewer C.S Sewell commented, "Bushman has a congenial role, which he handles to the satisfaction of his admirers...."

Voice of One

Release Date: Unknown. Mentioned in a June 1917 *Motion Picture Magazine* article. No other information found. Released in 1918 under the title *Cyclone Higgins, D.D.*

1918

Under Suspicion

Release Date: January 29, 1918. Metro Pictures Corporation. Distributed by Metro Pictures Corporation. Five reels. Director: Will S. Davis. Screenplay: Shelby De Vin. Adapted from the *Saturday Evening Post* short story *The Woolworth Diamonds* by Hugh S. Weir. Camera: R. J. Berquist. Cast: Beverly Bayne (Virginia Blake), Francis X. Bushman (Gerry Simpson), Sidney D'Albrook (Murphy), Eva Gordon (Mrs. Alice Woolworth), Franklyn Hanna (Chief of Detectives), Arthur Housman (Red Hogan), Hugh Jeffrey (Rogers), Frank Montgomery (Sweeney), Jack Newton (Cassidy).

Millionaire Gerry Simpson (Bushman) takes a job as a cub reporter to be near the woman he loves, reporter Virginia Blake (Bayne). While at a social reception, Alice Wentworth's (Gordon) jewelry is stolen and the only clue is a button torn off the burglar's coat by Mrs. Wentworth's pet monkey. Virginia sets out to solve the crime and discovers that Gerry's coat is missing a similar button. Upon searching his apartment, she discovers the missing jewels. Gerry's valet Rogers (Jeffrey), the real thief, finds her in the apartment and attacks Virginia. Gerry comes to the rescue, has Rogers arrested and purchases his sweetheart's newspaper, making himself the editor.

C.S. Sewell of *The Moving Picture World* found *Under Suspicion* "hardly up to the standard of the recent productions in which Francis X. Bushman and Beverly Bayne have appeared...."

The Brass Check

Release Date: March 11, 1918. Metro Pictures Corporation. Distributed by Metro Pictures Corporation. Five reels. Director: William S. Davis. Screenplay: June Mathis. Adapted from a short story by George Allen

England appearing in *All-Story Weekly*. Camera: R.J. Berquist. Cast: Beverly Bayne (Edith Everett), Francis X. Bushman (Richard Trevor), Syn De Conde, Ollie Cooper (Norma Glanor), Rudolph de Cordova (Cornelius Everett), Frank Currier (Silas Trevor), Hugh D'Arcy (J. Osborne Cole), Hugh Jeffrey (Blake), Frank Joyner (Henry Everett), Jack Newton (Robert Dexter), Augustus Phillips (Wellington Dix), John Smiley (William Roberts), Robert Williamson (Peter Glanor).

Richard Trevor (Bushman) takes the place of a detective and, after a series of thrilling adventures, obtains freedom from an insane asylum for Henry Everett (Joyner). He also gets financial compensation for inventor Everett from the powerful trust headed by his own father, Silas Trevor (Currier). Trevor also wins the hand of Everett's lovely sister Edith (Bayne).

As reported in *The Moving Picture World*, "... Bushman ... as the amateur detective ... appears in his favorite role of a vigorous son of wealth who is always ready to tackle any sort of odds—the bigger the better—and to lend a humorous touch to the proceedings by his coolness and nerve in moments of danger...."

With Neatness and Dispatch

Release Date: April 15, 1918. Metro Pictures Corporation. Distributed by Metro Pictures Corporation. Five reels. Director: William S. Davis. Screenplay: June Mathis and Luther Reed. Adapted from the *Saturday Evening Post* short story by Kenneth L. Roberts. Camera: R.J. Berquist. Cast: Ricca Allen (Aunt Letitia), Sylvia Arnold (Mary Ames), Adele Barker (Fanny), Beverly Bayne (Geraldine Ames), Francis X. Bushman (Paul Donaldson), John Charles ("Slim" Keegan), Frank Currier (Roger Burgess), Sidney D'Albrook (Daly), Arthur Houseman (Burns), Hugh Jeffrey (Inspector Corcoran), Walter Miller (John Pierce).

Police Commissioner Burgess' (Currier) nephew Paul (Bushman) is permitted to impersonate a house servant on a case involving a beautiful young woman, Geraldine Ames (Bayne). With neatness and dispatch, Donaldson foils a gang of crooks planning to rob Geraldine's Aunt Letitia's (Allen) home and he wins the heart of Geraldine.

"There is a lot of clean comedy which gets many laughs, and Bushman's handling of a broad comedy role will be a pleasant surprise to his admirers. Altogether, the picture provides good entertainment" (C.S. Sewell, *The Moving Picture World*).

Cyclone Higgins, D.D.

Release Date: May 13, 1918. Metro Pictures Corporation. Distributed by Metro Pictures Corporation. Five reels. Screenplay and Director: William Christy Cabanne. Camera: William Fildew. Cast: Sue Balfour (Widow

Pryor), Beverly Bayne (Sally Phillips), Eugene Borden (Owen Chase), Francis X. Bushman (Cyrus "Cyclone" Higgins), Robert Carson (Sheriff), Helen Dunbar (Mary Higgins), Charles Fang (Jonathan Moses Chi Wu Lung), Pop Kennard (Old Settler), John Prescott (Jasper Stone), Baby Ivy Ward (Dorothea). Produced under the working title *The Voice of One*.

Minister Cyrus Higgins (Bushman) arrives in a tough Southern town with his Chinese servant Johnathon Moses Chi Wu Lung (Fang) and the goal of bringing religion to the town. He incurs the hatred of Deputy Sheriff Stone (Prescott), whom he beats in a fight. He makes Stone apologize to Sally Phillips (Bayne) for a nasty insult. The fistfight earns the minister the respect of the townspeople and the nickname "Cyclone." Cyclone and Sally fall in love.

Reviewer C.S. Sewell (*The Moving Picture World*) remarked, "The roles of the two stars [Bushman and Bayne] differ materially from their previous efforts. The production is entertaining and there are a lot of good laughs combined with considerable heart interest.... Bushman does good work as Cyrus Higgins...."

Social Quicksands

Release Date: June 10, 1918, Metro Pictures Corporation. Distributed by Metro Pictures Corporation. Five reels. Director: Charles J. Brabin. Screenplay: Katharine Kavanaugh and June Mathis. Camera: R.J. Berquist. Cast: Rolinda Bainbridge (Mrs. Amos), Beverly Bayne (Phyllis Lane), Lila Blow (Mrs. Byrd Cutting), Francis X. Bushman (Warren Dexter), Jack Dunn, William Dunn (Jim), Mabel Fremyear (Mollie), Jack B. Hollis (Englishman), Elsie MacLeod (Miss "Nobody Home"), Armorel McDowell (The "Bullet Girl"), William Stone, Leslie Stowe (Dudley). Produced under the working title *The Heart of a Butterfly*.

Stood up by Warren Dexter (Bushman) at a social reception, Phyllis Lane (Bayne) vows to get Warren to the altar within a month. Exchanging clothes with Mollie (Fremyear), whom she caught stealing from Dexter's home, Phyllis pretends to be a thief forced by her father and brother to lead a life of crime. Warren takes on the challenge of converting this wayward but attractive thief and falls in love with her. She takes a job as his maid and helps prevent the real thieves from robbing his house. He proposes to Mollie and learns her true identity.

"The number as a whole is artistically presented and holds the interest firmly," concluded Robert C. McElravy, reviewer for *The Moving Picture World*.

A Pair of Cupids

Release Date: July 29, 1918. Metro Pictures Corporation. Distributed by Metro Pictures Corporation. Five reels. Director: Charles J. Brabin. Screenplay: Luther A. Reed. Camera: R.J. Berquist. Cast: Beverly Bayne (Virginia Parke), Thomas Blake (Bat Small), Francis X. Bushman (Peter

Warburton), Lou Gorey (Marie), Gerald Griffin (Michael McGroghan), Elwell Judge (Mary Ann McGroghan), John Judge (John Henry McGroghan), Edgar Norton (Martin), Jessie Stevens (Bridget McGroghan), Charles Sutton (Henry Burgess), Mrs. Turner (Lizette), Louis R. Wolheim (Dirk Thomas).

Stockbroker Peter Warburton (Bushman) and Virginia Parke (Bayne) are brought together via the devious workings of Warburton's uncle, Henry Burgess (Sutton). Burgess borrows his cleaning lady's twin children and leaves them (one each) on the doorsteps of Peter and Virginia. This diverts Peter's attention away from his business and Virginia's attention away from her poodle Frou Frou. The newfound parents form a bond and are about to become engaged when the twins' father hires some thugs to kidnap the children in order to collect a $25,000 ransom. Peter tracks down the kidnappers, recovers the twins and settles down with Virginia to have their own children.

Variety gave *A Pair of Cupids* a favorable review: "The Bushman-Bayne combination register admirably in polite drawing room comedy. The story is light and breezy with clever titles designed to create humor...."

The Poor Rich Man

Release Date: December 23, 1918. Metro Pictures Corporation. Distributed by Metro Pictures Corporation. Five reels. Director: Charles J. Brabin. Screenplay: Alert Shelby De Vin. Adapted from a story by Elaine Sterne. Camera: Frank D. Williams. Cast: Beverly Bayne (Arizona Brown), Francis X. Bushman (Vantyne Carter), Sally Crute (Edith Trentoni), William Frederic (Pecos Bill Brown), Stuart Holmes (Teddy Carter), C. Jay Williams (James Carter), Louis R. Wolheim (Wrestler). The working title for this production was *Little Miss Moneybags*. This was the last production by Metro Pictures Corporation featuring Bushman and Bayne. A later release, *God's Outlaw* (1919), was actually shot two years earlier. After Bushman and Bayne's fall from favor, Metro Pictures changed *God's Outlaw*'s dramatic subtitles and made it a comedic farce.

Millionaire James Carter (Williams) fakes his death to test his son Vantyne's (Bushman) ability to support himself. The father's will states that unless Vantyne can become self-sufficient within six months, he will not inherit his father's fortune, which will then go to his cousin Teddy (Holmes). Vantyne enlists the help of Arizona Brown (Bayne), with whom he has fallen in love, to turn a run-down farmhouse into a vibrant, fashionable resort. Teddy and Edith Trentoni (Crute) attempt to sabotage the operation by staging a kitchen strike and a robbery. The plan is foiled when James Carter appears to declare Vantyne and Arizona successful in their enterprise.

Walter K. Hill, reviewer for *The Moving Picture World*, commented, "There will be no question but what partisans of Francis X. Bushman and Beverly Bayne will be pleased with the result of their appearance…. It will not be through force of the story that *The Poor Rich Man* will most please.... It will be for the reason that Bushman and Bayne put their best effort into the swift-moving circumstances and thereby bring a generous measure of entertainment to apply...."

Gay and Festive Claverhouse

Release Date: Unknown. Metro Pictures Corporation. Five reels. Director: Charles J. Brabin. Screenplay: June Mathis. Adapted from the novel by Anne Warner French. Camera: Frank Williams. Cast: Beverly Bayne, Francis X. Bushman (Ernest Claverhouse). No other information known. This production may have been abandoned prior to completion.

1919

God's Outlaw

Release Date: July 7, 1919. Metro Pictures Corporation. Distributed by Metro Pictures Corporation. Five reels. Screenplay and Director: William Christy Cabanne. Camera: William Fildew. Cast: Beverly Bayne (Ruth Heatherly), Belle Bruce (Edith), Francis X. Bushman (Andrew Craig), Emily Chichester (Lonesome Lizzie), Helen Dunbar (Mrs. Heatherly), Charles A. Fang (Wu Sing), Samuel Kramer (Rufus Sanborn), Valentine Mott (Percy Smallwood). Metro Pictures Corporation's final release of a Bushman/Bayne film. In reality, it was filmed two years earlier as a serious drama. Metro rewrote the film's subtitles and turned the film into a farce, ridiculing the once great love team.

The original script featured Bushman as a young lawyer vowing never to enter a church again after his mother dies and his love turns down his marriage proposal because of her mother. He leaves town and becomes sheriff in another town. After false accusations and a vision, he is reunited with his love.

The Moving Picture World reviewer Robert C. McElravy remarked, "Some of the kidding sub-titles will bring laughs and the action also in some places, but on the whole, the offering has a tendency to drag...."

Daring Hearts

Release Date: August 28, 1919. Vitagraph Company of America. Distributed by Vitagraph Company of America. Six reels. Director: Henry Houry. Screenplay: Graham Baker. Camera: William McCoy, Arthur Quinn and Arthur Roff. Cast: Beverly Bayne (Louise de Villars), Francis X. Bushman (Hugh Brown), Karl Dane (Lt. Von Bergheim), Arthur

Donaldson (Burgomaster), Charles Kent (Count de Villars), George Des Lyon (Baptiste), L. Rogers Lytton (Baron Von Steinbach), Jean Paige (Suzette). After Metro Pictures and the Bushman/Bayne team parted ways, Vitagraph picked them up, starring them in this ill-fated production.

During World War I, American Hugh Brown (Bushman) of the French flying corps shoots down 30 enemy fighters before he is shot from the skies and captured. He escapes and makes his way to the house of Louise de Villars (Bayne), where he meets Baron Von Steinbach (Lytton), who orders him shot. Louise offers herself in return for Brown's release. When Von Steinbach moves in to collect his reward for releasing Brown, Louise kills him and flees with Brown to the trenches of friendly forces where they are married by a chaplain.

The *Harrison's Reports* review called *Daring Hearts* "extremely poor both as a production and as entertainment ... with serious inconsistencies, unskilled directing and amateurish acting."

1920

Smiling All the Way

Release Date: November 21, 1920. D.N. Schwab Production. Five reels. Director: Fred J. Butler. Screenplay: Paul Schofield. Adapted from the story "Alice in Underland" by Harry Payson Dowst. Cast: Beverly Bayne, Peggy Blackwood, Francis X. Bushman, David Butler, Jack Cosgrove, Harry Duffield, Rhea Haines, Leatrice Joy, J. Parker McConnell, Charles McHugh, Frances Raymond, Arthur Redden, Helen Scott, Charles Smiley, P. Dempsey Tabler, Lydia Yeamans Titus.

Harrison's Reports described *Smiling All the Way* as "an entertaining and amusing comedy-drama ... a first class attraction." The plot centers around a restaurant partnership between a lumberjack and a society girl.

1923

Modern Marriage

Release Date: April 7, 1923. F. X. B. Pictures. Distributed by American Releasing Corporation. Seven reels. Director: Lawrence C. Windom. Screenplay: Dorothy Farnum. Adapted from the novel *Lady Varley* by

Derek Vane. Camera: Edward F. Paul. Cast: Beverly Bayne (Denise Varley), Roland Bottomley (Frank Despard), Francis X. Bushman (Hugh Varley), Blanche Craig (Blossom Young), Pauline Dempsey (Mammy), Frankie Evans (Hugh, Jr.), Ernest Hilliard (Cort Maitland), Arnold Lucy (Elihu Simpson), Zita Moulton (Nita Blake). It is ironic that the great love team of Bushman and Bayne returned to the screen portraying a betrayed husband and unfaithful wife in this production.

An unfaithful wife, Denise Varley (Bayne), is implicated in the murder of her lover. Cort Maitland (Hilliard) knows about the affair and tries to steal Hugh Varley's (Bushman) invention but is shot in a struggle with Varley. Before dying, he confesses to killing Denise Varley's lover. Denise and Hugh reconcile.

1925

The Masked Bride

Release Date: December 13, 1925. MGM. Six reels. Director: William Christy Cabanne. Screenplay: Carey Wilson. Camera: Oliver Marsh. Cast: Francis X. Bushman (Grover), Chester Conklin (Wine Waiter), Roy D'Arcy (Prefect of Police), Mae Murray (Gaby), Pauline Neff (Grover's Sister), Basil Rathbone (Antoine), Fred Warren (Vibout), Leo White (Floor Manager).

Grover (Bushman) is an American millionaire researching French crime. He interviews Gaby (Murray), a dancer and thief, and falls in love with her. A wedding date is set but Gaby's former partner in crime, Antoine (Rathbone), forces her to steal a valuable necklace by threatening to kill Grover if Gaby does not comply. All is resolved with the Prefect of Police (D'Arcy) arresting Antoine and Grover understanding that Gaby stole the necklace to protect his life.

The New York Times commented, "Unconventional and pleasing touches in direction, clever titles and Mae Murray's iridescent charm serve to make [the film] quite an agreeable entertainment despite the weird story.... The hefty hero, who is not called upon to do anything hazardous but merely asked to have faith in the golden-haired dancer, is played by Francis X. Bushman, who knows his camera but who fails to impress one as a husband for Gaby...."

Ben-Hur

Release Date: December 30, 1925. MGM. Twelve reels. Producers: Louis B. Mayer, Samuel Goldwyn, Irving Thalberg. Director: Fred Niblo. Screenplay: Bess Meredyth, Carey Wilson. Adapted from the novel *Ben-*

Hur, a Tale of the Christ by Lew Wallace. Camera: René Guissart, Percy Hilburn, Karl Struss, Clyde De Vinna. Additional photography: E. Burton Steene, George Meehan. Trick Photography: Paul Eagler. Cast: Charles Belcher (Balthasar), Betty Bronson (Mary), Nigel De Bruiler (Simonides), Francis X. Bushman (Messala), Frank Currier (Arrius), Dale Fuller (Amrah), Winter Hall (Joseph), Kathleen Key (Tirzah), Mitchell Lewis (Sheik Ilderim), May McAvoy (Esther), Claire McDowell (Princess of Hur), Carmel Myers (Iras), Ramon Novarro (Ben-Hur), Leo White (Sanballat).

Ben-Hur was first staged at the Broadway Theater in New York City on November 29, 1899. The stage production featured Edward J. Morgan as Ben-Hur and William S. Hart as Messala. Kalem produced a one-reel version in 1907. Film production of this MGM version began in Italy in 1923 and encountered numerous delays. Charles Brabin was the original director and George Walsh the original Ben-Hur before production was relocated to Hollywood. By the time the finished film came out, the studio had spent over $4 million. During the filming, the Goldwyn Company merged with Louis B. Mayer and Metro Pictures to form Metro-Goldwyn-Mayer (MGM). An abbreviated version of *Ben-Hur* with synchronized music was released in 1931.

Ben-Hur begins with the appearance of the Star of Bethlehem and the journey of Mary and Joseph to the Cave of David after the innkeeper is unable to provide them with shelter. Twenty years later, Ben-Hur (Novarro) develops a relationship with the Roman Centurian Messala (Bushman). The friendship disintegrates when Messala arrests Ben-Hur's family for the death of the new governor, killed by a tile falling from their building. Ben-Hur is sentenced as a galley slave but is befriended by the ship's commander, Arrius (Currier). Ben-Hur saves Arrius' life after pirates scuttle their ship and in return Arrius grants Ben-Hur his freedom. Ben-Hur enters a chariot race against his arch-rival Messala. The Egyptian temptress Iras (Myers) attempts to seduce Ben-Hur but he resists her charms. Messala hires assassins to murder Ben-Hur but they fail. The chariot race transforms into a personal battle between Ben-Hur and Messala. Ben-Hur emerges victorious and Messala is killed. Ben-Hur reunites with his mother and sister and takes them to Christ to be cured. He learns of Christ's mission to save mankind. The reunited family returns to the Palace of Hur.

Variety and other trade papers proclaimed *Ben-Hur* a great success: "*Ben-Hur* in film form has been years in coming to the screen; millions have been spent on it; one large film corporation as a result of its production was compelled to merge with another; actors and directors lost their reputations as a result of it; likewise others, also actors and directors, have made theirs. And it was well worth waiting for all those years.... The word 'epic' has been applied to pictures time and again, but at the time that it was utilized there was no *Ben-Hur*, therefore you can scrap all the 'epics' that have been shown prior to the arrival of *Ben-Hur* and start a new book. This is the 'Epic' of motion picture achievement to date and don't let anyone tell you otherwise."

Variety went on to praise the actors: "Ramon Novarro, he may never have appealed in former productions, but anyone who sees him in this picture will have to admit that he is without a doubt a man's man and 100 percent of that. Novarro is made for all time by his performance here. Francis X. Bushman does a comeback in the role of the heavy that makes him stand alone. Don't let Bushy ever go back to the heroic stuff. He can land in that but if he will stick to heavies there is no doubt but with this background he will be the heavy of all times."

1926

The Marriage Clause

> Release Date: September 12, 1926. Universal. Eight reels. Screenplay and Director: Lois Weber. From the short story "Technic" by Dana Burnett. Camera: Hal Mohr. Cast: Francis X. Bushman (Barry Townsend), Andre Cheron (Critic), Grace Darmond (Mildred Le Blanc), Billie Dove (Sylvia Jordan), Robert Dudley (Secretary), Henri La Garde (Doctor), Charles Meakin (Stage Manager), Warner Oland (Max Ravenal), Oscar Smith (Sam), Caroline Snowden (Pansy).

A young country girl, Sylvia Jordan (Dove), achieves great success in the theater under the able direction of Barry Townsend (Bushman). In the process of working closely together, Sylvia and Townsend fall in love. But the more successful Sylvia becomes, the more tension arises between the two. Eventually Townsend leaves due to a misunderstanding over a non-marriage clause in her contract with producer Max Ravenal (Oland). Sylvia is heartbroken and, as a result, her health suffers. Townsend learns of her illness and returns to see her perform on stage. Knowing he is in the audience, she gives the performance of her life, collapsing on stage at the final curtain. She recovers from her illness and they marry.

The Marriage Clause earned rave reviews from the critics. *Harrison's Reports* said, "Miss Billie Dove has never looked prettier and has never done better work. The same can be said of Francis X. Bushman; he really acts ... he does not pose. The love affair between Francis Bushman and Billie Dove, as the hero and heroine respectively, is warmly sympathetic ... to such an extent that the spectator is made to feel sad that misunderstandings should creep in between them to bring about their separation; but he is gladdened when they are reunited."

1927

The Lady in Ermine

Release Date: January 9, 1927. First National Pictures. Seven reels. Director: James Flood. Screenplay: Benjamin Glazer. Adapted from the operetta "Die Frau im Hermelin" by Rudolph Schanzer and Ernst Welisch. Camera: Harold Wenstrom. Cast: Francis X. Bushman (Gen. Dostal), Ward Crane (Archduke Stephen), Corinne Griffith (Mariana Beltrami), Einar Hansen (Count Adrian Murillo), Jane Keckley (Mariana's Maid). Lorenz M. Hart and Jean Gilbert presented the first American adaptation and lyrics for the Schanzer–Welisch story in 1920.

Bushman plays another heavy role, Austrian Gen. Dostal, in *The Lady in Ermine*. The story is set in 1810 with the Austrian invasion of Italy. Countess Mariana Beltrami (Griffith) marries Count Adrian Murillo (Hansen) before he leaves for the front. Gen. Dostal (Bushman) makes the Beltrami castle his headquarters and pursues Countess Mariana's affections. Count Murillo returns to the castle after breaking through the Austrian lines. He is captured and ordered shot as a spy. Countess Mariana recalls a similar French invasion when her grandmother saved her husband by appearing in only an ermine coat before the enemy's general. Gen. Dostal, intoxicated by burgundy, dreams of a similar instance. He awakens and, believing that the experience occurred, spares Count Murillo's life.

The Thirteenth Juror

Release Date: September 3, 1927. Universal. Six reels. Director: Edwards Laemmle. Screenplay: Charles A. Logue. Adapted from the play *Counsel for the Defense* by Henry Irving Dodge. Camera: Ben Reynolds. Cast: Sidney Bracey (The Butler), Francis X. Bushman (Henry Desmond), Fred Kelsey (The Detective), Martha Mattox (The Housekeeper), Anna Q. Nilsson (Helen Marsden), Walter Pidgeon (Richard Mardsen), Sailor Sharkey (The Prisoner), George Siegmann (George Quinn, the Politician), Lloyd Whitlock (The District Attorney). Bushman received Best Performance of the Month ranking by *Photoplay*.

A political machine headed by politician George Quinn (Siegmann) attempts to ruin successful attorney Henry Desmond (Bushman) by leaking information about Desmond having an affair with Helen Marsden (Nilsson), the wife of his friend Richard (Pidgeon). Quinn and Desmond argue, and Quinn is killed. Marsden is arrested for the crime and Desmond refuses to defend him. Marsden is found guilty, but Desmond subsequently confesses his guilt. The Marsdens are reunited.

The Flag

Release Date: September 14, 1927. MGM. Two reels. Screenplay and Director: Arthur Maude. Cast: Francis X. Bushman (George Washington), Alice Calhoun (Betsy Ross), Johnny Walker.

Washington (Bushman) gathers the military leaders from the colonies to battle the British. When each leader demands that their standards lead the defending forces, Washington settles the argument by declaring that Betsy Ross (Calhoun) will create a new standard to lead the troops into battle.

1928

The Grip of the Yukon

Release Date: July 9, 1928. Universal. Seven reels. Director: Ernst Laemmle. Screenplay: Charles A. Logue. Adapted from "The Yukon Trail, a Tale of the North" by William MacLeod Raine. Camera: Jackson Rose. Cast: Francis X. Bushman (Colby MacDonald), James Farley (Sheriff), Neil Hamilton (Jack Elliott), Otis Harlan (The Doctor), June Marlowe (Sheila O'Neil), Burr McIntosh (Farrell O'Neil).

In the Yukon, prospectors Colby MacDonald (Bushman) and Jack Elliott (Hamilton) meet a half-crazed hermit, Farrell O'Neil (McIntosh). A fight ensues and the hermit is killed. The two prospectors take over the hermit's mining claim. O'Neil's daughter Sheila (Marlowe) arrives to find her father dead and takes a job in a dance hall to make a living. MacDonald and Elliott vie for Sheila's love. When she falls for Elliott, MacDonald bitterly tells the sheriff about the hermit's death. The sheriff rules it a case of self-defense and MacDonald accepts Elliott and Sheila as lovers.

Say It with Sables

Release Date: July 13, 1928. Columbia. Six reels. Director: Frank Capra. Screenplay: Dorothy Howell. Camera: Joe Walker. Cast: Francis X. Bushman (John Caswell), Helene Chadwick (Helen Caswell), Edna Mae Cooper (Maid), Alphonz Ethier (Detective Mitchell), Margaret Livingston (Irene Gordon), June Nash (Marie Caswell), Arthur Rankin (Doug Caswell).

Wealthy widower John Caswell (Bushman) ends an affair with his mistress Irene (Livingston) in order to wed a more suitable mate, Helen Caswell (Chadwick). The story takes a twist when Caswell's son Doug (Rankin) arrives home with his fiancée, none other than Irene. The father tells his son about his earlier affair with Irene and she is later found dead from a gunshot wound. Caswell confesses to Detective Mitchell that he murdered Irene. The son confesses to the murder to protect his father. However, Detective Mitchell has already found Mrs. Caswell's earring at the crime scene. He closes the case by claiming that Irene shot herself.

Harrison's Reports found *Say It with Sables* a worthy production: "Bushman is excellent as the father who wanted to shield his son whom he was very fond of; and so is Arthur Rankin, as the son."

Midnight Life

Release Date: August 28, 1928. Gotham Productions. Distributed by Lumas Film Corporation. Five reels. Director: Scott R. Dunlap. Screenplay: Adele Buffington. Adapted from "The Spider's Web" by Reginald Wright Kauffman. Camera: Ray June. Cast: Cosmo Kyrle Bellew (Harlan Phillips), Francis X. Bushman (Jim Logan), Eddie Buzzell (Eddie Delaney), Monte Carter (Steve Saros), Carlton King, Gertrude Olmstead (Betty Brown). Reportedly shot in only six days.

New York Police Lt. Jim Logan (Bushman) sets out to find the murderer of his best friend. A bloody trail of clues and assistance from nightclub dancer Betty Brown (Olmstead) lead Logan to Harlan Phillips (Bellew), the trigger man and leader of a gang of warehouse thieves. Logan outsmarts the gang leader, who gets killed in a trap he set for Logan.

The Charge of the Gauchos

Release Date: September 16, 1928. Ajuria Productions. Distributed by FBO Pictures. Six reels. Director: Alberty Kelly. Screenplay: W.C. Clifford. Camera: George Benoit, Nick Musuraca. Cast: Francis X. Bushman (Belgrano), Mathilde Comont (Aunt Rosita), Ligo Conley (Gomez), Gino Corrado (Moreno), Paul Ellis (Balcarce), Charles K. French (Salazar), Frank Hagney (Goyeneche), Olive Hasbrouck (Mariana), John Hopkins (Lezica), Henry Kolker (Viceroy), Jacqueline Logan (Monica Salazar), Charles Hill Mailes (Saavedra), Jack Ponder (George Gordon), Guido Trento (Monteros).

Bushman plays another Washingtonesque character in *The Charge of the Gauchos*. Belgrano (Bushman), the Washington of the Argentines, leads his people in revolt against the tyrannical Spaniards. He achieves stunning victories against the Spanish Loyalists with his ragtag army despite overwhelming odds.

He is aided in his military maneuvers by the secret messages sent by his sweetheart Monica Salazar (Logan). When she is arrested for treason and sentenced to be beheaded, Belgrano rescues her from death. Belgrano and Monica wed after the revolution.

1930

The Call of the Circus

Release Date: January 15, 1930. Pickwick Pictures. Distributed by C.C. Burr Pictures. Six reels. Director: Frank O'Connor. Screenplay: Maxine Alton. Camera: Louis Physioc. Cast: Francis X. Bushman (The Man), Ethel Clayton (The Woman), Dorothy Gay (The Girl-at-the-Well), William Cotton Kirby (The Boy), Sunburnt Jim Wilson (The Shadow), Joan Wyndham (The Girl). Bushman made his "talkie" debut in this feature.

Bushman portrays a retired clown who takes up horticulture. He saves a young girl and misinterprets her gratefulness for affection. The young girl later falls in love with the retired clown's son. The older man realizes his foolishness and he makes up with his wife.

The Dude Wrangler

Release Date: June 1, 1930. Sono-Art Productions. Six reels. Director: Richard Thorpe. Screenplay: Robert N. Lee. Adapted from "The Dude Wrangler" by Caroline Lockhart. Cast: Lina Basquette (Helen Dane), Francis X. Bushman (Canby), Aileen Carlyle, Clyde Cook (Pinkey Fripp), Alice Davenport (Dude Guest), George Duryea (Wally McCann), Julia Swayne Gordon (Dude Guest), Wilfred North (The "Snorer"), Fred Parker, Louis Payne, Jack Richardson, Virginia Sale (Dude Guests), Margaret Seddon (Aunt Mary), Kamiyama Sojin (Wong), Ethel Wales (Mattie). According to "In Search of Hollywood, Wyoming," Caroline Lockhart wrote "The Dude Wrangler" in 1921. An attempt was made to produce the film in 1922 with movie hopeful Tim McCoy of Thermopolis, Wyoming. Plans by Mountain Plains Enterprise Company of Denver, Colorado, to construct the Sunshine Studios at McCoy's Owl Creek Dude Ranch fell through and the project was abandoned. Lockhart delivered the film property to the Wallace Reid Production Company with these stipulations: production was to begin no later than September 1, 1927, the leading roles were to be played by actors of national reputation and the exterior shots were to be filmed in or around Cody, Wyoming. *The Dude Wrangler* was eventually released by Sono-Art Productions. Caroline Lockhart died in Cody, Wyoming, in 1962 at the age of 91.

A rich youth, Wally McCann (Duryea), purchases a ranch in Wyoming to impress his girlfriend Helen (Basquette). One of the dude ranch's guests, Canby (Bushman), falls in love with Helen and plans a series of escapades with the Chinese cook, Wong (Sojin), in order to drive away guests and win over Helen. The plan backfires with McCann rising to the occasion by standing up to Canby and winning Helen's affection.

Once a Gentleman

Release Date: September 1, 1930. James Cruze Productions. Distributed by Sono-Art World Wide Pictures. Nine reels. Director: James Cruze. Screenplay: Walter Woods. Adapted from a story by George F. Worts. Camera: Jackson Rose. Cast: King Baggot (Van Warner), Estelle Bradley (Gwen), Francis X. Bushman (Bannister), Cyril Chadwick (Jarvis), Charles Coleman (Wuggins), Drew Demarest (Timson), George Fawcett (Colonel Breen), William F. Holmes (Ogelthorpe), Edward Everett Horton (Oliver), William O'Brien (Reeves), Evelyn Pierce (Natalie), Gertrude Short (Dolly), Frederic Sullivan (Wadsworth), Emerson Treacy (Junior), Lois Wilson (Mrs. Mallin). King Baggot and Bushman appear together in *Once a Gentleman* 16 years after Bushman beat out Baggot, Maurice Costello, Jack Kerrigan and other leading men in "The *Ladies' World* Hero Contest" and earned the opportunity to portray John D. Curtis in *One Wonderful Night,* which boosted Bushman's rising career into the stratosphere.

House servant Oliver (Horton) gets a well-deserved vacation after years of faithful service to Mr. Van Warner (King Baggot). While on leave, he is mistaken for an Indian gentleman and close friend of Col. Breen (Fawcett). The comedy builds as Oliver lets the misconception continue. He is invited to Mr. Bannister's (Bushman) home and falls in love with the widowed Mrs. Mallin (Wilson), the maid. After a series of escapades, Oliver is exposed as a fraud. However, he is allowed to return to his former employer, with his Mrs. Mallin joining him.

The New York Times commented, "*Once a Gentleman* created no small amount of merriment...." It praised Edward Everett Horton and the strange and laughable situations in which the butler found himself. "In support of Mr. Horton's excellent work ... King Baggot in the role of Mr. Warner and Francis X. Bushman as Bannister ... merit praise for their acting."

1932

Watch Beverly

Release Date: 1932. Sound City at Shepperton, Great Britain. Director: Arthur Maude. Screenplay: Baring Pemberton, John Cousins. Based on the play by Cyril Champion. Camera: George Dudgeon Stretton. Cast: Dorothy Bartham (Audrey Thurloe), Edith Barker Bennett, Francis X. Bushman (President Orloff), Vincent Clive, Antony Holles (Arthur Briden), Henry Kendall (Victor Beverly), Frederic de Lara (Rachmann), Patrick Ludlow (Patrick Nolan), Aileen Pitt Marsden (Anne Markham), Charles Mortimer (Sir James Briden), Colin Pole (George), Ernest Stidwell (Inspector Roberts). Although many of Bushman's early films were distributed in Great Britain, he was billed as Cecil Stanhope.

Diplomat Victor Beverly (Kendall) takes offense upon discovering that a rich British businessman has obtained lucrative oil drilling rights in exchange for the promise of a large payment to a foreign dictator. In retaliation, Beverly impersonates the dictator, obtains the money and donates it to a British charity. Bushman played yet another presidential role as President Orloff.

1934

The Film Parade

Release Date: January 12, 1934. J. Stuart Blackton's Cavalcade of Motion Pictures. Narrated by J. Stuart Blackton, founder of Vitagraph Company of America, and featuring 150 of the world's greatest motion picture stars. Blackton traces the history of motion pictures starting with an Egyptian temple built by Ramses around 1600 B.C. Carvings of a goddess embellished the temple. The different poses of the goddess made her appear to move as warriors rode past in their chariots. The movie featured clips of early Essanay players such as Broncho Billy Anderson, Bushman, Charlie Chaplin, Gloria Swanson and Ben Turpin. Blackton dedicated the collection to Thomas Alva Edison.

1936

Hollywood Boulevard

Release Date: August 21, 1936. Paramount. Eight reels. Director: Robert Florey. Screenplay: Marguerite Roberts. Camera: Karl Struss, George Clemens. Cast: Oscar Apfel (Dr. Inslo), Irving Bacon (Gus the Bartender), Edmond Burns (Guest), Francis X. Bushman (Director of Desert Scene), Ed Cecil (Butler), Ruth Clifford (Nurse), Betty Compson (Betty), Albert Conti (Mr. Sanford), Gary Cooper (Man at Bar), Maurice Costello (Director), Robert Cummings (Jay Wallace), Esther Dale (Martha), Roy

D'Arcy (The Sheik), Ed Dearing (Motor Policeman), William Desmond (Guest), Lowell Drew (Doorman at Trocadero), Eddie Dunn (Grip), Joanne Dudley (Girl in Pullman), William Farnum, Hyman Fink (Snapshot "Hymie"), Johnny Fletcher (Vendor), James Ford (Guest), Mabel Forrest (Mother), Gregory Gaye (Russian writer), C. Henry Gordon (Jordan Winslow), Creighton Hale (Man at Bar), John Halliday (John Blakeford), Margaret Harrison (Guest), Robert E. Homans (Gray), Marsha Hunt (Patricia Blakeford), Frieda Inescourt (Alice Winslow), Thomas Jackson (Detective), Tom Kennedy (Bouncer), Lois Kent (Little Girl), Rita La Roy (Nella), Mae Marsh (Carlotta Blakeford), Frank Mayo (Himself), Kitty McHugh (Secretary), Francis Morris (Moran's Secretary), Charles Morton (Guest), Jack Mower (Frank Stucky), Jack Mulhall (Man at Bar), Harry Myers (Himself), Pat O'Malley (Dancer), Jane Novak (Mrs. Steinman), Franklin Parker (Brown Derby Workman), Richard Powell (Pete Moran), Purnell Pratt (Mr. Steinman), Hal Prince (Police Radio Dispatcher), Esther Ralston (Flora Moore, Actress), Herbert Rawlinson (Manager of Graumann's Chinese Theater), Charles Ray (Charlie Smith, Assistant Director), Bert Roach (Scenarist), Matty Roubert (Newsboy), Gertrude Simpson (Gossip), John Sylvester (Brown Derby Workman), Phil Tead (Master of Ceremonies), Monte Vandergrift (Electrician), Bryant Washburn (Robert Martin), William Wayne (Brown Derby Workman), Eleanore Whitney (Herself), Charles Williams (Reporter), Otto Yamaoka (Thomas).

A behind-the scenes glimpse of Hollywood. Washed-up star John Blakeford (Halliday) must take any role to keep his sordid life together. Jordan Winslow (Gordon) offers Blakeford $25,000 for his autobiography to appear in serial form in Winslow's gossip rag *Modern Truth*. Blakeford is shocked when he sees the distorted, sensationalized version. Ironically, Winslow's wife Alice (Inescourt) proves to be "the other woman" in Blakeford's life and she unsuccessfully tries to stop publication of the autobiography for fear her affair with Blakeford will be discovered. She shoots Blakeford after an argument during which he insists he must continue writing the autobiography. Blakeford's daughter Patricia (Hunt) is arrested for the shooting but her fiancé Jay Wallace (Cummings) discovers a recording of the confrontation between Blakeford and Alice Winslow and clears Patricia. Winslow agrees not to print any more of the autobiography after Blakeford says he will claim that the gunshot wound was accidentally self-inflicted.

The storyline must have given Bushman and other silent movie stars making cameo appearances shivers down their spines considering how high some of their popularities soared before a fickle public found new stars to replace them. *The New York Times* said it best: "We felt pathetically embarrassed for the former stars and featured players who appeared as extras, bit players and background. Hollywood, having neglected them all these years, at least should have had the decency and good taste not to make them parade themselves as Exhibits A, B and C of the Forgotten Men and Women of Filmdom. *Hollywood Boulevard* is hardly a sporting gesture."

1937

Dick Tracy (Serial)

Release Date: 1937. Republic. 15-episode serial. Directed by Ray Taylor, Alan James. Screenplay: Winston Miller, Barry Shipman. Adapted from the comic strip series by Chester Gould. Cast: Richard Beach (Gordon Tracy, Before) Smiley Burnette (Mike McGurk), Francis X. Bushman (Chief of Police Anderson), Ralph Byrd (Dick Tracy), John Dilson (Brewster), Byron K. Foulger (Korvitch), Harrison Greene (Cloggerstein), Fred Hamilton (Steve), Kay Hughes (Gwen), Theodore Lorch (Paterno), George de Normand (Flynn), Wedgewood Nowell (Clayton), Oscar and Elmer (Themselves), John Piccori (Dr. Moloch), Buddy Roosevelt (Burke), Edwin Stanley (Odette), Lee Van Atta (Junior), Herbert Weber (Martino), Carleton Young (Gordon Tracy, After).

Chester Gould's comic strip series *Dick Tracy* debuted on October 12, 1931, for the Chicago Tribune-New York News Syndicate. Republic Pictures launched the first *Dick Tracy* serials in 1937. Republic revived the popular detective hero in 1938, 1939 and 1941. Over the years, Republic, RKO and Touchstone have produced ten *Dick Tracy* films and serials stretching from 1937 through 1990. Ralph Byrd, the original Dick Tracy, also portrayed the detective in the 1951-1952 *Dick Tracy* TV show. Byrd died in 1952 at the age of 43 from a heart attack. In the 1937 serial, Dick Tracy (Byrd) is assigned by Chief Anderson (Bushman) to halt the terrorist activities of the notorious Spider Gang, headed by a sinister figure who calls himself "The Spider." The gang captures Dick Tracy's brother Gordon (Beach) and the evil. Dr. Moloch (Piccori) performs an operation on him, rendering him a mindless slave with no memory of the past and unable to determine right from wrong. He is completely at the mercy of the Spider's orders. The Spider uses Gordon (now played by Young) as a pawn to keep Dick Tracy off balance, although the ace detective persists in narrowing the gap between himself and the master criminal. The Spider employs all kinds of weaponry to achieve his aims, the most impressive of which is a powerful death ray mounted on his futuristic aircraft, the Flying Wing.

Episodes:
1. The Spider Strikes
2. The Bridge of Terror
3. The Fur Pirates
4. Death Rides the Sky
5. Brother Against Brother
6. Dangerous Water
7. The Ghost Town Mystery
8. Battle in the Clouds
9. The Stratosphere Adventure
10. The Gold Ship
11. Harbor Pursuit
12. The Trail of the Spider
13. The Fire Trap
14. The Devil in White
15. Brothers United

Thoroughbreds Don't Cry

Release Date: December 3, 1937. MGM. Eight reels. Director: Alfred E. Green. Assistant Director: Horace Hough. First Assistant Director: Charles O'Malley. Screenplay: Lawrence Hazard. Based on a story by Eleanore Griffin and J. Walter Ruben. Camera: Leonard Smith. Cast: Marie Blake (Operator), Charles D. Brown ("Click" Donovan), Francis X. Bushman (Race Steward), George Chandler (Usher), Elisha Cook, Jr. (Boots Maguire), Frankie Darro ("Dink" Reid), Edgar Dearing (Policeman), James Flavin (Timmie's Agent), Judy Garland (Cricket West), Forrester Harvey (Wilkins), Henry Kolker ("Doc" Godfrey), Jack Norton (Man with Monocle), Mickey Rooney (Timmie Donovan), Ronald Sinclair (Roger Calverton), C. Aubrey Smith (Sir Peter Calverton), Helen Troy (Hilda), Sophie Tucker (Mother Ralph).

Judy Garland received top billing for the first time in this film. Jockey Timmie Donovan (Mickey Rooney) throws a horse race in order to pay for his father's operation. He is thrown out of racing despite proof that his father deceived him. More riding and romance ensues before the happy resolution.

1941

Mr. Celebrity

Release Date: 1941. Producers Releasing Corporation. Director: William Beaudine. Screenplay: Martin Mooney. Story: Martin Mooney and Charles Samuels. Cast: Francis X. Bushman (Himself), Johnny Burke, Doris Day, William Halligan (Grandfather), Robert "Buzzy" Henry (Orphan), Jim Jeffries (Himself), James Seay (Uncle), Laura Treadwell (Grandmother), Clara Kimball Young (Herself).

An orphan (Henry) and his veterinarian uncle (Seay) hide out on the horse racing circuit to avoid receiving legal papers filed by the boy's grandparents in a custody suit over the boy's guardianship.

The boy and his uncle arrive at Celebrity Farm and help save it from foreclosure by staging horse races. The uncle is given a horse breeding contract enabling him to retain custody of his nephew.

Celebrities at the farm include Bushman, Jim Jeffries and Clara Kimball Young.

Harrison's Reports rated *Mr. Celebrity* as pleasant entertainment suitable for all viewers, adding, "Many persons will be touched at seeing again the old favorites, Francis X. Bushman and Clara Kimball Young, who appear throughout the picture."

FILMOGRAPHY

1942

Silver Queen

Release Date: November 13, 1942. United Artists. Director: Lloyd Bacon. Screenplay: Cecil Kramer, Bernard Schubert. Story: Forrest Halsey, William Allen Johnston. Camera: Harry Neumann. Cast: Roy Barcroft (Dan Carson), Janet Beecher (Mrs. Forsythe), George Brent (James Kincaid), Frederick Burton (Dr. Hartley), Francis X. Bushman (Creditor), Bruce Cabot (Gerald Forsythe), Marietta Canty (Ruby), Ed Cassidy (Colonel), Spencer Charters (Doc Stonebraker), George Eldredge (Admirer), Franklyn Farnum (Creditor), Earle Hodgins (Desk Clerk), Arthur Hunnicutt (Editor Brett), Cy Kendall (Sheriff), Priscilla Lane (Coralie Adams), Sam McDaniel (Toby), Lynne Overman (Hector Bailey), Eugene Pallette (Steve Adams), Herbert Rawlinson (Judge), George Renavent (Maitre d' Andres), Jason Robards, Sr. (Bank Teller), Eleanor Stewart (Millicent Bailey), Fred "Snowflake" Toones (Butler), Guinn "Big Boy" Williams (Blackie). Bushman plays a small part.

Society girl Coralie Adams (Lane) is forced to take up gambling after her father dies penniless due to gambling away a fortune and his deed to a silver mine, the "Silver Queen." Adams plans to marry wealthy Gerald Forsythe (Cabot) to regain her social status but first travels to San Francisco to become the Barbary Coast gambling queen. Professional gambler James Kincaid (Brent), who won the deed to the silver mine, gives the deed to Forsythe as a wedding present for Adams. Unscrupulous Forsythe never tells her about the deed. Adams sends back profits from her saloon to Forsythe with instructions to pay off the family debts. Instead, he puts the money into the silver mine operations. Kincaid finds out about Forsythe's deception, regains the money and silver mine for Adams, and they marry.

1944

Wilson

Release Date: February 26, 1944. Twentieth Century–Fox. Director: Henry King. Screenplay: Lamar Trotti. Camera: Leon Shamroy. Cast: George Anderson (Secretary Houston), Mary Anderson (Eleanor Wilson), John Ardell, Robert Barron (Senator Meredith), Sidney Blackmer (Josephus Daniels), Clifford Brooke (Lloyd George), Jess Lee Brooks, Francis X. Bushman (Bernard M. Baruch), Harry Carter, Ken Christy, Davidson Clark (Champ Clark), Russ Clark, Charles Coburn (Prof. Henry Holmes), Marcel Dalio (Clemenceau), Frank Dawson, Ralph Dunn (La

Follette), Guy D'Ennery, Paul Everton (Judge Westcott), William Eythe (George Felton), Antonio Filauri, Geraldine Fitzgerald (Edith Wilson), Madeleine Forbes (Jessie Wilson), William Forrest, Eddie Foy, Jr. (Eddie Foy), Russell Gaige (Secretary Colby), Gus Glassmire, Gilson Gowland (Senator), Jesse Graves, Jessie Grayson, Joseph J. Greene (Chief Justice White), Reed Hadley (Usher), Thurston Hall (Senator E.H. Jones), Charles Halton (Colonel House), Sir Cedric Hardwicke (Henry Cabot Lodge), Josh Hardin, Major Sam Harris (Gen. Bliss), Del Henderson, Tony Hughes, John Ince (Senator Watson), Gladden James, Cy Kendall (Charles F. Murphy), J.M. Kerrigan (Edward Sullivan), Alexander Knox (Woodrow Wilson), Ralph Linn, Katherine Locke (Helen Bones), Stanley Logan (Secretary Lansing), Arthur Loft (Secretary Lane), George Macready (McCombs), Aubrey Mather, George Matthews, Edwin Maxwell (William Jennings Bryan), Larry McGrath, Robert Middlemass (Secretary Garrison), Charles Miller (Senator Bromfield), Thomas Mitchell (Joseph Tumulty), Matt Moore (Secretary Burleson), Ed Mundy, Ruth Nelson (Ellen Wilson), Anne O'Neal (Jennie), Frank Orth (Smith), Hilda Plowright (Jeanette Rankin), Vincent Price (William G. McAdoo), Isabel Randolph, James Rennie (Jim Beeker), Stanley Ridges (Admiral Grayson), Roy Roberts (Ike Hoover), Dewey Robinson (Worker), Harold Schlickemeyer, Tonio Selwart (Von Bernstorff), Jamesson Shade (Secretary Payne), Reginald Sheffield (Secretary Baker), Arthur Space (Francis Sayre), Ferris Taylor, Harry Tyler, John Whitney.

Darryl F. Zanuck created a stunning tribute to President Woodrow Wilson and American history in Wilson. The film opened in New York City and was critically acclaimed. *The New York Herald Tribune* said, "A challenging segment of American history has been reconstructed with great honesty and imagination...."

In excess of $3 million was spent on the production, including a lavish reproduction of the White House. Unfortunately, the film proved to be a box office disaster.

Bushman portrayed a stately Bernard M. Baruch but much of his performance was left on the cutting room floor. In a newspaper interview years later, Bushman remarked that he felt he did some of his best work in *Wilson* but for political reasons surrounding Baruch, much of Bushman's performance was cut out.

1945

The Good Old Days

Release Date: 1945. A cavalcade of silent films. No other information was found.

1951

Hollywood Story

Release Date: June 1951. Universal-International. Director: William Castle. Screenplay: Fred Brady, Frederick Kohner. Camera: Carl Guthrie. Cast: Julia [Julie] Adams (Sally Rousseau), Jim Backus (Mitch Davis), Francis X. Bushman (Himself), Betty Blythe (Herself), Paul Cavanagh (Roland Paul), Fred Clark (Sam Collyer), Richard Conte (Larry O'Brien), Richard Egan (Lt. Lennox), William Farnum (Himself), Helen Gibson (Herself), Henry Hull (Vincent St. Clair), Louis Lettieri (Jimmy), Joel McCrea (Himself), Katherine Meskill (Mary), Houseley Stevenson (Mr. Miller). In conjunction with the release of *Hollywood Story*, there was a tribute to silent movie stars at the Academy Award Theater. Bushman, Helen Gibson and Hank Mann were among the silent stars who attended the tribute. Extras who worked on *Hollywood Story* received $15.56 for a day's work. The silent movie stars such as Bushman, who provided cameo appearances with some speaking parts, received payment in recognition and $55 for their day's work, not much of a tribute.

The storyline centers around a murder of a silent movie director and was taken loosely from the real-life, never-solved 1922 murder of Hollywood director William Desmond Taylor in 1922. Producer Larry O'Brien (Conte) arrives in Hollywood to make a movie about the murder of a silent film director. O'Brien hires scriptwriter Vincent St. Clair (Hull) to produce the script. Despite death threats, O'Brien continues work on the production and discovers clues about the unsolved murder. In the end, O'Brien proves that St. Clair is the dead man's brother and murdered him during a jealous rage.

Harrison's Reports called *Hollywood Story* an "interesting murder mystery melodrama, set against a Hollywood background.... As an added treat, four old-time stars [Bushman, Betty Blythe, William Farnum and Helen Gibson] appear briefly...."

David and Bathsheba

Release Date: August 13, 1951. Twentieth Century-Fox. Director: Henry King. Screenplay: Phillip Dunne. Based on the book by Dr. Theodore Isaac Rubin and the chronicles in the Second Book of Samuel. Camera: Leon Shamroy. Cast: Gilbert Barnett (Absalom), John Burton (Priest), Francis X. Bushman (King Saul), Harry Carter (Executioner), James Craven (Court Announcer), John Duncan (Jesse's Third Son), Lumsden Hare (Old Shepherd), Susan Hayward (Bathsheba), Holmes Herbert (Jesse), Dennis Hoey (Joab), Teddy Infuhr (Jonathan), James Robertson Justice (Abishai), Raymond Massey (Nathan), Jayne Meadows (Michal), Richard Michelson (Jesse's First Son), Kieron Moore (Uriah), Paula Morgan (Adultress), Paul Newlan (Samuel), Gregory Peck (David), Leo Pessin (David as a Boy), Robert Stephenson (Executioner), Allan Stone (Amnon), John Sutton (Ira), Walter Talun (Goliath), Dick Winters (Jesse's Second Son), George Zucco (Egyptian Ambassador). Much of the movie was filmed on location near Nogales, Arizona, where Darryl F. Zanuck had a mud-and-plaster reproduction of ancient Jerusalem constructed.

A Biblical saga centering around David's (Peck) love affair with the beautiful Bathsheba (Hayward). David falls in love with Bathsheba, Uriah's (Moore) wife. David sends Uriah off to war where he is killed in action. That leaves David free to marry Bathsheba and discard his wife, Michal (Meadows), the daughter of King Saul (Bushman). A baby is born shortly after the marriage but soon dies. Nathan (Massey) stirs up discontent and leads a group of dissidents to the palace to demand that Bathsheba pay for her adultery. David is tempted to flee with Bathsheba but accepts responsibility for his actions after he prays at the Ark of the Covenant and sees a vision of King Saul. The rain starts and drought ends. David returns to Bathsheba and they pledge to carry out the Lord's work.

The New York Times praised Gregory Peck's portrayal of David as both "outstanding and singular. However, Susan Hayward's lush Titian-haired Bathsheba has physical attributes and no character and her blandishments are standard and strangely modern despite her surroundings."

1952

Apache Country

Release Date: 1952. Columbia. Director: George Archainbaud. Screenplay: Norman Shannon Hall. Camera: William Bradford. Cast: Gene Autry (Himself), Greg Barton (Luke Thorn), Francis X. Bushman (Commander Latham), Pat Buttram (Himself), Carolina Cotton (Herself), Byron Foulger (Bartlett), Harry Lauter (Dave Kilrain), Tom London (Patches), Sydney Mason (Walter Rayburn), Frank Matts (Steve), Mary Scott (Laura Rayburn), Mickey Simpson (Tom Ringo).

A Gene Autry Western in which Autry and his sidekicks round up the bad guys for the government. Bushman plays a stately Commander Latham. In a letter from Gene Autry, he described Bushman as "very effective in *Apache Country*. We also knew him from the Masquers Club (we were both members), and other Hollywood get-togethers. He was an important part of Hollywood history."

The Bad and the Beautiful

Release Date: 1952. MGM. Director: Vincente Minnelli. Screenplay: Charles Schnee. Story: George Bradshaw. Camera: Robert Surtees. Cast:

Stanley Andrews (Sheriff), Ben Astar (Joe), Madge Blake (Mrs. Rosser), Vanessa Brown (Kay Amiel), Robert Burton (McDill), Francis X. Bushman (Eulogist), Louis Calhern (Voice on the Recording), Marietta Canty (Ida), Leo G. Carroll (Henry Whitfield), Jonathan Cott (Assistant Director), Kirk Douglas (Jonathan Shields), Bess Flowers (Joe's Friend at Party), Steve Forrest (Leading Man), Kathleen Freeman (Miss March), Gloria Grahame (Rosemary Bartlow), Peggy King (Singer), Lucille Knoch (Blonde), George Lewis (Actor in Screen Test), Harold Miller, Alyce May, Dorothy Patrick (Arlene), William "Bill" Phillips (Assistant Director), Walter Pidgeon (Harry Pebbel), Dick Powell (James Lee Bartlow), Gilbert Roland (Victor "Gaucho" Ribera), Perry Sheehan (Secretary), Elaine Stewart (Lila), Paul Stewart (Syd Murphy), Barry Sullivan (Fred Amiel), Ivan Triesault (Von Ellstein), Dee Turnell (Linda), Lana Turner (Georgia Lorrison), Karen Verne (Rosa), Sammy White (Gus).

Jonathan Shields (Douglas) gathers together Hollywood greats to revive his failing studio. Over the years, Shields has walked over these actors and more on his way to the top. Each actor treats the audience to a flashback of their experiences with Shields. Reportedly, the film portrays the real-life movie mogul David O. Selznick.

Harrison's Reports praised *The Bad and the Beautiful*: "Thanks to the masterful direction, the fine-screenplay, the exceptionally good dialogue and the excellent performances of everyone in the star-studded cast, *The Bad and the Beautiful* emerges as a first-rate adult drama, with a powerful dramatic impact and a quality that keeps one's eyes riveted to the screen."

1954

Sabrina

Release Date: 1954. Paramount. Producer and Director: Billy Wilder. Screenplay: Ernest Lehman, Samuel Taylor, Billy Wilder. Based on the play *Sabrina Fair* by Samuel Taylor. Camera: Charles Lang, Jr. Cast: David Ahdar (Ship Steward), Marjorie Bennett (Margaret the Cook), Humphrey Bogart (Linus Larrabee), Francis X. Bushman (Mr. Tyson), Colin Campbell (Board Member), Ellen Corby (Miss McCardle), Marcel Dalio (Brown), Harvey Dunn (Man with Tray), Otto Forrest (Elevator Operator), Walter Hampden (Oliver Larrabee), Charles Harvey (Spiller), Paul Harvey (Doctor), Audrey Hepburn (Sabrina Fairchild), Marcel Hillaire (The Professor), William Holden (David Larrabee), Martha Hyer (Elizabeth Tyson), Nancy Kulp (Jenny the Maid), Kay Kuter (Houseman), Bill Neff (Man with Linus), Emory Parnell (Charles the Butler), Kay Riehl (Mrs. Tyson), Marion Ross (Spiller's Girl), Greg Stafford (Man with David), Emmett Vogan (Board Member), Joan Vohs (Gretchen Van Horn), Nella Walker (Maude Larrabee), John Williams

(Thomas Fairchild). Hepburn, Bogart and Holden all won Academy Awards for their performances in this romantic comedy.

Chauffeur's daughter Sabrina Fairchild (Hepburn) gets romantically involved with two wealthy brothers, David Larrabee (Holden) and Linus Larrabee (Bogart). Sabrina is first enthralled by David but Linus interferes with that romance to prevent it from getting in the way of a major business deal. Unexpectedly, he also falls in love with Sabrina. *The New York Times* commented, "We might as well say it and get it over with, *Sabrina* is in our wistful estimation, the most delightful comedy-romance in years...."

1957

The Story of Mankind

Release Date: 1957. Warner Brothers. Director: Irwin Allen. Screenplay: Irwin Allen, Charles Bennett. Based on the book by Hendrik Willem Van Loon. Camera: Nick Musuraca. Cast: Jim Ameche (Alexander Graham Bell), David Bond (Early Christian), Francis X. Bushman (Moses), John Carridine (Khufu), Charles Coburn (Hippocrates), Ronald Colman (Spirit of Man), Melville Cooper (Major Domo), Nick Cravat (Apprentice), Dani Crayne (Helen of Troy), Richard Cutting (Court Attendant), Henry Daniell (Bishop of Beauvais), Helmut Dantine (Anthony), Anthony Dexter (Columbus), Reginald Gardiner (Shakespeare), Toni Gerry (Wife), Austin Green (Lincoln), Sir Cedric Hardwicke (High Judge), Major Sam Harris (Noble in Queen Elizabeth's Court), Eden Hartford (Laughing Water), Dennis Hopper (Napoleon), Edward Everett Horton (Sir Walter Raleigh), Hedy Lamarr (Joan of Arc), Alexander Lockwood (Promoter), Peter Lorre (Nero), Chico Marx (Monk), Groucho Marx (Peter Minuit), Harpo Marx (Isaac Newton), Melinda Marx (Early Christian Child), Bart Mattson (Cleopatra's Brother), Virginia Mayo (Cleopatra), Don Megowan (Early Man), Marvin Miller (Armana), Nancy Miller (Early Woman), Agnes Moorehead (Queen Elizabeth), Leonard Mudie (Chief Inquisitor), Cathy O'Donnell (Early Christian Woman), Tudor Owen (Court Clerk), Franklin Pangborn (Marquis de Varennes), Vincent Price (Devil), Ziva Rodann (Concubine), Cesar Romero (Spanish Envoy), Angelo Rossitto (Dwarf), Harry Ruby (Indian Brave), William Schallert (Earl of Warwick), Reginald Sheffield (Ceasar), Abraham Sofaer (Indian Chief), George E. Stone (Waiter), Bobby Watson (Hitler), Marie Wilson (Marie Antoinette), Marie Windsor (Josephine).

The Story of Mankind flopped despite an all-star cast. While Vincent Price as the Devil and Francis X. Bushman as Moses are believable, Harpo Marx as Isaac Newton and Dennis Hopper as Napoleon represent some of the worst casting in movie history. The film was lambasted in reviews across the country and rightfully earns its status as one of *The Fifty Worst Films of All Time*.

1960

Twelve to the Moon

Release Date: 1960. Columbia. Director: David Bradley. Screenplay: DeWitt Bodeen. Story: Fred Gebhardt. Camera: John Alton. Cast: Phillip Baird (Dr. Rochester), Tema Bey (Dr. Selim Hamid), Francis X. Bushman (Narrator), Ken Clark (Capt. John Anderson), Tom Conway (Dr. Feodor Orloff), Cory Devlin (Dr. Asmara Makonen), Anthony Dexter (Dr. Luis Vargas), Michi Kobi (Dr. Hideko Murata), Anna-Lisa (Dr. Sigrid Beomark), Robert Montgomery, Jr. (Roddy Murdock), Roger Til (Dr. Etienne Martel), Richard Weber (Dr. David Ruskin), John Wengraf (Dr. Erik Heinrich).

An ill-fated voyage to the Moon and an even more ill-fated movie venture.

1961

The Phantom Planet

Release Date: December 13, 1961. A Four Crown Production. Released by American International Pictures. Director: William Marshall. Screenplay: Fred Gebhardt. Camera: Elwood J. Nicholson. Cast: Francis X. Bushman (Sesom), Mel Curtis (Lt. Cutler), Anthony Dexter (Herron), Dolores Faith (Zetha), Dean Fredericks (Capt. Frank Chapman), Coleen Gray (Liara), Dick Haynes (Col. Lansfield), John Herrin (Capt. Beecher), Al Jarvis (Judge Eden), Richard Kiel (Solarite), Lori Lyons (Radar Officer), Michael Marshall (Lt. White), Earl McDaniel (Pilot Leonard), Akemi Tani (Communications Officer), Marion Thompson, Richard Weber (Lt. Makonnen), Jimmy Weldon (Navigator Webb).

Another science-fiction story by Gebhardt which fails to lift off the ground. The only bit of originality stems from Bushman's character's name, Sesom, which is Moses spelled backwards.

1965

Peer Gynt

Release Date: September 15, 1965. Willow Corporation. Distributed by Brandon Films. Director: David Bradley. Associate Director: Thomas A.

Blair, Roy Aggert, Jr. Based on the verse drama by Henrik Ibsen. Camera: David Bradley, Richard Roth, Robert Cooper. Cast: Rose Andrews (Anitra), Alice Badgerow (Cowherd Girl), Anty Ball (Cowherd Girl), Betty Barton (Ingrid), Thomas A. Blair (Button Moulder/Thin Person), David Bradley (Herr Trumpeterstraale/Bailiff), Francis X. Bushman (Boyg, a Voice in the Darkness), Robert Cooper (Man in Mourning), Alan Eckhart (Mads Moen), Roy Eggert, Jr. (Dovre-King/Mons. Ballon/Priest), Katherine Elfstrom (Solveig), Betty Hanisee (Aase), Alan Heston (Ugly Urchin), Charlton Heston (Peer Gynt), Mrs. Herbert Hyde (Old Woman), Rod Maynard (Lad), Warren McKenzie (MacPherson), Sarah Merrill (Woman in Green, as a Hag), George B. Moll (Drunk/Bedouin Chief), Charles Paetow (Aslak), Lucille Powell (Kari), Sue Straub (Old Woman), Audrey Wedlock (Woman in Green), Morris Wilson (Haegstad), Jane Wilimovsky (Old Woman).

Originally filmed in 1941 as a Northwestern University film project. Re-edited with a voice-over by Francis X. Bushman. Charlton Heston's first movie appearance at age 16.

Solveig (Elfstrom) rejects Peer Gynt's (Heston) love. For spite, he abducts a young maiden and takes her to the mountains where he seduces her and then abandons her. He is taken captive by a band of trolls after the Troll King's daughter, the Woman in Green, discovers him asleep in the forest. He escapes and returns to live with Solveig. He leaves Solveig and travels the world, becoming rich and stealing a sacred robe. Years later, he returns home to see a funeral with the corpse bearing his own image. Solveig's love saves Peer and he vows to reform his wicked ways.

1966

Ghost in the Invisible Bikini

Release Date: April 6, 1966. American International Pictures. Director: Don Weis. Screenplay: Louis M. Heyward, Elwood Ullman. Story: Louis M. Heyward. Camera: Stanley Cortez. Cast: Frank Alesia (Boy), Elena Andreas, Herb Andreas (Statues), George Barrows (Monstro), Jerry Brutsche (Boy), Francis X. Bushman (Malcom), Patti Chandler (Girl), Alan Fife (Rat Pack), Bobby Fuller Four (Themselves), Ed Garner (Boy), Sue Hamilton (Girl), Susan Hart (The Ghost), Bob Harvey (Rat Pack), Luree Holmes (Shirl), Mary Hughes (Girl), Boris Karloff (The Corpse), Patsy Kelly (Myrtle Forbush), Aron Kincaid (Bobby), Tommy Kirk (Chuck Phillips), Harvey Lembeck (Eric Von Zipper), John Macchia (Rat Pack), Claudia Martin (Lulu), Alberta Nelson (Alberta), Quinn O'Hara (Sinistra), Piccola Pupa (Piccola), Basil Rathbone (Reginald Ripper), Andy Romano (J.D.), Myrna Ross (Rat Pack), Benny Rubin (Chicken

Feather), Salli Sachse (Girl), Bobbi Shaw (Princess Yolanda), Nancy Sinatra (Vivki), Deborah Walley (Lili Morton), Jesse White (J. Sinister Hulk).

A lightweight "haunted house" comedy.

Radio Appearances

First Nighter

1931 CBS production in Chicago featuring Bushman.

One Man's Family

Bushman landed a spot in the NBC production *One Man's Family*, which ran from 1932 to 1959. It was the longest-running serial drama in radio history on a calendar basis (3,256 episodes) and the first serial to originate in San Francisco. Bushman played the role of the Rev. McArthur. The show ran 30 minutes.

Betty and Bob

Betty and Bob first appeared on NBC Blue in 1932, originating in Chicago. Bushman portrayed Peter Standish. The radio serial ran on NBC from 1932 to 1936, on CBS from 1936 to 1938 and again on NBC from 1938 to 1940. The show ran 15 minutes. The show depicted the married life of Betty and Bob Drake.

Rin-Tin-Tin

Rin-Tin-Tin began on the NBC Blue network in 1930 and ran to 1934. Bushman starred as the owner of Rin-Tin-Tin. The 15-minute episodes featured the heroic exploits of the famous canine.

The Story of Mary Marlin

The Story of Mary Marlin originated from Chicago on October 3, 1934. The 15-minute CBS broadcast covered the life of Senator Mary Marlin. Bushman portrayed Michael Dorne.

Stepmother

Bushman played the lead male role of banker John Fairchild in *Stepmother*, which originated in Chicago in 1938 and ran for four years. The storyline centers around John Fairchild's second wife Kay and her success in her new role as stepmother to John's children. The broadcast lasted 15 minutes. The Columbia Broadcasting System's *Stepmother* press release described Bushman as follows: "The handsome Bushman profile still rises jauntily above a pair of shoulders that remind one of his days as professional strong man, wrestler and six-day bike racer...."

Margo of Castlewood

A short-lived 15-minute 1938 broadcast on the Blue network featuring Bushman as the husband of Margo Carver (Barbara Luddy), the 79-year-old matriarch of the Carver family.

Those We Love

Those We Love originated in 1937 and ran on the Blue network and NBC through 1945. Bushman played the role of John Marshall, father of twins Kathy and Kit, around whom the story revolved.

Valiant Lady

Bushman played a supporting role in the opening episodes of *Valiant Lady*, which premiered on March 7, 1938, on CBS, later moving to NBC.

The Little Theater Off Times Square

Robert L. Bushman remembers his Uncle Frank hosting *The Little Theater Off Times Square* during his Chicago radio years. Bushman was the host, Mr. First Nighter.

The Adventures of Nero Wolfe

The original detective radio show *The Adventures of Nero Wolfe* began broadcasting in 1943 with Santos Ortega. Bushman took over the role of detective Nero Wolfe from 1945 through 1946 under the title *The New Adventures of Nero Wolfe*. Perpetual bad guy Sidney Greenstreet assumed Nero Wolfe's mantle in another resurrection of the show from 1950 until its final demise in 1951. The show appeared in 30-minute segments on the Blue, ABC, MBS and NBC networks.

This Is My Best: Miss Dilly Says No

A 1944–45 CBS broadcast originating from Columbia's Playhouse in Hollywood. The show was hosted by Orson Welles and featured an all-star cast. Welles portrayed Mr. Horatio, Ann Sothern played Miss Dilly, Rita Hayworth portrayed Mirella and Bushman was Mr. Gladstone.

Masquerade

This NBC radio serial broadcast from January 14, 1946, to August 29, 1947, as part of *The General Mills Hour*. The show originated in Chicago and moved in mid–1946 to California, where Bushman joined the cast.

Johnny Madero, Pier 23

Jack Webb primed himself for *Dragnet* with his starring role in *Johnny Madero, Pier 23*. Despite a solid cast, including Bushman, the 30-minute waterfront crime drama broadcast only ran during the summer of 1947 on MBS.

The Dan Carson Story

Bushman teamed up with Pat O'Brien and Lynn Bari in the 1947 production of *The Dan Carson Story* on NBC for *The Rexall Summer Theater*. Bushman played crotchety Major Carson. In a *New York Times* September 7, 1947, interview, Bushman commented, "I enjoy radio because I am now a lazy man. It is a more intense, more exacting medium than movies because mistakes cannot be corrected with retakes, but no advance study is necessary. Hours are easy. There are no waits for lights or scenes to be set up. One starts and stops rehearsals and programs on the dot of prescribed times. I like it." The September 22, 1947, *Time* called Bushman a hit in his role as Major Carson: "He oozed kindly wisdom persuasively enough to insure himself a berth on that show for some years to come...."

Let's Talk About Hollywood

Bushman appeared with Celeste Holm and Eddie Bracken in the July 25, 1948, 30-minute broadcast of *Let's Talk About Hollywood* on NBC.

Lux Radio

In 1950, Bushman appeared on *The Lux Radio Theater* with Greer Garson and Walter Pidgeon. Louis B. Mayer happened to be on the set and Bushman described the meeting: "After the scene he threw his arms around me."

Movie Town Radio Theater

Bushman appeared in a 30-minute segment titled "Encore" in 1951.

New Theater

In 1951, Bushman appeared with Ramsey Hill in a 30-minute segment called "After Many a Summer a Swan Dies."

The Railroad Hour

Gordon MacRae hosted *The Railroad Hour*, which ran from 1948 to 1954 on NBC. Bushman appeared in a 30-minute segment called "Sari" on March 17, 1952.

Suspense

This CBS mystery series featured guest appearances by many of the world's biggest names. Bushman appeared in "The City That Was" on November 17, 1957.

In the sixties, Bushman hosted a radio show with his fourth wife, Iva, once a week in Glendale, California, on KIEV. They discussed events in the entertainment world.

Television Appearances

Toast of the Town

When Victor Borge substituted for vacationing Ed Sullivan on the CBS series *Toast of the Town* in August 1951, Les Paul and Mary Ford headlined the show while Bushman and Norma Thorton gave a demonstration of the contrasting ways a movie scene would be played in silent movies versus today. Bushman also put in a plug for the newly released *David and Bathsheba*, in which he played King Saul.

Pepsi Cola Playhouse

Pepsi Cola Playhouse ran on ABC from October 2, 1953, to June 26, 1955, presenting dramatic productions. Bushman appeared on the April 16, 1954, episode "Home Sweet Home."

Schlitz Playhouse of Stars

Irene Dunne hosted the *Schlitz Playhouse of Stars*, which was broadcast on CBS from October 5, 1951, through March 27, 1959. Bushman appeared in "The Secret" on September 10, 1954.

George Burns and Gracie Allen Show

Bushman appeared on a October 22, 1956, segment called "The Interview."

The Big Surprise

The New York Times as well as local papers carried news of Bushman's role as contestant on NBC's quiz show *The Big Surprise*. For eight weeks starting on October 23, 1956, he answered questions on his chosen topic, "Love Poetry." "It's appropriate," he remarked. "After all, didn't I once have the reputation of being one of the world's great lovers? Furthermore, I like poetry and read a lot of it…. We shall be rich, if I can remember my poetry."

With $30,000 in winnings and a chance to turn that amount into $100,000, he left the decision whether to go ahead up to his wife Iva. Her response: "No!" With their $30,000 in hand, they flew back to Hollywood where Bushman was playing Moses in *The Story of Mankind* for Warner Brothers. The *Baltimore Sun* reported that people were so taken with the Bushman charm shown on the quiz show that new Bushman fan clubs emerged shortly thereafter, with a mixture of both old and young members. In a November 27 interview with Louella Parsons, Bushman credited Iva with his success on the quiz show. "She coached and coached me…. Iva said she was sure when the questions became harder they would ask me a Latin poem by Ernest Dowson, 'Non Sum Qualis Eram Bonae Sub Regno Cynarae,' Sure enough it happened."

Mr. Adams and Eve

Ida Lupino and Howard Duff starred in the situation comedy *Mr. Adams and Eve*, which appeared on CBS from January 4, 1957, through September 23, 1958. Bushman appeared in the episode "The Business Manager" on March 1, 1957.

The Bob Hope Show

Bushman appeared on the Bob Hope NBC variety show special on November 24, 1957. Afterward, actors such as Bushman, Danny Thomas and Tennessee Ernie Ford attended a party at Hope's home.

Court of Last Resort

Bushman appeared in the episode "The Steve Hardlika Case" on January 24, 1958.

77 Sunset Strip

Efram Zimbalist, Jr., and Edd Byrnes solved mysteries on and near Sunset Strip from October 1958 through September 1964 on ABC. Appropriately, Bushman played a role in the "All Our Yesterdays" episode on November 21, 1958. The November 21, 1958, *Los Angeles Times* reported, "Bushman co-stars ... on a program generally occupied with murder and skullduggery, *77 Sunset Strip*, the new mystery series. Yet tonight's play, according to Bushman, is a lovely story—no violence, nothing of that sort in it...." Other cast members included Doris Kenyon, John Carridine, Merry Anders.

The Danny Thomas Show

Bushman appeared on Danny Thomas' long-running sitcom on October 12, 1959.

Hedda Hopper's Hollywood

Bushman appeared in a 1959 episode of *Hedda Hopper's Hollywood* that enraged Ed Sullivan, who aired on an opposing network. Sullivan complained to Ronald Reagan, president of the Screen Actors Guild, that Hopper was paying $4,000 while he was spending over $42,000 for talent. Reportedly Sullivan had to pay Charlton Heston $10,000 for an appearance on his show while Hopper got Heston to agree to appear in a *Ben-Hur* sketch with Bushman and Ramon Novarro for only $210.

The Many Loves of Dobie Gillis

For "The Flying Millicans" episode (February 2, 1960), Bushman wore the same sandals and leather wristlets he wore as Messala in *Ben-Hur*.

Perry Mason

Bushman made two appearances on the popular *Perry Mason* drama series starring Raymond Burr. "The Case of the Flying Father" was broadcast on June 11, 1960, and "The Case of the Nine Dolls" followed on November 11, 1960. He portrayed a hard-bitten oil tycoon who meets a granddaughter he didn't know existed in "The Case of the Nine Dolls."

Theater

Bushman appeared in the episode "The Weekend Nothing Happened" on February 10, 1961.

Peter Gunn

Bushman was in "The Last Resort" episode on May 15, 1961. The ABC series starred Craig Stevens as detective Peter Gunn and featured original jazz themes by Henry Mancini.

The Golden Years of Hollywood

Gene Kelly hosted this special Hollywood documentary, appearing in November 1961. Bushman and "Golden Girl" JoAnne Quackenbush graced the cover of the *Herald/Express TV Week* while they looked over some of the films from "the old days."

G.E. Theater

Bushman appeared in "The Other Wise Man" episode on December 25, 1961. Ronald Reagan hosted the popular and long-running *General Electric The-*

ater through nearly all of its stay on CBS from February 1, 1953, through September 16, 1962.

Dr. Kildare

Bushman visited the set of *Dr. Kildare* as a guest actor numerous times. The show ran on NBC from September 28, 1961, through August 30, 1966. Bushman's appearances on the medical drama series included "The Bell in the Schoolhouse Tolls" (September 27, 1965), "Life in the Dance Hall" (September 28, 1965), "Some Doors Are Slamming" (October 5, 1965), "Enough *La Boheme* for Everybody" (October 11, 1965), "Now, the Mummy" (October 12, 1965) and "A Pyrotechnic Display" (October 18, 1965).

Batman

Bushman portrayed Van Jones in the back-to-back episodes "Death in Slow Motion" and "The Riddler's False Notion" on April 27 and 28, 1966.

Voyage to the Bottom of the Sea

In his last television appearance on October 16, 1966 (which came out after his death on August 24, 1966 at age 83), Bushman played an old man on the *Voyage to the Bottom of the Sea* episode, "The Terrible Toys." The science fiction series appeared on ABC from September 14, 1965 through September 15, 1968.

Stars of the Silents Saluted

Merv Griffin hosted the January 14, 1971, CBS special *Stars of the Silents Saluted*. Filmage from *Ben-Hur* was shown. Beverly Bayne and other living silent movie stars made appearances.

You Bet Your Life

Francis X. Bushman also appeared on Groucho Marx's long-running *You Bet Your Life* quiz show (broadcast date unknown). On that episode he told Groucho about the many statues for which he had posed.

Appendix I.
Lenore Bushman Filmography

Lenore was a strikingly beautiful woman. Her film credits include the 1927 silent film *The Love Wager* and two talkies. *Just a Gigolo* (1931) and *Red River Range* (1938). She appeared with such big stars as Ray Milland and John Wayne. In one of her uncredited bit parts, she reportedly gave Clark Gable his first movie kiss. She was quoted as saying, "I thought he was very capable, but, of course nobody dreamed how far he would go in the movies."

1927

The Love Wager

Release Date: February 21, 1927. Platinum Pictures. Distributed by Hollywood Pictures. Six reels. Screenplay and Director: Clifford Slater Wheeler. Camera: Earl Walker. Cast: Lucy Beaumont, Lenore Bushman, Gaston Glass, Jane Grey, Sheldon Lewis, Arthur Rankin, Dorothea Raynor, W.W. Watson.

A man sentenced to 20 years in prison for accidentally killing his mother receives a letter of introduction to a wealthy woman from his cellmate, who commits suicide. Upon release from prison, he meets the woman and becomes involved in a love wager.

APPENDIX I

1931

Just a Gigolo

Release Date: June 6, 1931. MGM. Seven reels. Director: Jack Conway. Adaptation and Dialogue: Hans Kraly, Richard Schayer and Claudine West. Adapted from the play *Dancing Partner* by Alexander Engel and Alfred Grunwald. Camera: Oliver T. Marsh. Cast: Maria Alba (A French Wife), Yola d'Avril (Pauline), Lilian Bond (Lady Agatha Carrol), Lenore Bushman (Gwenny), Albert Conti (A French Husband), Gerald Fielding (Tony), Charlotte Granville (Lady Jane Hartley), William Haines (Lord Robert Brummel), Ray Milland (Freddie), Irene Purcell (Roxana Hartley), C. Aubrey Smith (Lord George Hampton).

Irene Purcell played the role of Roxana Hartley in both the stage production and this movie version. William Haines, who portrayed Lord Robert Brummel, also assisted with the art direction for the film. *Just a Gigolo* was a bit controversial at the time. The Hays Office advised MGM that it objected to Brummel's clear intent to seduce Roxana.

Lord Robert Brummell (Haines) pretends to be a gigolo in order to escape the marriage being planned for him by his uncle, Lord George Hampton (Smith), to Roxana Hartley (Purcell), the daughter of a well-to-do friend. He poses as a gigolo to prove that his future wife will be unfaithful to him. He pursues Roxana in a variety of attempts to seduce her but fails. The two fall in love with each other after a series of comic charades. Lenore Bushman played Gwenny, Roxana's friend.

1938

Red River Range

Release Date: December 22, 1938. Republic Pictures. Six reels. Director: George Sherman. Screenplay: Stanley Roberts. Based on characters created by William Colt MacDonald. Camera: Jack Marta. Cast: Earl Askam (Morton), Stanley Blystone (Randall), Lenore Bushman (Evelyn Maxwell), Burr Caruth (Pop Mason), Edward Cassidy, Ray Corrigan (Tucson Smith), Olin Francis (Kenton), Kirby Grant (Tex Reilly), Lorna Gray (Jane Mason), Perry Ivins (Hartley), Theodore Lorch, Bob McKenzie, Sammy McKim (Tommy Jones), Jack Montgomery, Polly Moran (Mrs. Maxwell), William Royle (Payne), Al Taylor, Max Terhune (Lullaby Joslin), Fred "Snowflake" Toones (Bellhop), John Wayne (Stoney Brooke), Roger Williams (Sheriff).

Appendix I

Red River Range was part of the long-running Western series *The Three Mesquiteers*. This episode features the Red River Cattlemen's Association hiring mesquiteers Stoney Brooke (Wayne), Tucson Smith (Corrigan) and Lullaby Joslin (Terhune) to apprehend a gang of cattle rustlers. Lenore Bushman played Evelyn Maxwell, who "teaches" Brooke how to ride at a dude ranch. Brooke infiltrates the gang pretending to be a wanted killer and the ruse pays off with the eventual capture of the rustlers.

Appendix II. Francis X. Bushman, Jr., Filmography

The young Bushman began his career under his given name, Ralph Bushman. He first took to the stage with *When Love Is Young,* which played for 57 weeks on the Keith-Orpheum circuit. He made an impressive presence on stage and in films with his six-foot-four frame, blue eyes and brown hair.

At first he resisted the temptation to bill himself as Francis, Jr. "Dad gave me my own name, and if I can't make it amount to something, it's my own fault," he said. "Dad made his fame through his own efforts, and I don't intend to try to get some place by borrowing his name. I intend to work hard in this business because it's the thing I like, but if I ever get anyplace it will be as Ralph, not as Junior."

Nevertheless, Ralph Bushman took the name of Francis X. Bushman, Jr., after he had made his mark in the movies and signed a major studio contract. A number of the movies he appeared in were directed by Jack Conway, Bushman's son-in-law, who directed for MGM. Understandably, a number of films listed in various Francis X. Bushman, Jr., filmographies are in fact his father's films. We have made every effort to clear up this confusion. For the purposes of this filmography, we will identify Ralph Bushman as Francis X. Bushman, Jr., since that is how he was credited throughout most of his movie career.

Films are listed alphabetically under year of release.

1920

It's a Great Life

Release Date: August 29, 1920. Eminent Authors Pictures, Inc. Distributed by Goldwyn Distributing Corporation. Six reels. Director: E. Mason Hopper. Screenplay: Edward T. Lowe, Jr. Based on the short story *The*

Empire Builders by Mary Roberts Rinehart which appeared in *The Saturday Evening Post.* Camera: John Mescall. Cast: Francis X. Bushman, Jr. (Big Graham), Howard Halston (The Wop), Otto Hoffman (Prof. Mozier), Clara Horton (Lucille Graham), John Lynch (Watchman), E.J. Mack (Small), Molly Malone (Eloise Randall), Tom Pierce (Prof. Randall).

A lighthearted comedy of schoolboy love. A pearl discovered in an oyster spurs thoughts of South Sea adventure and school romance.

1923

The Man Life Passed By

Release Date: December 24, 1923. Metro Pictures Corporation. Seven reels. Director: Victor Schertzinger. Screenplay: Winifred Dunn. Camera: Chester A. Lyons. Cast: Andre de Beranger (Leo Friend), Hobart Bosworth ("Iron Man" Moore), Francis X. Bushman, Jr. (Jerry), Larry Fisher (Peters), William Humphrey (The Lawyer), Lydia Knott (John's Mother), Cullen Landis (Harold Trevis), Percy Marmont (John Turbin), Eva Novak (Joy Moore), Jane Novak (Hope Moore), Gertrude Short (Paula), George Siegmann (Crogan), Lincoln Stedman (Muggsy).

Industrialist "Iron Man" Moore (Bosworth) steals inventor John Turbin's (Marmont) plans. Turbin vows vengeance against Moore for causing his destitute situation. However, he forgives Moore after being befriended by Moore's daughters, Hope (Jane Novak) and Joy (Eva Novak).

Our Hospitality

Release Date: November 3, 1923. Joseph M. Schenck Productions. Distributed by Metro Pictures Distributing Corporation. Seven reels. Directors: Bustor Keaton, John Blystone. Screenplay: Jean Havez, Joseph Mitchell, Clyde Bruckman. Camera: Elgin Lessley, Gordon Jennings. Cast: Kitty Bradbury (Aunt Mary), Francis X. Bushman, Jr. (Clayton Canfield), Leonard Clapham (James Canfield), Monte Collins (Reverend Benjamin Dorsey), Edward Coxen (John McKay), James Duffy (Sam Gardner), Jean Dumas (Mrs. McKay), Buster Keaton (William McKay), Buster Keaton, Jr. (The Baby), Joseph Keaton (Lem Doolittle), Joe Roberts (Joseph Canfield), Natalie Talmadge (Virginia Canfield), Craig Ward (Lee Canfield). Buster Keaton both co-directed and starred in this classic comedic melodrama. Other Keaton family members in this film include Buster's wife Natalie Talmadge, their infant son, Buster Keaton, Jr., and Buster's father Joseph Keaton.

William McKay (Buster Keaton) returns home after many years and finds himself in the custody of the other faction in a Kentucky feud. However, he is promised "our hospitality" while he is in their territory. Naturally, he falls in love with the daughter of the leader of the Canfield clan. After a series of Keatonesque routines, McKay escapes and marries Virginia Canfield (Talmadge), settling the long-standing feud.

1925

Away in the Lead

Release Date: October 8, 1925. Goodwill Pictures. Five reels. Cast: Francis X. Bushman, Jr. No other information found on this film.

Never Too Late

Release Date: November 12, 1925. Goodwill Pictures. Five reels. Director: Forrest Sheldon. Screenplay: Samuel M. Pyke. Camera: Frank Cotner. Cast: Charles Belcher (Arthur Greystone), Francis X. Bushman, Jr. (Johnny Adams), Gino Corrado (Count Gaston La Rue), Lorimer Johnson ("The Boss" John Kemp), Ollie Kirby (Mabel Greystone), Roy Laidlaw (Robert Leland), Harriet Loweree (Helen Bentley). This film represented one of the first starring roles for Ralph Bushman and it was during this period that he switched to using the name Francis X. Bushman, Jr.

Johnny Adams (Bushman) rescues Helen Bentley (Loweree) from kidnappers and smashes their smuggling ring.

The Pride of the Force

Release Date: September 11, 1925. Rayart Pictures. Five reels. Director: Duke Worne. Screenplay: Arthur Hoerl. Cast: Francis X. Bushman, Jr. (Jack Griffen), Edythe Chapman (Mother Moore), Joseph Girard (Police Captain), Gladys Hulette (Mary Moore), Crauford Kent (Charley Weldon), James Morrison (Jimmy Moore), Tom Santschi (Officer Moore).

Officer Danny Moore (Santschi) is passed over for promotion after he stops to help an injured child and lets crooks escape. He redeems himself when he foils a bank robbery. Unfortunately, one of the people he arrests is his own daughter, Mary Moore (Hulette). Jack Griffen (Bushman), who is in love with Mary, proves her innocence.

Who's Your Friend

Release Date: December 16, 1925. Goodwill Pictures. Five reels. Screenplay and Director: Forrest K. Sheldon. Camera: Roland Price. Cast: Jimmy Aubrey (Bilkins, Lanning's Valet), Francis X. Bushman, Jr. (Ken Lanning), Hazel Howell (Yvette), Laura La Verne (Aunty), William Moran (Reverend Jenkins), Patricia Palmer (Alice Stanton), Erwin Renard (Gregory), Hal Thompson (Mr. Stanton).

The parents of Alice Stanton (Palmer) call off her wedding to Ken Lanning (Bushman) when another woman, Yvette (Howell), is discovered in his apartment. Rival suitor Gregory (Renard), who placed Yvette in Ken's apartment, proposes marriage to Alice, who believes that Ken has two-timed her. A number of false starts of the wedding provide comedy as does the actual marriage high above the city on a construction hoist.

1926

Brown of Harvard

Release Date: April 5, 1926. MGM. Eight reels. Director: Jack Conway. Screenplay: A.P. Younger. Camera: Ira H. Morgan. Cast: Mary Alden (Mrs. Brown), Mary Brian (Mary Abbott), Francis X. Bushman, Jr. (Bob McAndrews), Edward Connelly (Prof. Abbott), Ernest Gillen (Reggie Smythe), William Haines (Tom Brown), Jack Pickford (Jim Doolittle), David Torrence (Mr. Brown), Guinn Williams (Hal Walters). John Wayne made his first appearance in this film as a bit player. In the January 26, 1976, *The New York Times,* Wayne remarked on his 50 years in the movie business, "The average actor has a career of about 20 years. Well, 50 years ago this summer, I did my first scene, doubling Francis X. Bushman, Jr., in a football picture...."

Bob McAndrews (Bushman) and Tom Brown (Haines) vie for the attention of Prof. Abbott's (Connelly) daughter Mary (Brian). Tom makes unwanted advances toward Mary and Bob intervenes. Tom joins the football team only to sit on the bench. In an important game against rival Yale, Tom and Bob team up to score the winning points. Tom wins Mary's affections. The film was shot on location at Harvard and featured footage from the prior year's Harvard game.

The picture received good reviews and *Harrison's Reports* commented, "Francis X. Bushman, Jr., as the hero's rival, acts well...."

Dangerous Traffic

Release Date: June 7, 1926. Otto K. Schreier Productions. Distributed by Goodwill Pictures. Five reels. Screenplay and Director: Bennett Cohn.

Camera: Dwight Warren. Cast: Francis X. Bushman, Jr. (Ned Charters), Mildred Harris (Helen Leonard), Ethan Laidlaw (Foxy Jim Stone), Tom London (Marc Brandon), Jack Perrin (Tom Kennedy), Hal Walters (Harvey Leonard).

Seaside Record reporter Ned Charters (Bushman) helps revenue agent Tom Kennedy (Perrin) break up a smuggling gang.

Eyes Right

Release Date: June 29, 1926. Otto K. Schreier Productions. Distributed by Goodwill Pictures. Five reels. Director: Louis Chaudet. Screenplay: Leslie Curtis. Camera: Allen Davey. Cast: Francis X. Bushman, Jr. (Ted Winters), Dora Dean (Alice Murdock), Flobelle Fairbanks (Betty Phillips), Robert Hale (Lt. Smith), Larry Kent (Cadet-Major Snodgrass), Frederick Vroom (Col. Thomas A. Davis).

Former high school football star Ted Winters (Bushman) takes a job in the kitchen of the San Diego Military Academy because he cannot afford the tuition. The commandant, Col. Davis (Vroom), sees him playing a game of pickup football and arranges for him to attend the academy. Winters falls in love with Betty Phillips (Fairbanks), the commandant's niece. Jealous Cadet-Major Snodgrass (Kent) frames Winters on a drinking charge and he is dismissed from the academy. Betty pleads his case, Winters is reinstated and he leads the team to victory. Snodgrass is expelled for his misdeeds.

Midnight Faces

Otto K. Schreier Productions. Distributed by Goodwill Pictures. Five reels. Screenplay and Director: Bennett Cohn. Camera: King Grey. Cast: Charles Belcher (Samuel Lund), Francis X. Bushman, Jr. (Lynn Claymore), Nora Cecil (Mrs. Hart), Eddie Dennis (Useless McGurk), Larry Fisher (Red O'Connor), Al Hallett (Otis), Kathryn McGuire (Mary Bronson), Edward Peil, Sr. (Suie Chang), Jack Perrin (Richard Mason), Martin Turner (Trohelius Snapp), Andy Waldron (Peter Marlin).

Lynn Claymore (Bushman) inherits a deserted house in the Florida Everglades from an unknown uncle. A gang of crooks in cahoots with the butler and the maid kidnap Mary Bronson (McGuire). A Chinaman, Suie Chang (Peil), turns out to be an undercover agent who captures the crooks. Lynn and Mary are reunited.

1927

The Understanding Heart

Release Date: February 26, 1927. Cosmopolitan Productions. Distributed by MGM. Seven reels. Director: Jack Conway. Screenplay: Edward T. Lowe, Jr. Story: Pewter Bernard Kyne. Camera: John Arnold. Cast: Francis X. Bushman, Jr. (Tony Garland), Richard Carle (Sheriff Bentley), Harvey Clark (Uncle Charley), Joan Crawford (Monica Dale), Rockcliffe Fellowes (Bob Mason), Jeff Miley (Bardwell), Carmel Myers (Kelcey Dale). *The Understanding Heart* features Joan Crawford in an early starring role.

Forest ranger Bob Mason (Fellowes) kills Bardwell (Miley) in self-defense. However, he is convicted of murder due to Kelcey Dale's (Myers) false testimony. Mason escapes and is hidden from the authorities by Kelcey's sister Monica (Crawford), who is in love with forest ranger Tony Garland (Bushman). Tony goes for help when a fire endangers the party. Kelcey admits her perjury and Mason is exonerated. Monica and Tony profess their love for each other.

1928

Four Sons

Release Date: February 13, 1928. Fox Film Corporation. Ten reels. Director: John Ford. Screenplay: Philip Klein. Adapted from *The Saturday Evening Post* story *Grandmother Bernle Learns Her Letters* by Ida Alexa Ross Wylie. Camera: George Schneiderman, Charles G. Clark. Cast: Lt. George Blagoi (Officer), Stanley Blystone (Officer), Carl Boheme (Officer), Francis X. Bushman, Jr. (Franz Bernle), June Collyer (Ann, the American Girl), Earle Foxe (Von Stomm), Constant Franke (Officer), Hans Furberg (Officer), Albert Gran (Letter Carrier), James Hall (Joseph Bernle), Tibor von Janny (Officer), Leopold Archduke of Austria (German Captain), Hughie Mack (Innkeeper), Margaret Mann (Grandma Bernle), Michael Mark (Von Stomm's Orderly), George Meeker (Andres Bernle), Ruth Mix (Johann's Girl), Charles Morton (Johann Bernle), L.J. O'Connor (Aubergiste), Robert Parrish (Child), Jack Pennick (Joseph's American Friend), Wendell Phillips Franklin (James Henry), Capt. John Porters (Officer), Frank Reicher (Schoolmaster), Ferdinand Schumann-Heink (Officer), August Tollaire (Burgomaster). Background footage filmed in Germany. *Four Sons* is considered one of director John Ford's best early films.

Anti-war film about a Bavarian mother who loses three sons in the war and moves to the United States with her only remaining son.

Marlie the Killer

Release Date: March 4, 1928. Fred J. McConnell Productions. Distributed by Pathé Exchange. Five reels. Director: Noel Mason Smith. Screenplay: George W. Pyper. Camera: Harry Cooper. Cast: Richard Alexander (Sam McKee), Francis X. Bushman, Jr. (Bob Cleveland), Joseph W. Girard (John Cleveland), Klondike (Marlie, a Dog), Sheldon Lewis (Tom Arnold), Blanche Mehaffey (Marion Nichols).

Bob Cleveland (Bushman) is sent by his father (Girard) to their construction site to fire the foreman of the dam project. The foreman forces Bob's car off a cliff but he is rescued by passersby. Bob and his dog, Marlie prevent the foreman from blowing up the dam.

Haunted Island

Release Date: 1928. A Universal serial remake of the 1918 Universal Pictures production *Brass Bullet.* Ten episodes. Director: Robert F. Hill. Cast: Francis X. Bushman, Jr., Grace Cunard, Jack Daugherty, Helen Foster, Al Ferguson, Myrtis Grinley, Scotty Mattraw, Carl Miller, John T. Price.

The serial is loosely adapted from the pirate story *Pleasure Island.* No other information was found.

The Scarlet Arrow

Release Date: 1928. Universal Pictures. Ten episodes. Director: Ray Taylor. Cast: Francis X. Bushman, Jr. (Bob North), Charles Comstock, Al Ferguson, Bess Flowers, Aileen Goodwin, Hazel Keener.

Bob North (Bushman) of the Royal Canadian Mountain Police is featured in serial episodes involving the Canadian fur trade, gold mines and desperadoes.

1929

Father's Day

Listed in the *1929 Film Book.* No other information was found. See the discussion of the 1930 production of *Sins of the Children.*

1930

The Girl Said No

Release Date: March 15, 1930. MGM. Ten reels. Director: Sam Wood. Adaptation: Sarah Y. Mason. Story: A.P. Younger. Camera: Ira Morgan. Cast: Clara Blandick (Mrs. Ward), Francis X. Bushman, Jr. (McAndrews), Junior Coghlan (Eddie Ward), Phyllis Crane (Alma Ward), Marie Dresser (Hettie Brown), William Haines (Tom Ward), Leila Hyams (Mary Howe), William Janney (Jimmie Ward), William V. Mong (Mr. Ward), Polly Moran (Hildegarde).

Football hero Tom Ward (Haines) returns home after graduation from college. He turns his affections on Mary Howe (Hyams), who is infatuated with her employer McAndrews (Bushman). Ward kidnaps Mary from the altar and she realizes how much he loves her.

Sins of the Children

Release Date: June 28, 1930. Cosmopolitan Productions. Distributed by MGM. Nine reels. Director: Sam Wood. Adaptation: Samuel Ornitz. Based on the play *Father's Day* by J.C. Nugent and Elliott Nugent. Camera: Henry Sharp. Cast: Henry Armetta (Tony), Clara Blandick (Martha Wagenkampf), Francis X. Bushman, Jr. (Ludwig), James Donlan (Bide Taylor), Mary Doran (Laura), Dell Henderson (Ted Baldwin), Leila Hyams (Alma), Lee Kohlmar (Dr. Heinrich Schmidt), Louis Mann (Adolf), Robert McWade (Joe Higginson), Robert Montgomery (Nick Higginson), Elliott Nugent (Johnnie), Jane Reid (Katherine), Jane Wood (Muriel Stokes). Elliott Nugent, who played the role of Johnny, wrote the original story with his father, J.C. Nugent. Produced and reviewed under the title *The Richest Man in the World*. This film was a sequel to the 1929 MGM production *Father's Day*.

Immigrant barber Adolf Wagenkampf (Mann) uses his life's savings to send his son Ludwig (Bushman) to a sanitarium for his health. His other son Johnnie (Nugent) steals from his employer and disappears, leaving his father to cover the shortage. Johnnie later becomes a successful inventor and the family is reunited.

They Learned About Women

Release Date: January 31, 1930. MGM. Eleven reels. Directors: Jack Conway, Sam Wood. Screenplay: Sarah Y. Mason, Arthur Baer. Story: A.P. Younger. Camera: Leonard Smith. Cast: Francis X. Bushman, Jr. (Haskins), Mary Doran (Daisy), Tom Dugan (Tim), Eddie Gribbon (Brennan), Bessie Love (Mary), J.C. Nugent (Stafford), Benny Rubin (Sam), Joseph T. Schenck (Jack), Gus Van (Jerry). This baseball show business film featured vaudeville headliners Gus Van and Joseph T. Schenck and a number of show songs. This was Bushman, Jr.'s, first talking picture. The story was remade in 1949 as the more successful *Take Me Out to the Ball Game*.

Jack (Schenck) and Jerry (Van) give up professional baseball to become successful vaudeville singers. They both love Mary (Love) but a vamp, Daisy (Doran), ends up breaking up their singing team. They return to baseball and play in the World Series. Mary ends up with her true love, Jack.

Way Out West

Release Date: August 2, 1930. MGM. Eight reels. Director: Fred Niblo. Screenplay: Byron Morgan, Alfred Block. Camera: Henry Sharp. Cast: Francis X. Bushman, Jr. (Steve), Cliff Edwards (Trilby), William Haines (Windy), Vera Marsh (La Belle Rosa), Charles Middleton (Buck), Polly Moran (Pansy), Leila Hyams (Molly), Jack Pennick (Pete), Buddy Roosevelt (Tex), Jay Wilsey (Hank). *Ben-Hur* director Fred Niblo teams up with another Bushman. This was Niblo's last film for MGM.

Windy (Haines), a crooked carnival gambler, cheats some cowhands and is forced to work off his debt on a ranch owned by Molly (Hyams). He falls in love with Molly but is beaten in a fight by ranch hand Steve (Bushman), who is also in love with her. Windy saves Molly and she falls in love with him.

Spell of the Circus

Release Date: October 23, 1930–February 2, 1931. Universal. Ten episodes. Director: Robert F. Hill. Cast: Francis X. Bushman, Jr., Tom London, Monte Montague, Bobby Nelson, Albert Vaughn. A mystery story taking place under the Big Top.

Episodes:
1. A Menacing Monster. October 23, 1930.
2. The Phantom Shadow. October 23, 1930.
3. Racing With Death. October 23, 1930.
4. A Scream of Terror. December 8, 1930.
5. A Leap for Life. December 9, 1930.
6. A Fatal Wedding. January 6, 1931.
7. A Villain Unmasked. January 6, 1931.
8. The Baited Trap. January 19, 1931.
9. The Terror Tent. January 21, 1931.
10. The Call of the Circus. February 2, 1931.

1931

The Cyclone Kid

Release Date: October 28, 1931. Big 4 Film Corporation. Six reels. Director: J.P. McGowan. Assistant Director: William Nolte. Screenplay: George Morgan. Camera: Edward Kull. Cast: Ted Adams (Joe Clarke), Buzz Barton (Buddy Comstock), Francis X. Bushman, Jr. (Steve Andrews), Silver Harr (Sheriff), Caryl Lincoln (Rose Comstock), Lafe McKee (Harvey Comstock), Nadja (Pepita), Blackie Whiteford (Pete). The first of a series of three unsuccessful Buzz Barton Westerns. Bushman also appeared in the other two Buzz Barton Westerns, *Human Targets* and *Tangled Fortunes*, both released by Big 4 Film Corporation in 1932.

Steve Andrews (Bushman), a ranch foreman, is in love with ranch owner Harvey Comstock's (McKee) daughter Rose (Lincoln). Steve and Rose's brother Buddy (Barton) are on the trail of a band of outlaws rustling the Comstock Ranch's cattle. When Rose is kidnapped by the desperadoes, Buddy and Steve gather a posse of ranch hands and rescue her. Rose promises to marry Steve.

Galloping Ghost

Release Date: 1931. Mascot Pictures Corporation. Twelve episodes. Director: B. Reeves "Breezy" Eason. Cast: Ernie Adams (Brady), Frank Brownlee (Tom), Francis X. Bushman, Jr. (Buddy Courtland), Tom Dugan (Jerry), Stepin Fetchit (Snowball), Harold "Red" Grange (Himself), Dorothy Gulliver (Barbara), Eddie Hearn (Harlow), Gwen Lee (Irene), Tom London (Mullins), Theodore Lorch (The Mystery Man), Walter Miller (Elton). Director Eason previously assisted in the direction of the chariot race in the 1925 *Ben-Hur*.

This serial used the popularity of Red Grange and his football career as a basic premise. Grange takes the blame for accepting a bribe from a gambling syndicate to protect his teammate, Buddy Courtland (Bushman). The main storyline centered around the battling of two taxi cab companies. Prior to *The Galloping Ghost*, Grange had acted in two silent films, *One Minute to Play* (1926) and *Racing Romeo*.

Episodes:
1. The Idol of Clay.
2. Port of Peril.
3. The Master Mind.
4. The House of Secrets.
5. The Man Without a Face.
6. The Torn $500 Bill.

7. When the Lights Went Out.
8. The Third Degree.
9. Sign in the Sky.
10. The Vulture's Lair.
11. The Radio Patrol.
12. The Ghost Comes Back.

1932

Human Targets

Release Date: January 19, 1932. Big 4 Film Corporation. Six reels. Director: J.P. McGowan. Screenplay: George Morgan. Camera: Edward Kull. Cast: Ted Adams (Deputy), Buzz Barton (Buzz Dale), Francis X. Bushman, Jr. (Bart Travis), Edward Cobb (Duke Remsden), Franklin Farnum (Sheriff), Helen Gibson (Mrs. Dale), John Ince (Doctor), Leon Kent (Pop Snyder), Edgar Lewis (Recorder), Pauline Parker (Nellie Dale), Nanci Price (Marjorie Stockton), Rin-Tin-Tin (Himself), Fred Toones (Snowflake). Rin-Tin-Tin appears in this Buzz Barton Western. In the 1930s, Francis X. Bushman played in Rin-Tin-Tin radio episodes.

Buzz Dale (Barton), Bart Travis (Bushman) and Rin-Tin-Tin battle outlaws led by Duke Remsden (Cobb) over a gold claim. Stagecoach robberies and posse chases add to the action.

The Last Frontier

Release Date: 1932. RKO Radio. Twelve episodes. Directors: Spencer Gordon Bennet, Thomas L. Storey. Screenplay: George Plympton, Robert F. Hill. Cast: Judith Barrie, Joe Bonomo, Fred Burns, Francis X. Bushman, Jr., Yakima Canutt, Creighton (Lon) Chaney (Jr.), Slim Cole, Benny Corbett, Mary Jo Desmond, William Desmond, Fritzi Fem, Dorothy Gulliver, Frank Lackteen, LeRoy Mason, Pete Morrison, Richard Neill, Bill Nestell, Claude Peyton. *The Last Frontier* proved to be RKO's only foray into serial production. RKO also released a cutdown 65 minute version titled *The Black Ghost*.

The Black Ghost (Chaney) pursues a gang of outlaws headed by Bushman.

Tangled Fortunes

Release Date: 1932. Big 4 Film Corporation. Six reels. Director: J.P. McGowan. Screenplay: Frank Howard Clark. Camera: Edward Kull. Cast:

Frank Ball (John "Pap" Davis), Buzz Barton (Buzz Davis), Francis X. Bushman, Jr. (Jim Collins), Fargo Bussey (Chris), Edmund Cobb (Buck Logan), Francis Ford (Matt Higgins), Charles W. Hertzinger (Andy Wiggins), Carly Lincoln (Sally Martin), Jack Long (Lefty), Ezell Poole (Betty).

"Pap" Davis (Ball) is shot by Buck Logan's (Cobb) gang when he refuses to disclose the location of his mine. Buzz Davis (Barton) vows to avenge his father's death. A kidnapping, hidden gold and a shoot-out add to the excitement.

1933

The Three Musketeers

Release Date: 1933. Mascot Pictures Corporation. Twelve episodes. Directors: Armand Schaeffer, Colbert Clark. Screenplay: Norman Hall, Colbert Clark, Wyndham Gittens, Ben Cohn. Based on the novel by Alexandre Dumas. Cast: Hooper Atchley (El Kadur), Noah Beery, Jr. (Stubbs), Francis X. Bushman, Jr. (Schmidt), Yakima Canutt (Arab), Ken Cooper (Arab), Creighton (Lon) Chaney (Jr.) (Armand Corday), Gordon DeMain (Colonel Duval), William Desmond (Captain Boncour), Al Ferguson (Ali), Robert Frazer (Major Booth), Ruth Hall (Elae Corday), Raymond Hatton (Renard), Wilfred Lucas (El Shaitan), George Magrill (El Maghreb), Merrill McCormick (Henchman), Jack Mulhall (Clancy) Edward Piel (Ratkin), Robert Warwick (Col. Brent), John Wayne (Tom Wayne). Francis X. Bushman, Jr., and John Wayne meet again in Wayne's last serial. Also released as the feature *Desert Command*.

John Wayne stars and Bushman plays one of the Legionnaires in this production of Alexandre Dumas' classic *The Three Musketeers*.

Episodes:
1. The Fiery Circle.
2. One for All and All for One.
3. The Master Spy.
4. Pirates of the Desert.
5. Rebels' Rifles.
6. Death's Marathon.
7. Naked Steel.
8. The Master Strikes.
9. The Fatal Cave.
10. Trapped.
11. The Measure of a Man.
12. The Glory of Comrades.

1934

Death on the Diamond

Release Date: September 14, 1934. MGM. Seven reels. Director: Edward Sedgwick. Second Unit Director: John Waters. Assistant Director: Edward Woehler. Screenplay: Harvey Thew, Joe Sherman, Ralph Spence. Based on the novel *Death on the Diamond: A Baseball Mystery Story* by Cortland Fitzsimmons. Camera: Milton Krasner. Second Unit Camera: Ray Binger, Leonard Smith. Cast: Walter Brennan (Hot Dog Vendor), Herman Brix (Bruce Bennett), Don Brodie (Man on Ticket Line), Edward Brophy (Grogan), Francis X. Bushman, Jr. (Pitcher Sam Briscoe), Heinie Conklin (Hot Dog Vendor), James Ellison (Cincinnati Pitcher Sherman), Madge Evans (Frances), Franklin Farnum (Fan), Pat Flaherty (Coach Pat), Sam Flint (Baseball Commissioner), Sumner Getchell (Man on Ticket Line), C. Henry Gordon (Karnes), Fred Graham (Cardinal Player), Ted Healy (O'Toole), DeWitt Jennings (Patterson), Paul Kelly (Jimmie), David Landau (Pop Clark), Jack Norton (The Gambler), Dennis O'Keefe (Radio Announcer), Robert Livingston (Higgins), Nat Pendleton (Hogan), Jack Raymond (Man on Ticket Line), Willard Robertson (Cato), Mickey Rooney (Mickey), Joe Sauers [Sawyer], Harry Semels (Barber Customer), Max Wagner (Hot Dog Vendor), Bobby Watson (Radio Announcer), the Cincinnati Reds, the Chicago Cubs, the St. Louis Cardinals.

The St. Louis Cardinals are in the running for the pennant. As they close in, several players are injured and killed. Pitcher Larry (Young) spots someone placing an explosive in the dugout and beans him with the baseball. It turns out that the man is the groundskeeper who is in cahoots with the Cardinals owner's business rival. The Cardinals go on to win the pennant.

The Girl from Missouri

Release Date: August 3, 1934. MGM. A Jack Conway Production. Distributed by MGM. Eight reels. Directors: Jack Conway, Sam Wood. Assistant Director: Al Shenberg. Screenplay: Anita Loos, John Emerson. Camera: Ray June, Hal Rosson. Cast: Norman Ainsley (Second Butler), Lionel Barrymore (T.B. Paige), Clara Blandick (Miss Newberry), William "Stage" Boyd (Eadie's Stepfather), James Burke (Policeman), Francis X. Bushman, Jr. [listed as Ralph Bushman] (Doorman), Lane Chandler (Doorman), Hale Hamilton (Charles Turner), Jean Harlow (Eadie), Howard Hickman (Senator), Russell Hopton (Bert), Gladys Hulette (Secretary), Patsy Kelly (Kitty Lennihan), Fuzzy Knight (Cameraman), Henry Kolker (Senator Titcombe), Alice Lake (Manicurist), Marion Lord (Wardrobe Mistress), Alan Mowbray (Lord Douglas), Dennis O'Keefe (Dance Extra), Nat Pendleton (Lifeguard), Lee Phelps (Policeman), Bert Roach (Willie), Desmond Roberts (Butler), Larry Steers (Extra in Stateroom), Lewis Stone

(Frank Cousins), Carol Tevis (Baby Talker), Franchot Tone (Tom Paige), Richard Tucker (Office Manager), Charles Williams (Cameraman), C. Wilson (Lieutenant).

Frank Cousins (Stone) pleads with T.R. Paige (Barrymore) for financial assistance, but Paige refuses. Cousins gives chorus girl Eadie (Harlow) a pair of golden cufflinks and then commits suicide. The police believe Eadie is involved in Cousins' death but Paige clears her. Eadie follows Paige to Florida with hopes of marrying the rich man but falls in love with his son Tom (Tone) instead. To prevent his son from marrying the golddigger, Paige sets her up in a compromising situation. Tom eventually sees through his father's plot and marries Eadie.

Paris Interlude

Release Date: July 27, 1934. MGM. Eight reels. Director: Edwin L. Marin. Assistant Director: Les Selander. Screenplay: Wells Root. Based on the play *All Good Americans* by S.J. and Laura Perelman. Camera: Milton Krasner. Cast: Maurice Brierre (Intern), Edward Brophy (Ham), Francis X. Bushman, Jr., Fred Cravens (Reporter), James Donlin (Jones), Madge Evans (Julie Bell), Madeline Field (Fat Girl), Constant Franke (Intern), Ted Healy (Jimmy), Eddie Hearn (Reporter), Louise Henry (Mary Louise), Pauline High (Nurse), Otto Kruger (Sam Colt), Gus Leonard (Beggar), George Meeker (Rex Fleming), Una Merkel (Cassie), Gene Perry (Doctor), Bert Roach (Noble), Dan Roberts (Reporter), Rolfe Sedan (Waiter), Maude Truax (Duchess), Richard Tucker (Stevens), Carlos J. de Valdez (Doctor), Charles Warren (Reporter), Billy West (Reporter), Robert Young (Pat Wells).

American journalists in Paris vie for the affection of Julie Bell (Evans). The older, more experienced Sam Colt (Kruger) gains the upper hand but leaves on a foreign assignment to China, callously leaving Julie without saying goodbye. Despite this, Julie remains faithful. Word comes back of Sam's death at the hands of Chinese bandits and Julie and young reporter Pat Wells (Young) drown their sorrows together. She rejects Pat's marriage proposal and instead agrees to marry American stockbroker Rex Fleming (Meeker). Pat tries again and is successful in driving off Rex as a suitor. On the day set for Pat and Julie's marraige, Sam returns from China, near death. After he recuperates, he proposes to Julie. In the end, Pat and Julie marry and Sam heads off on another adventure, this time to the South Pole with Admiral Byrd.

Viva Villa

Release Date: April 10, 1934. MGM. Twelve reels. Directors: Jack Conway, Howard Hawks. Fill-in Director: William Wellman. Assistant Directors: John Waters, Red Golden, Arthur Rosson. Second Unit Director:

Arthur Rosson, Dick Rosson. Screenplay: Ben Hecht. Based on the book *Viva Villa* by Edgecump Pinchon and O. B. Stade. Camera: James Wong Howe, Charles G. Clarke. Cast: Henry Armetta (Mendoza Brother), Mischa Auer (Military Attache), Wallace Beery (Pancho Villa), William Von Brincken (German Reporter), Nigel De Brulier (Political Judge), Francis X. Bushman, Jr. (Calloway), Leo Carrillo (Sierra), Shirley Chambers (Wrong Girl), Emil Chautard (General), Andre Cheron (French Reporter), Steve Clemento (Member of Pascal's Staff), Donald Cook (Don Felipe), Phillip Cooper (Pancho, the Boy), Harry Cording (Majordomo), John Davidson (Statesman), Dan Dix (Drunkard), David Durand (Bugler Boy), Stuart Erwin (Johnny Sykes), Sam Godfrey (Prosecuting Attorney), Anita Gordiana (Dancer), Brandon Hurst (Statesman), Nick De Ruiz (Peon), James Martin (Mexican Officer), Francis McDonald (Villa's Man), Bob McKenzie (Bartender), John Merky (Pascal's Aide), Katherine de Mille (Rosita), Belle Mitchell (Spanish Wife), Leonard Mudie (Statesman), Chris Pin Martin (Peon), Herbert Prior (General), Frank Puglia (Villa's Father), George Regas (Don Rodrigo), Pedro Regas (Member of Pascal's Staff), Charles Requa, (Grandee), Tom Ricketts (Grandee), Julian Rivero (Telegraph Operator), Adrian Rosley (Mendoza Brother), Hector Sarno (Mendoza Brother), Joseph Schildkraut (General Pascal), Harry Semels (Soldier), Paul Stanton (Newspaper Man), Charles Stevens (Member of Pascal's Staff), George E. Stone (Emilio Chavita), Arthur Thalasso (Butcher), Arthur Treacher (English Reporter), Carlos De Valdez (Old Man), Michael Visaroff (Russian Reporter), Henry B. Walthall (Francisco Madero), Clarence Hummel Wilson (Jail Official), Fay Wray (Teresa).

Pancho Villa's rise from a petty bandit to Mexico's revolutionary leader. Wallace Beery was voted "Best Actor" at the Venice Film Festival for his portrayal of Pancho Villa.

When Lightning Strikes

Release Date: 1934. Fleuter Productions. Distributed by Regal Distributing Corporation. Six reels. Directors: Burton King, Harry Revier. Assistant Director: Bartlett Carre. Screenplay: J.P. McGowan. Camera: Edward Kull. Cast: Francis X. Bushman, Jr. (Matt Caldwell), Alice Dahl (Helen Stevens), William Desmond (Marshall Stevens), J.P. McGowan (Lafe Broderick), Lightning, the Wonder Dog (Himself), Tom London (Wolf), Murdock MaQuarrie (Jim Caldwell), Marin Sais (Mrs. Stevens), Blackie Whiteford (Hunky).

Lightning, the Wonder Dog, aides a father (MaQuarrie) and son (Bushman) fight off a rival (McGowan).

Appendix II

1935

Don't Bet on Blondes

Release Date: July 13, 1935. Warner Brothers. Seven reels. Director: Robert Florey. Screenplay: Isabel Dawn, Boyce De Gaw. Camera: William Rees. Cast: Vince Barnett (Brains), Herman Bing (Prof. Gruber), Daisy Bufford (Maid), Francis X. Bushman, Jr. [listed as Ralph Bushman] (Youth), Walter Byron (Dwight Boardman), Hobart Cavanaugh (Philbert O. Slemp), George Chandler (Henry), Spencer Charters (Doc), Andre Cheron (Albert), Clay Clement (T. Everett Markham), Joseph Crehan (Doctor), H. Dickinson (Telephone Man), Claire Dodd (Marilyn Young), Maude Eburne (Ella Purdy), Florence Fair (Nurse), Paul Fix (Youth), Errol Flynn (David Van Dusen), William Gargan (Numbers), Roger Gray, Harrison Green, Grace Hale (Matron), Winter Hall (Minister), Sam Hayes (Announcer's Voice), Ben F. Hendricks (Gangster), Selmer Jackson, Jack Kenny (Telephone Man), Guy Kibbee (Col. Youngblood), George Meeker, Milton Kibbee (Cashier), Marc Lawrence (Gangster), Jack Low (Gangster), Bob Montgomery (Telephone Man), Jack Norton (Slade), Jack Pennick (Gangster), Elsa Peterson, George H. Reed (Butler), Jack H. Richardson (Elevator Man), Cyril Ring (Second Man), Constantine Romanoff (Gangster), Ferdinand Schumann-Heink (Laboratory Assistant), Harry Seymour (Telephone Man), Eddie Shubert (Steve), Pat Somerset (Usher), Mary Treen (Switchboard Operator), Warren William (Odds Owen), Buddy Williams (Black Man), Tammany Young (Tout).

Former bookie Odds Owen (Williams) opens an insurance business and issues a policy guaranteeing payment if Col. Youngblood's (Kibbee) Broadway star daughter Marilyn Young (Dodd) marries within three years. To keep from paying off on the policy, Owen chases off potential suitors and starts dating Marilyn himself. He falls in love with her but she finds out about the policy and thinks he is only dating her because of the policy. She plans to marry T. Everett Markham (Clement), an old rival of Owen's, but Owen eventually prevails and wins the heart of Marilyn.

I Found Stella Parrish

Release Date: November 16, 1935. Warner Brothers. Nine reels. Director: Mervyn LeRoy. Assistant Director: William Cannon. Screenplay: Casey Robinson. Camera: Sid Hickox. Cast: Eddie Acuff (Dimmy), Harry Beresford (James), Harlan Briggs (Theater Manager), Elsa Buchanan (Maid), Francis X. Bushman, Jr. [listed as Ralph Bushman] (Erik), Rita Carlyle (Woman), Edward Cooper (Caligula), Phyllis Coghlan (London Operator), John Dilson (Producer's Assistant), Vernon Downing (Slave), Elspeth Dudgeon (Woman), Gordon "Bill" Elliott (Reporter), Charles Evans (Old Actor), Kay Francis (Stella Parrish), Lew Harvey (Reporter),

Ian Hunter (Keith Lockridge), Hugh Huntley (Cemelius), Olaf Hytten (Butler), Sybil Jason (Gloria Parish), Alice Keating (New York Operator), Crauford Kent (Lord Chamberlain), Milton Kibbee (Costumer), Walter Kingsford (Reeves), Lotus Liu (Mabel), Paul Lukas (Stephen Norman), Barton MacLane (Clifford Jeffords), Ferdinand Munier (Andrews), Vesey O'Davoren (Deck Steward), Tempe Pigott (Woman), James Ralph (Nana), Joseph Sawyer (Chuck), Shirley Simpson (Woman), Vernon Steele (Slave), Robert Strange (Jed Duffy), Lotus Thompson (Secretary), Mary Treen (Sob Sister), Emmett Vogan (Reporter), Mane Wells (Hotel Operator).

Successful actress Stella Parish (Francis) flees from her past (her daughter was born in prison after she was wrongly convicted of a murder her husband committed) when her husband Clifton Jeffords (MacLane) tries to blackmail her. To make a living she appears in burlesque.

Murder Man

Release Date: July 12, 1935. MGM. Seven reels. Director: Tim Whelan. Assistant Director: Dave Friedman. Screenplay: Ted Whelan, John C. Higgins. Camera: Lester White. Cast: Stanley Andrews (Police Commissioner), Lionel Atwill (Capt. Cole), Irving Bacon (Merry-Go-Round Man), William Norton Bailey (Welch), Robert Barrat (Robins), Alan Bridge (Judge), Virginia Bruce (Mary Shannon), James P. Burtis (Police Sergeant), Francis X. Bushman, Jr. [listed as Ralph Bushman] (Pendleton), George Chandler (Sol Hertzbereger), Davison Clark (Warden Powell), William Collier, Sr. ("Pop" Grey), Charles Coleman (Doorman), Jack Daley (Desk Sergeant), Charles E. Delaney (Policeman), William Demarest ("Red" Maguire), John Dilson (Meltzer), James Donlon (Bartender), Theodor von Eltz (J. Spencer Halford), James Flavin (Policeman), Robert Frazer (Doctor), George Guhl (Miller), Louise Henry (Lillian Hopper), Howard C. Hickman (Jennings), Joe Irving (Tony), Selmer Jackson (Vallist), Edward Keane (Editor), Fuzzy Knight ("Buck" Hawkins), Lucien Littlefield (Rafferty), Wilbur Mack (Bartender), Bob Murphy (Policeman), Milton Owen (Waiter), Reginald Pasch (Third Mate), Jeanie Roberts (Mable), John Sheehan (Sweeny), Harvey Stephens (Henry Mander), James Stewart ("Shorty"), Ben Taggart (Prison Guard), Spencer Tracy (Steve Grey), Harry Tyler (Doc Warren), Robert Warwick (Colville), Bobby Watson (Carey Booth). Spencer Tracy's first film for MGM, and James Stewart's film debut.

Homicide reporter Steve Grey (Tracy) keeps ahead of the police in solving the murder of a crooked businessman. He delivers an airtight case against con man Henry Mander (Stephens) and Mander is sentenced to death for the crime. In reality, Grey planned and committed the murder (Stephens ruined his father and caused the death of his estranged wife). In the end, Grey realizes he cannot send an innocent man to prison and confesses.

1936

Caryl of the Mountains

Release Date: March 27, 1936. Reliable Pictures. 61 minutes. Director: Bernard B. Ray. Assistant Director: R.G. Springsteen. Screenplay: Tom Gibson. Camera: Bill Hyer. Cast: Francis X. Bushman, Jr. (Sgt. Brad Sheridan), George Chesebro (Constable O'Brien), Steve Clark (Capt. Edwards), Earl Dwire (Inspector Bradshaw), Jack Hendricks (Constable Gary), Rin-Tin-Tin, Jr. (Rinty), Josef Swickard (Jean Foray), Robert Walker (Enos Colvin), Lois Wilde (Caryl Foray).

Rinty (Rin-Tin-Tin, Jr.) and Mountie Sergeant Brad Sheridan (Bushman) clear Caryl Foray (Wilde) of embezzlement and track down the murderer of Caryl's father and stealer of the bonds, Enos Colvin (Walker).

Fury

Release Date: June 5, 1936. MGM. Nine reels. Director: Fritz Lang. Assistant Directors: Horace Hough, Les Selander. Screenplay: Bartlett Cormack, Fritz Lang. Camera: Joseph Ruttenberg. Cast: Walter Abel (District Attorney Adams), Frank Albertson (Charlie Wilson), Erville Alderson (Plumber), Ricca Allen (Horsefaced Woman), Herbert Ashley (Oscar), Leila Bennett (Edna Hopper), Clara Blandick (Judge's Wife), Ward Bond (First Objector in Movie Theater), Edwin J. Brady (Dawson's Friend), Walter Brennan ("Bugs" Meyers), Ray Brown (Farmer), Frederick Burton (Judge Hopkins), Francis X. Bushman, Jr. [listed as Ralph Bushman] (Young Teacher), Theresa Brown (Woman Gossip), Bruce Cabot (Kirby Dawson), Nora Cecil (Albert's Mother), George Chandler (Milton Johnson), Harvey Clark (Pippen), Charles Coleman (Innkeeper), Jane Corcoran (Praying Woman), Jules Cowles (Lockup Keeper), Alexander Cross (Outgoing Watchman), Esther Dale (Mrs. Whipple), Jack Daley (Factory Foreman), Belle Donovan (Sheriff's Secretary), Edward Ellis (Sheriff Thaddeus Hummel), Helen Flint (Franchette), Mary Foy (Angular Woman), Roger Gray (Stranger), Bud Flanagan (Reporter), Jonathan Hale (Defense Attorney), Ben Hall (Goofy), Sherry Hall (Court Clerk), Edna Mae Harris (Black Woman), Lew Harvey (Mug in Poolroom), Raymond Hatton (Hector), Harry Hayden (Jailer), Sam Hayes (Announcer), Daniel Haynes (Taxi Driver), Dutch "O.G." Hendrian (Miner), Al Herman (Dawson's Friend), Howard Hickman (Governor), Robert E. Homans (Incoming Watchman), Arthur Hoyt (Grouch), Si Jenks (Hillbilly), Clarence Kolb (Mr. Pippin), Gwen Lee (Mrs. Garrett), Edward LeSaint (Doctor), Wally Maher (Chief Cameraman), Tom Mahoney (Bailiff), Murdock MacQuarrie (Dawson's Friend), Carlos Martin (Donelli), Edwin Maxwell (Vickery), Mira McKinney (Hysterical Woman), Frank Mills (Dawson's Friend), Esther Muir (Girl in the Night Club), Billy Newell (Hotdog Stand Owner), Elsa

Newell (Hotdog Stand Owner's Wife), George Offerman, Jr. (Defendant), Franklin Parker (Cameraman), Jack Perry (Man in Poolroom), Victor Potel (Jorgeson), James Quinn (Dawson's Friend), Ruth Renick (Sally Humphries), Bert Roach (Waiter), Christian Rub (Ahem), Sylvia Sidney (Katherine Grant), Lucille Stafford (Woman Gossip), Will Stanton (Drunk), Carl Stockdale (Hardware Man), Arthur Stone (Durkin), Everett Sullivan (New Deputy), Frank Sully (Miner), Gertude Sutton (Mrs. Tuttle), Albert Taylor (Old Timer), Tommy Tomlinson (Reporter), Spencer Tracy (Joe Wilson), Minerva Urecal (Fanny), Guy Usher (Assistant Defense Attorney), Morgan Wallace (Fred Garrett), George Walcott (Tom Wilson), William Wayne (Cameraman), Dick Wessel (Bodyguard), Huey White (Bus Driver), Dorothea Wolbert (Barber's Wife), Duke York (Taxi Driver), Janet Young (Prim Woman). Another Spencer Tracy vehicle, also featuring early appearances of Walter Brennan and Ward Bond.

Joe Wilson (Tracy) is mistakenly arrested on a kidnapping charge. His girlfriend Katherine (Sidney) goes to his assistance but arrives as an enraged lynch mob sets fire to the jail. Wilson escapes unnoticed and goes into hiding. Bitter, he seeks revenge. In the meantime, the real kidnappers are apprehended. The lynch mob is tried and found guilty of Wilson's murder. Katherine pleads with him to come forward and he relents, allowing the lynch mob members to be freed.

1937

Bad Guy

Release Date: August 27, 1937. MGM. Eight reels. Director: Edward Cahn. Assistant Director: Dolph Zimmer. Screenplay: Earl Felton, Harry Ruskin. Based on the story *High Voltage* by J. Robert Bren, Kathleen Shepard, Hal Long. Camera: Lester White. Cast: Ernie Alexander (Drunk), Richard Allen (Guard), Barbara Bedford (Mrs. LeClair), George Billings (Urchin), James Blaine (Detective), Don Brodie (Banker), Francis X. Bushman, Jr. [listed as Ralph Bushman] (Driver), Bruce Cabot (John "Lucky" Walden), Joe Caits (Footsie), Jean Chatburn (Betty Ryan), Clay Clement (Bronson), G. Pat Collins (Griffith), Roger Converse (Detective), Baldwin Cook (Spectator), Jules Cowles (Bartender), Richard Cramer (Dr. Wilson), Alan Curtis (Operator), Bob Davis (Linesman), Mary Dees (Girl), Drew Demarest (One-Arm Bill), John Dilson (Dr. Logan), Lester Dorr (Interne), Don Douglas (Instructor), Charles Dunbar (Spectator), Eddie Dunn (Joe LeClair), Cliff Edwards ("Hi-Line"), Paul Everton (Judge), Huntley Gordon (District Attorney), Ray Gordon (Blochman), Charley Grapewin (Dan Gray), Jack Grey (Conductor), Virginia Grey (Kitty Ryan), George Guhl (Cop), John Hamilton (Warden Summers), Mahlon Hamilton (Prison Doctor), Eddie Hart (Linesman), Dutch Hendrian (Bouncer), Warren Hymer ("Shorty"), Harry Jans (O'Neill), Ethan Laidlaw (Bouncer), Charles Lane (Lucky's Attorney),

Hal Le Seuer (Operator), Horace MacMahon (Malone), Charles McMurphy (Cop), Ivan Miller (Detective), Roger Moore (Clerk), Edward Norris (Steve Carroll), Frank O'Connor (Cop), Paddy O'Flynn (Repair Man), Garry Owen (Ned Burns), Leonard Penn (Detective), Lee Phelps (Repair Man), Dick Rich (Earl), Dutch Schlickenmayer (Bouncer), Harry Semels (Manelli), Philip G. Sleeman (Convict), Gertrude Simpson (Spectator), Ben Taggart (Desk Sergeant), Edith Trivers (Girl), Jerry Tucker (Urchin), Harry Tyler (Convict), Monte Vandergrift (Candy Salesman), Polly Vann (Spectator), E. Alyn Warren (Night Watchman), Bobby Watson (Wheel Chair Operator), Norman Willis (Edwards).

Linesman "Lucky" Walden (Cabot) kills another man over a gambling debt and is sentenced to be executed. Ned Burns (Owen) testifies that the killing was in self-defense and the governor commutes Walden's sentence to life imprisonment. After Lucky saves a fellow prisoner's life, the governor obtains a parole for him. Lucky again runs afoul of the law and convinces his brother Steve (Norris) to break him out of jail using electricity from the jail elevator to burn the bars. The police corner Steve and Lucky at a power station. Lucky gets electrocuted trying to escape while the police arrest Steve, proving crime does not pay.

Big City

Release Date: September 3, 1937. A Frank Borzage Production. MGM. Eight reels. Director: Frank Borzage. Assistant Director: Lew Borzage. Screenplay: Dore Schary, Hugo Butler. Camera: Joseph Ruttenberg. Cast: Abdullah Abbas, Eadie Adams (Eddie's Wife), Lowden Adams (Butler), Monya Andre, Stanley Andrews (Detective Bennett), John Arledge (Buddy), Sam Ash (Man Who Gets Punched), Herbert Ashley (First Detective), Irving Bacon (Jim Sloane), Snowy Baker (Himself), Barbara Bedford (Screaming Woman), Janet Beecher (Sophie Sloan), Clem Bevans (Granpa Sloan), Robert Brister (Comet Cab Driver), Helen Brown (Nora), Francis X. Bushman, Jr. [listed as Ralph Bushman] (Doorman), Orville Caldwell (Comet Cab Driver), George Chandler (Mr. Briggs), Jules Cowles (Janitor), Joseph Crehan (Curtis), Jack Daley (Mounted Policeman), Man Mountain Dean (Himself), Edgar Dearing (Tom Reilley), William Demarest (Beecher), Leigh DeLacy (Landlady), Jack Dempsey (Himself), Lester Dorr (Petty Officer), Jack Dougherty (Started), Frank DuFrane (Purser), Tom Dugan (Policeman), Jackie Fields (Himself), Paul Fix (Night Watchman), Edward James Flanagan (Cab Driver Stanley), James Flavin (Comet Cab Driver), Grace Ford (Mary Reilley), Edward Gargan (Dumb Cop), Natalie Garson, Maine Geary (Independent Cab Driver), Neal Glisby (Athlete), George Godfrey (Himself), Charley Grapewin (The Mayor), Jack C. Grey (Detective), Eddie Gribbon (Dumb Detective), Taski Hagio (Himself), Frank S. Hagney (Comet Cab Driver), Mahlon Hamilton (Doorman), Lew Harvey (Comet Cab Driver), Paul Harvey (District Attorney Gilbert), Russell Hopton (Buddy), Jack Hutchinson (Clerk), Gladden James (Mayor's Secretaries), James J. Jeffries (Himself), Joseph King (Jackson), Mitchell Lewis (Detective Haley), Ruth March (Mayor's Secretary), Don Sugai Matsuda (Athlete), Matt McHugh (Cab Driver), Robert McKenzie (Frank Turner), Jimmy McLarin (Himself), Charles McMurphy (Heller), Bull Montana (Himself), Paul Newman (Comet Cab Driver), Lillian Nicholson (Immigrant), Robert O'Connor (Comet Cab Driver), Oscar O'Shea (John C. Anderson), Jack Pennick (Comet Cab Driver), Lee Phelps (Immigration Officer Adams), Alonzo Price (Detective Meyers), Eddie Quillan (Mike Edwards), Luise Rainer (Anna Benton), Dick Rich (Comet Cab Driver), Joe Rivers (Himself), Dewey Robinson (Fuller), Maxie Rosenbloom (Himself), Matty Roubert (Newsboy), Dick Rush (Doorman), Harry Semels (Counter Man), George Skuttesky (Priest), Gus Sonnenberg (Himself), Will Stanton, Lander Stevens (Ship Captain), Nick Thompson (Counter Man), Jim Thorpe (Himself), Andrew J. Tombes (Inspector Matthews), Regis Toomey (Fred Hawkins), Spencer Tracy (Joe Benton), Helen Troy (Lola Johnson), Richard Tucker (Dr. Franklin), Victor Varconi (Paul Roya), Ray Walker (Eddie Donogan), Cotton Warburton (Himself), Larry Wheat (Minor Official), Alice White (Peggy Devlin), Guinn Williams (Danny Devlin), Eric Wilton (Butler), Harry Woods (Miller), Lillian Worth (Immigrant), Frank Wykoff (Himself).

Another Spencer Tracy vehicle. Features a number of notable prize fighters, including James C. Jeffries, who appeared with Francis X. Bushman decades earlier. Paul Newman plays a bit part in this film.

New York City independent cabbie Joe Bennett (Tracy) and his brother-in-law, Paul Roya (Varconi), battle large rival Comet Cab Company. Roya is killed by a night watchman who thinks he planted explosives. Anna Benton (Rainer), Joe's wife, is also implicated in the planting of the bomb and is to be deported. Joe discovers the real bomber and clears everything up before Anna sets sail for Europe. Jack Dempsey and the other fighters teach the Comet Cab Company cabbies a lesson they won't soon forget.

My Dear Miss Aldrich

Release Date: September 17, 1937. MGM. Eight reels. Director: George B. Seitz. Assistant Director: E.J. Babille. Screenplay: Herman J. Mankiewicz. Camera: Charles Lawton, Jr. Cast: William Norton Bailey (Dupont), Don Barclay (Second Drunk), Jack Baxley (Customer), Janet Beecher (Mrs. Sinclair), Arthur Belasco (Press Man), Margaret Bert (Boy's Mother), Marie Blake (Telephone Operator), Sunny Bupp (Little Boy), Francis X. Bushman, Jr. [listed as Ralph Bushman] (Hauser), Leonard Carey (Butler William), Roger Converse (Ted Martin), Marcelle Corday (Madame Sada), George Davis (Waiter), Bud Fine (Doctor), James Flavin (Doctor), Robert Greig (The Major Domo), Paul Harvey (Mr. Sinclair), Selmer Jackson (Captain), Rita Johnson (Ellen Warfield), Walter Kingsford (Mr. Talbot), Leonid Kinskey (Waiter), Adia Kuznetzoff (Servant), Gwen Lee (Hat Saleswoman), Edward J. LeSaint (American), Hal Le Suer (Reporter), Lya Lys (The Queen), J. Farrell MacDonald ("Doc" Howe), Wally Maher (Mechanic), Clive Morgan (Doorman), Paul Newlan

(Husky Man), George Noisom (Office Boy), Jack Norton (First Drunk), Edna May Oliver (Mrs. Atherton), Maureen O'Sullivan (Martha Aldrich), Garry Owen (Cop), Walter Pidgeon (Ken Morley), Renie Riano (Maid), Brent Sargent (Gregory Stone), Leonid Snegoff (Equerry), Carl Stockdale (Apartment House Manager), Charles Waldron (Mr. Warfield, Ex-Governor), Guinn Williams (Attendant), Harry Tyler (Taxi Driver James Joseph McElarney), E. Alyn Warren (Doctor), Billy Wayne (Joe). This film was Walter Pidgeon's first lead role at MGM.

Schoolteacher Martha Aldrich (O'Sullivan) takes control of the *New York Globe-Leader* after the death of her uncle. She butts heads with editor Ken Morley (Pidgeon), who refuses to hire women. She scoops Morley on a big story and takes a job as a reporter on the paper. A series of comical situations develop as they fall in love and Ken realize she is a crack reporter.

1938

Love Is a Headache

Release Date: January 14, 1938. MGM. Eight reels. Director: Richard Thorpe. Screenplay: Marion Parsonnet, Harry Ruskin, William R. Lipman. Suggested by a story by Lou Heifetz, Herbert Klein. Camera: John Seitz. Cast: Ernie Alexander (Johnson), Sam Ash (Headwaiter), George Billings (Kid), Marie Blake (Hillier's Secretary), Sidney Bracy (Waiter), June Brewster (Chorus Girl), (Don Brodie (Reporter), Francis X. Bushman, Jr. [listed as Ralph Bushman] (Guard), Chester Clute (Salesman), Jules Cowles (Doorman), Richard Cramer (Process Server), Edgar Dearing (Detective Reardon), Sarah Edwards (Mrs. Warden), James Farley (Sergeant), Chester Gann (Louie), Gladys George (Carlotta "Charlie" Lee), Ted Healy (Jimmy Slattery), Howard Hickman (Editor Williams), Leyland Hodgson (George), Fay Holden (Mary), Frank Jenks (Joe Cannon), Leonard Kilbrick (Kid), Henry Kolker (Mr. Ellinger), Leigh de Lacy (Older Woman), Hal LeSeur (Hocky Gent), Robert Middlemass (Police Commissioner), Ralph Morgan (Reggie Odell), Bea Nigro, Jack Norton (Bartender), Oscar O'Shea (Pop), Barnett Parker (Hotchkiss), Gll Patrick (Reporter), Jessie Ralph (Janet Winfield), Lillian Read (Hat Check Girl), Cyril Ring (Reporter), Mickey Rooney ("Mike" O'Toole), Buster Slaven (Kid), Julius Tannen (Mr. Hillier), Phillip Terry (Radio Man in Café), Franchot Tone (Peter Lawrence), Virginia Weidler ("Jake" O'Toole).

Critic Peter Lawrence (Tone) continually lambastes Broadway star Carlotta "Charlie" Lee's (George) performances despite being in love with her. Her agent, Jimmy Slattery (Healy), has her adopt orphaned children as a ploy to attract good publicity. At first she objects, but gradually she grows to love the kids. After Slattery places a story about them in the papers, Lawrence threatens to take them to the child welfare bureau. To keep the kids, Carlotta promises to marry millionaire Reggie Odell (Morgan). Slattery then arranges a fake kidnapping to garner more publicity. To keep Carlotta out of trouble with the police, Reggie promises to get the children away from her. She flees to a country motel with the children and Lawrence tracks her down. Carlotta pleads that she must marry in order to keep the children. Janet Winfield (Ralph), owner of the motel and justice of the peace, overhears Carlotta's predicament and marries Carlotta and Lawrence while keeping a shotgun aimed at Lawrence.

Man-Proof

Release Date: January 7, 1938. MGM. Eight reels. Director: Richard Thorpe. Assistant Director: Edward Woehler. Screenplay: Vincent Lawrence, Waldemar Young, George Oppenheimer. Based on the story *The Four Marys* by Fanny Heaslip Lea. Camera: Karl Freund. Cast: Eric Alden (Man in Drawing Room), Irving Bacon (Drug Clerk), May Beatty (Landlady), Marie Blake (Telephone Operator), Betty Blythe (Country Club Woman), Nana Bryant (Meg Swift), Francis X. Bushman, Jr. (Young Man at Fight), George Chandler (Third Reporter), Naomi Childers (Secretary), Harvey Clark (Artist), Diane Cook (Bridesmaid), Henry Davenport (Old Man Hitchhiker), Bob Davis (Man in Drawing Room), Bob Evans (Kid Nestor), Jean Fenwick (Bridesmaid), Grace Hayle (Second Woman), Edward Hearn (Ticket Man), John Hiestand (Radio Announcer), Arthur Houseman (Sour Puss), Mary Howard (First Girl), Ruth Hussey (Jane), Rita Johnson (Florence), Claude King (Man at Party), Gwen Lee (Girl at Fight), Hal LeSeuer (Man in Drawing Room), Myrna Loy (Mimi Swift), Matt McHugh (First Reporter), Claire Meyers (Bridesmaid), John Miljan (Tommy Gaunt), Julius Molnar, Jr. (Office Boy), Jack Norton (Drunk at Fight), Oscar O'Shea (Bartender Gus), Leonard Penn (Bob), Walter Pidgeon (Alan Whyte), Aileen Pringle (First Woman), Frances Reid (Second Girl), Rosalind Russell (Elizabeth Kent Wythe), Clarice Sherry (Bridesmaid), William Stack (Minister), Jerome Storm (Poolroom Man), Dan Toby (Fight Announcer), Franchot Tone (Jimmy Kilmartin), Laura Treadwell (Third Woman), Dorothy Vaughn (Matron), Charles Williams (Second Reporter), Dick Winslow (Messenger Boy), Duke York (Referee). All-star cast with Myrna Loy, Rosalind Russell, Franchot Tone, and Walter Pidgeon.

Mimi Swift (Loy) pines for playboy Alan Whyte (Pidgeon) despite his having married Elizabeth Kent (Russell). Newspaper artist and friend Jimmy Kilmartin (Tone) helps her get a job as an illustrator on his paper in the hope that she will forget Whyte. When Whyte returns from his honeymoon, Mimi makes a play for him. Elizabeth tells Mimi that Whyte is too selfish to love anyone but himself. Heartbroken, Mimi consoles herself with Jimmy. They realize they are in love with each other.

The Shining Hour

Release Date: November 18, 1938. MGM. A Frank Borzage Production. Eight reels. Director: Frank Borzage. Assistant Director: Lew Borzage.

Screenplay: Jane Murfin, Ogden Nash. Based on the play by Keith Winter. Camera: George Folsey. Cast: Frank Albertson (Benny Collins), Fay Bainter (Hannah Linden), Harry Barris (Bertie), Granville Bates (Man), Francis X. Bushman, Jr. (Doorman), George Chandler (Press Agent), Charles C. Coleman (Butler), Jim Conlin (Man), Roger Converse (Clerk), Joan Crawford (Olivia Riley), Tony De Marco (Olivia's Dance Partner), Melvyn Douglas (Henry Linden), Sarah Edwards (Woman), Bess Flowers (Burse), Grace Goodall (Mrs. Smart), Grace Hayle (Mrs. Briggs), Allyn Joslyn (Roer Franklin), Hattie McDaniel (Belvedere), Buddy Messenger (Elevator Boy), Oscar O'Shea (Charlie Collins), Claire Owen (Stewardess), Frank Puglia (Headwaiter), Jack Raymond (Farmer), Cyril Ring (Candid Cameraman), Edwin Stanley (Minister), Margaret Sullavan (Judy Linden), Jacques Vanaire (Waiter), E. Alyn Warren (Leonard), Robert Young (David Linden).

Nightclub entertainer Olivia Riley (Crawford) marries wealthy farmer Henry Linden (Douglas) not for love but for social status. They move to the family farm, where she falls in love with Henry's brother, David (Young), who also feels attraction for Olivia. David's wife, Judy, rushes into a burning building after she discovers David's affections for Olivia. Olivia rescues Judy (Sullavan). David returns to his wife, and Henry and Olivia go to live elsewhere.

Three Comrades

Release Date: June 3, 1938. MGM. A Frank Borzage Production. Ten reels. Director: Frank Borzage. Assistant Director: Lew Borzage. Screenplay: F. Scott Fitzgerald, Edward E. Paramore. Camera: Joseph Ruttenberg, Karl Freund. Cast: Ricca Allen (Housekeeper), Stanley Andrews (Officer Giving Toast), Jessie Arnold (Nurse), Lionel Atwill (Breuer), Barbara Bedford (Rita), Walter Bonn (Adjutant), Henry Brandon (Man with Patch), Francis X. Bushman, Jr. [listed as Ralph Bushman] (Comic), George Chandler (Comic), Spencer Charters (Herr Schultz), Harvey Clark (Baldheaded Man), Roger Converse (Becker's Assistant), Henry Hull (Dr. Heinrich Becker), Charley Grapewin (Local Doctor), William Haade (Younger Vogt Man), Donald Haines (Kid), Elva Kellogg (Singer in "Yankee Ragtime College Jazz" Number), Guy Kibbee (Alfons), Priscilla Lawson (Frau Brunner), Mitchell Lewis (Boris), Marjorie Main (Old Woman), Claire McDowell (Frau Zalewska), Edward McWade (Major Domo), Esther Muir (Frau Schmidt), Ferdinand Munier (Burgomaster), George Offerman, Jr. (Adolph), Sarah Padden (Frau Schultz), Leonard Penn (Tony), St. Luke's Choristers, Margaret Sullavan (Patricia Hollmann), Robert Taylor (Erich Lohkamp), Phillip Terry (Soldier Who Embraces Father), Franchot Tone (Otto Koster), E. Alyn Warren (Bookstore Owner), Norman Willis (Eldest Vogt Man), Morgan Wallace (Owner of Wrecked Car), Monty Woolley (Dr. Felix Jaffe), Robert Young (Gottfried Lenz), George Zucco (Dr. Plauten). An all-star cast with Margaret Sullavan, Robert Taylor, Franchot Tone, and Robert Young starring in a stark, co-scripted screenplay by F. Scott Fitzgerald.

Three German soldiers, Erich (Taylor), Otto (Tone), and Gottfried (Young), start an automobile repair business after the war. Erich meets and falls in love with Hollmann (Sullavan). They marry but their bliss is short-lived because she suffers from tuberculosis. Gottfried is killed by thugs and Hollmann succumbs to her disease. The movie ends with the spirits of Hollmann and Gottfried visiting Otto and Erich as they leave the cemetery.

Too Hot to Handle

Release Date: September 16, 1938. MGM. Eleven reels. Director: Jack Conway. Second Unit Director: Richard Rosson. Assistant Director: Joseph Newman, Harold Weinberger. Screenplay: Laurence Stallings, John Lee Mahin. Based on a story by Len Hammond. Camera: Harold Rosson. Cast: Ernie Alexander (Projectionist), Eddie Arden (Cycle Messenger), William Broadus (Medicine Man), Francis X. Bushman, Jr. [listed as Ralph Bushman] (Newsreel Man), Bill Carey (Elevator Boy), Leo Carrillo (Joselito), Thomas Carr, Steve Carruthers (Radio Operator), Luke Chan (Wong), Lane Chandler (Cameraman), Betty Ross Clarke (Mrs. Harding), Walter Connolly ("Gaby" MacArthur), Ray Cooke (Cycle Messenger), Nick Copeland (Still Cameraman), Nell Craig (Todd's Secretary), Joseph Crehan (Advertising Man), Hal K. Dawson (Cutter), John Dilson (Laboratory Foreman), Drew Demorest (Still Man), Mimi Doyle (Sob Sister), Charles Dunbar (Expressman), Eddie Dunn (Newsreel Man), William Dunn (Native Chief), Frank Faylen (Assistant Dubber), James Flavin (Reporter), Harry Fleischmann (Newsreel Man), Jessie Fung (Chinese Specialty Dancer), Willie Fung (Willie), Clark Gable (Chris Hunter), Chester Gan (Chinese Sergeant), Natalie Garson (Stewardess), Gregory Gaye ("Popoff"), John Hamilton (Fairfield), Johnny Hines (Parsons), Selmer Jackson (Coast Guard Captain), Robert Emmett Keane (Foreign Editor), David Kerman (Still Man), Paul King (Bell Hop), Henry Kolker ("Pearly" Todd), Paul Kruer (Policeman), Eddie Lee (Officer), Richard Loo (Charlie), Myrna Loy (Alma Harding), George Peter Lynn (Harry Harding), Marjorie Main (Miss Wayne), Wilbur Mar (Chinese Specialty Dancer), Philo McCullough (Cameraman), Bud McTaggart (Cycle Messenger), Buddy Messenger (Cycle Messenger), Walter Miller (First Flier), Roger Moore (Still Man), Albert Morin (Newsreel Man), Lillie Mui ("Tootsie"), Kenneth Nolan (Reporter), Patsy O'Connor ("Fake" Hulda Harding), Ted Oliver (Newsreel Man), Edwin Parker (Coast Guard Attendant), Franklin Parker (Attendant), Edward Peil, Sr. (Newsreel Man), Lee Phelps (Policeman), Walter Pidgeon (Bill Dennis), Chris Pin Martin (Pedro), Aileen Pringle (Mrs. MacArthur), Cyril Ring (Cameraman), Don Roberts (Reporter), William H. Royle (Second Flier), Al Shean (Gumpel), Charles Sherlock (Cameraman), Edwin Stanley (Advertising Man), Charles Sullivan (Gunman), Stanley Taylor (Newsreel Man), Harry Tyler (Newsreel Man), Monte Vandergrift (Policeman), Ray Walker (Sound Mixer), George Webb (Mr. Rodney, Attorney), Virginia Weidler (Hulda Harding), Robert Whitmen (Newsreel Man), Josephine Whittell ("Fake" Mrs. Harding), Martin Wilkins (Native Guide), Ernest Wilson (Medicine Man). Top movie draws Clark

Appendix II

231

Gable and Myrna Loy team up in a newsreel photographer story, directed by Jack Conway.

Parsons (Hines), the brother of aviatrix Alma Harding (Loy), is missing in a South American jungle. Harding convinces rival newsreel men Chris Hunter (Gable) and Bill Dennis (Pidgeon) to search for him. They track him down and discover he is the captive of a voodoo cult. Hunter uses photography as his own brand of "Black Magic" to distract the tribe. Harding and Dennis assist in the escape aboard a seaplane. Hunter scoops Dennis with his newsreel footage and gets the girl.

1939

Let Freedom Ring

Release Date: February 24, 1939. MGM. Nine reels. Director: Jack Conway. Second Unit Director: John Waters. Assistant Director: Horace Hough. Screenplay: Ben Hecht. Based on original story by Ben Hecht. Camera: Sidney Wagner. Cast: Luis Alberni (Tony), Maude Allen (Hilda), C.E. Anderson (Sheriff Hicks), Edward Arnold (Jim Wade), Trevor Bardette (Gagan), Lionel Barrymore (Thomas Logan), Billy Bevan (Cockney), Virginia Bruce (Maggie Adams), Francis X. Bushman, Jr. [listed as Ralph Bushman] (Gagan Henchman), Charles Butterworth (The Mackerel), Eddie Dunn ("Curly"), Nelson Eddy (Steve Logan), Harry Fleischmann (Gagan Henchman), George F. Hayes (Jerry "Pop" Wilkie), Louis Jean Heydt (Ned Wilkie), Tenen Holtz (Hunky), Guy Kibbee (Judge David Bronson), Aida Kuznetzoff (Pole), Mitchell Lewis (Joe), Philo McCullough (Gagan Henchman), Sarah Padden ("Ma" Logan), Emory Parnell (Swede), Victor Potel (Second Swede), Dick Rich ("Bumper" Jackson), Constantine Romanoff (Russian), Lionel Royce (German), Syd Saylor (First Surveyor), Ted Thompson (Second Surveyor), Raymond Walburn (Underwood), H.B. Warner (Rutledge).

Steve Logan (Eddy) outwits Jim Wade (Arnold), the head of the railroad trying to take over Logan's small western hometown of Culver City. He pretends to ally himself with Wade but saves the town from tyranny by working underground.

1941

Honky Tonk

Release Date: 1941. MGM. Ten reels. Director: Jack Conway. Screenplay: Marguerite Roberts, John Sanford. Camera: Harold Rosson. Cast: Erville

Alderson (Man with Rail), Demetrius Alexis (Tug), Hooper Atchley (Senator Ford), Dorothy Ates (Dance Hall Girl), Don Barclay (Man with Gun), Jack Baxley (Citizen), Art Belasco (Pallbearer), Betsy Blythe (Mrs. Wilson), Veda Ann Borg (Pearl), Ed Brady (Waiter), Alan Bridge (Man in Meeting House), Francis X. Bushman, Jr. [listed as Ralph Bushman], John "Jack" Carr (Brazos' Henchman), Edward Cassidy (Citizen), Tom Chatterton (Citizen), Heinie Conklin (Dental Patient), Sheila Darcy (Louise), Albert Dekker (Brazos Hearn), Joe Devlin (Miner), John Farrell (Man with Feathers), Clark Gable (Candy Johnson), Dorothy Granger (Saloon Girl), Eddie Gribbon (Pallbearer), Earl Gunn (Miner), William Haade (Miner), Lew Harvey (Blackie), Russell Hicks (Dr. Otis), Al Hill (Miner), Fay Holderness (Bricklayer), Lew Kelly (Miner), Cy Kendall (Man with Tar), Marjorie Main (Reverend Mrs. Varner), John Maxwell (Kendall), Charles McAvoy (Miner), Art Miles (Dealer), Frank Mills (Pallbearer), Howard Mitchell (Citizen), Monte Montague (Miner), Frank Morgan (Judge Cotton), Esther Muir (Prostitute), Horace Murphy (Butler), Tiny Newlan (Gentleman), Ted Oliver (Miner), Gordon O'Malley (Guest), Anne O'Neal (Nurse), Henry O'Neill (Daniel Wells), William Pagan (Citizen), Ralph Peters (Pallbearer), Lee Phelps (Man in Meeting House), Henry Roquemore (Butcher), Dick Rush (Dentist), Syd Saylor (Pallbearer), Harry Semels (Pallbearer), John Sheehan (Citizen), Jack C. Smith (Citizen), Carl Stockdale (Citizen), Charles Sullivan (Miner), Elliott Sullivan (Candy's Man), Ray Teal (Poker Player), Bill Telaak (Citizen), Claire Trevor ("Gold Dust" Nelson), Lana Turner (Elizabeth Cotton), Malcolm Waite (Miner), Morgan Wallace (Adams), Eddy Waller (Train Conductor), Chill Wills (The Sniper), Douglas Wood (Governor Wilson), Harry Worth (Harry Gates), Will Wright (Man in Meeting House). Gable and Turner heat up the action in this western setting. Gable's wife, Carole Lombard, appeared on set to make sure the romance stayed on screen.

Crooked gambler Candy Johnson (Gable) charms the daughter, Elizabeth (Turner), of corrupt Judge Cotton (Morgan). He marries Elizabeth and opens a saloon. Despite his own past corruption, Judge Cotton threatens to expose Johnson as a crook. Cotton dies and Elizabeth, hearing of her father's death, falls from her buggy. Her child is stillborn. Johnson leaves town in mourning. Realizing she loves him more than ever, Elizabeth follows.

Love Crazy

Release Date: May 23, 1941. MGM. Director: Jack Conway. Screenplay: William Ludwig, Charles Lederer, David Hertz. Based on story by William Ludwig, David Hertz. Camera: Ray June. Cast: Dick Allan (Detective), Jimmy Ames (Taxi Driver), Joan Barclay (Telephone Operator), Florence Bates (Mrs. Cooper), Barbara Bedford (Secretary), Sidney Blackmer (George Hennie), Wade Boteler (Detective Captain), Aldrich Bowker (Doorman), Francis X. Bushman, Jr. [listed as Ralph Bushman] (Guard), Jack Carson (Ward Willoughby), Ken Christy (Guard), Elisha Cook, Jr. (Elevator Boy), Joseph Crehan (Judge), Jay

Appendix II

Eaton (Guest), Fern Emmett (Martha), Harry Fleischmann (Driver), Pat Gleason (Detective), Roy Gordon (Doctor), Jesse Graves (Butler), George Guhl (Driver), Sara Haden (Cecilia Landis), Eddie Hart (Detective), George Irving (Doctor), Selmer Jackson (Doctor), Richard Kipling (Guest), Bill Lally (Guard), Kathleen Lockhart (Mrs. Bristol), George Lolier (Detective), Myrna Loy (Susan Ireland), Donald MacBride ("Pinky" Grayson), George Magrill (Guard), Philo McCullough (Detective), Charles McMurphy (Detective), James H. McNamara (Guest), George Meeker (DeWest), James Millican (Detective), Jack Mulhall (Court Clerk), Clarence Muse (Robert), Broderick O'Farrell (Guest), Paul Palmer (Detective), Gail Patrick (Isobel Grayson), Ed Peil, Sr. (Detective), Lee Phelps (Guard), James Pierce (Detective), William Powell (Steven Ireland), Kai Robinson (Detective), Sig Rumann (Dr. Wuthering), Byron Shores (Doctor), Vladimir Sokoloff (Dr. Klugle), Larry Steers (Guest), Rudy Steinbock (Detective), Harry Strang (Sergeant), William Tannen (Attendant), Edward Van Sloan (Doctor), Emmett Vogan (Doctor), Ian Wolfe (Doctor), Douglas Wood (Doctor). William Powell and Myrna Loy, famous as Nick and Nora Charles, team up for a change of pace in this romantic comedy.

Steven Ireland (Powell) and his wife, Susan (Loy), are about to celebrate their fourth anniversary, but a series of misconceptions causes them to break up. Steven fakes insanity to prevent his wife from divorcing him, but the ruse backfires and the judge commits him to an insane asylum. He escapes with the police in hot pursuit. He evades them by dressing in drag. All ends well with Steven and Susan reunited after many comical situations unfold.

1942

Crossroads

Release Date: 1942. MGM. Director: Jack Conway. Screenplay: Gus Trosper. Based on story by John Kafka, Howard Emmett Rogers. Camera: Joseph Ruttenberg. Cast: Enrique Acosta (Associate Judge), Felix Bressart (Dr. Andre Tessler), Francis X. Bushman, Jr. (Giant Policeman), Jack Chefe (Reporter), Frank Conroy (Defense Attorney), Armand Cortes (Clerk), Alex Davidoff (Detective), George Davis (Clerk), Jean Del Val (Court Clerk), Guy D'Enery (Reporter), William Edmunds (Driver), Adolph Faylauer (Associate Judge), Budd Fine (Paris Policeman), Harry Fleischmann (Assistant Defense Attorney), Christian J. Frank (Guard), Octavio Giraud (Associate Judge), Gibson Gowland (Reporter), Grace Hayle (Patient), Adrian Kerbrat (Boy), Jo Jo LaSavio (Boy), Hedy Lamarr (Lucienne Talbot), Fritz Leiber (Deval), Bertram Marburgh (Landers), Alphonse Martell (Headwaiter), Shirley McDonald (Reporter), Philip Merivale (Commissionaire of Police), Torgen Meyer (Old Man), Louis Montez (Associate Judge), Frank Morales (Boy), Sandra Morgan

(Reporter), Ferdinand Munier (Fat Man), John Mylong (Baron de Lorraine), Louis Natheaux (Reporter), Anna Q.Nilsson (Madame Deval), Reginald Owen (Concierge), Edith Penn (Reporter), John Picorri (Waiter), Guy Bates Post (President of Court), William Powell (David Talbot), Theodore Rand (Orchestra Leader), Basil Rathbone (Henri Sarrow), James Rennie (Martin), Billy Roy (Boy), Sig Rugman (Dr. Alex Benoit), John St. Polis (Professor), Hector Sarno (Organ Grinder), Lester Sharpe (Paris Policeman), Irene Shirley (Maid), Vladimir Sokoloff (LeDuc), Claire Trevor (Michelle Allaine), Alice Ward (Nurse Receptionist), H.B. Warner (Prosecuting Attorney), Paul Weigel (Old Man), Marek Windheim (Clerk at Airport), Margaret Wycherly (Mme. Pelletier), Jack Zoller (Student). William Powell and Hedy Lamarr star in this mystery suspense thriller.

LeDuc (Sokoloff) blackmails French diplomat David Talbot (Powell) for his supposed past as a criminal. Talbot takes LeDuc to court for extortion, but LeDuc claims that Talbot is really Jean Pelletier, a notorious criminal who borrowed money from LeDuc. Talbot remembers nothing from his earlier life due to an injury. Michelle Allaine (Trevor), a cabaret singer, testifies that she knows Talbot to be Pelletier, her long-lost lover. A surprise witness, Henri Sarrow (Rathbone), destroys LeDuc's case by testifying that he was with Pelletier when he died. After the trial is dismissed, Sarrow visits Talbot, explaining that he lied at the trial and Talbot is Pelletier after all. As proof, he produces a photo of Talbot and Allaine in an intimate pose. At first Talbot is convinced he is the criminal, but a meeting with Dr. Andre Tessler (Bressart) discloses that the photo is a current one and not from the past since Talbot now parts his hair on the other side due to the injury. Sarrow and Allaine are brought to justice.

Bibliography

Books

American Film Institute. *The American Film Institute Catalog of Motion Pictures Produced in the United States: Feature Films 1911–1920*. Berkeley: University of California Press, 1988.
_____. *The American Film Institute Catalog of Motion Pictures Produced in the United States: Feature Films 1921–1930*. Berkeley: University of California Press, 1988.
_____. *The American Film Institute Catalog of Motion Pictures Produced in the United States: Feature Films 1931–40*. Berkeley: University of California Press, 1993.
Applebaum, Stanley. *Silent Movies: A Picture Quiz Book*. New York: Dover, 1974.
Atkinson, Brooks. *Broadway*. New York: Macmillan, 1970.
Balshofer, Fred, and Arthur C. Miller. *One Reel a Week*. Berkeley: University of California Press, 1967.
Barbour, Alan G. *Days of Thrills and Adventure*. New York: Macmillan, 1970.
Behlmer, Rudy. *Hollywood's Hollywood*. Secaucus NJ: Citadel, 1976.
Berg, A. Scott. *Goldwyn: A Biography*. New York: Knopf, 1989.
Billips, Connie J., and Arthur Pierce. *Lux Presents Hollywood: A Show-by-Show History of the Lux Radio Theatre and the Lux Video Theatre 1934–1957*. Jefferson NC: McFarland, 1995.
Blum, Daniel. *A Pictorial History of the Silent Movies*. Spring Books, 1961.
Bodeen, De Witt. *From Hollywood*. South Brunswick NJ.: Barnes, 1976.
_____. *More from Hollywood*. South Brunswick NJ: Barnes, 1977.
Bowers, Ronald L., and James Robert Parish. *The MGM Stock Company: The Golden Era*. New Rochelle: Arlington House, 1973.
Bowser, Eileen. *History of the American Cinema: The Transformation of Cinema 1907–1915*. New York: Scribner's, 1990.
_____, and Richard Griffith, and Arthur Mayer. *The Movies*. New York: Simon and Schuster, 1981.
Brooks, Tim, and Earle Marsh. *The Complete Directory to Prime Time TV Shows 1946–Present*. New York: Ballantine, 1985.
Brown, Pamela Ann, and Peter Harry Brown. *The MGM Girls: Behind the Velvet Curtain*. New York: St. Martin's, 1983.
Brownlow, Kevin. *Behind the Mask of Innocence*. Berkeley: University of California Press, 1992.
_____, with photographs selected by John Kobal. *Hollywood: The Pioneers*. New York: Knopf, 1979.

_____. *The Parade's Gone By*. New York: Knopf, 1979.
Bushnell, Brooks. *Directors and Their Films*. Jefferson NC: McFarland, 1993.
Butler, Ivan. *Silent Magic*. New York: Ungar, 1988.
Buxton, Frank, and Bill Owen. *The Big Broadcast 1920–1950*. New York: Viking, 1972.
Carey, Gary. *All the Stars in Heaven: Louis B. Mayer's MGM*. New York: Dutton, 1981.
Carpozi, George. *The Matinee Idols*. New York: Manor, 1978.
Carroll, David. *The Matinee Idols*. New York: Galahad, 1974.
Cline, William C. *In the Nick of Time: Motion Picture Sound Serials*. Jefferson NC: McFarland, 1984.
Cocchi, John. *Second Feature*. Secaucus NJ: Citadel, 1991.
Cross, Robin. *2,000 Movies: The 1950s*. New York: Arlington House, 1989.
Crowther, Bosley. *Hollywood Rajah: The Life and Times of Louis B. Mayer*. New York: Holt, Rinehart & Winston, 1960.
D'Agostino, Annette M. (comp.). *An Index to Short and Feature Film Reviews in the Moving Picture World: The Early Years 1907–1915*. Westport, CT: Greenwood, 1995.
De Cordova, Richard. *Picture Personalities: The Emergence of the Star System in America*. Urbana: University of Illinois Press, 1990.
Dimmitt, Richard B. *An Actor Guide to the Talkies: A Comprehensive Listing of 8,000 Feature Length Films from January 1949 Until December 1964*. Metuchen NJ: Scarecrow, 1968.
_____. *A Title Guide to the Talkies*. Metuchen NJ.: Scarecrow, 1965.
Dooley, Roger. *From Scarface to Scarlett*. New York: Harcourt Brace Jovanovich, 1981.
Drew, Bernard Alger. *Motion Picture Series and Sequels: A Reference Guide*. New York: Garland, 1990.
Dreyfuss, Randy, and Henry Medved. *The Fifty Worst Films of All Time (And How They Got That Way)*. New York: Warner, 1984.
Dunning, John. *Tune-In Yesterday: The Ultimate Encyclopedia of Old-Time Radio, 1925–1976*. Englewood Cliffs NJ: Prentice Hall, 1976.
Eames, John Douglas. *The MGM Story: The Complete History of Fifty Roaring Years*. New York: Crown, 1977.
_____. *The Paramount Story*. London: Octopus, 1985.
Eells, George. *Hedda and Louella*. New York: Putnam, 1972.
Elley, Derek. *The Epic Film: Myth and History*. London and Boston: Routledge & Kegan Paul, 1984.
Everson, William K. *American Silent Films*. New York: Oxford University Press, 1978.
Fernett, Gene. *American Film Studios: An Historical Encyclopedia*. Jefferson NC: McFarland, 1988.
Fetrow, Alan. *Sound Films, 1927–1939*. Jefferson NC.: McFarland, 1992.
Film Review Index. Monterey Park: Audio-Visual Associates, 1972.
Finch, John R. *Close-Ups from the Golden Age of the Silent Cinema*. Cranbury NJ: Barnes, 1978.
Finler, Joel W. *The Hollywood Story*. New York: Crown, 1988.
Flamini, Roland. *Thalberg: The Last Tycoon and the World of MGM*. New York: Crown, 1994.
Franklin, Joe. *Classics of the Silent Screen*. Secaucus NJ: Citadel, 1959.
Gaige, Crosby. *Footlights & Highlights*. New York: Dutton, 1948.
Gertner, Richard, and Martin Quigley. *Films in America 1929–1969*. New York: Golder, 1970.
Glut, Donald F., and Jim Harmon. *The Great Movie Serials: Their Sound and Fury*. Garden City NY: Doubleday, 1972.
Gomery, Douglas. *The Hollywood Studio System*. New York: Macmillan, 1986.

Goodgold, Ed, and Ken Weiss. *To Be Continued*. New York: Crown, 1972.
Goodman, Ezra. *The Fifty-Year Decline of Hollywood*. New York: Simon and Schuster, 1961.
Grau, Robert. *The Theatre of Science: A Volume of Progress and Achievement in the Motion Picture Industry*. New York: Blom, 1969.
Green, Abel, and Joe Laurie, Jr. *Show Biz: From Vaudeville to Video*. New York: Holt, 1951.
Griffith, Richard. *The Talkies*. New York: Dover, 1971.
Halliwell, Leslie. *The Filmgoer's Companion*. New York: Avon, 1977.
_____. *Hollywood Film and Video Guide*. New York: Harper Perennial, 1996.
Hampton, Benjamin B. *History of the American Film Industry: From Its Beginning to 1931*. New York: Dover, 1970.
_____. *A History of the Movies*. New York: Arno, 1970.
Harrison, P.S. *Harrison's Reports and Films Reviews : 1919–1962*. Hollywood: Hollywood Film Archives.
Hay, Peter. *Movie Anecdotes*. New York: Oxford University Press, 1990.
Heisner, Beverly. *Hollywood Art: Art Directors in the Days of the Great Studios*. Jefferson NC: McFarland, 1990.
Hirschhorn, Clive. *The Columbia Story*. New York: Crown, 1990.
_____. *The Universal Studio*. London: Octopus, 1986.
_____. *The Warner Bros. Story*. London: Octopus, 1986.
Hudson, Richard M., and Raymond Lee. *Gloria Swanson*. New York: Castle, 1970.
Huey, William R. *In Search of Hollywood, Wyoming: 1894–The Silent Years–1929*. Wyoming: Huey, 1985.
Huff, Theodore. *Charlie Chaplin*. New York: Arno, 1972.
Hurst, Walter E. *Film Superlist: 20,000 Motion Pictures in the U.S. Public Domain*. Hollywood: 7 Arts Press, 1986.
Kaduck, John M. *Grandma's Scrapbook of Silent Movie Stars*. Des Moines: Wallace-Homestead, 1976.
Katchmer, George A. *Eighty Silent Film Stars*. Jefferson NC: McFarland, 1991.
Katz, Ephraim. *The Film Encyclopedia*. New York: Putnam, 1979.
Kerr, Laura, and Allen Rivkin. *Hello, Hollywood*. New York: Doubleday, 1962.
Kinnard, Roy. *Fifty Years of Serial Thrills*. Metuchen NJ: Scarecrow, 1983.
Kobal, John. *Hollywood: The Years of Innocence*. New York: Abbeville, 1985.
Koszarski, Richard. *Hollywood Directors 1914–1940*. New York: Oxford University Press, 1976.
_____, ed. *The Rivals of D.W. Griffith: Alternate Auteurs 1913–1918*. Minneapolis: Walker Art Center, 1976.
Lahue, Kalton C. *Continued Next Week: A History of the Moving Picture Serial*. Norman: University of Oklahoma Press, 1964.
_____. *Gentlemen to the Rescue: The Heroes of the Silent Screen*. New York: Castle, 1972.
Lambert, Gavin. *Norma Shearer: A Life*. New York: Knopf, 1990.
Langman, Larry. *A Guide to Silent Westerns*. New York: Greenwood, 1992.
Lawton, Richard. *A World of Movies: 70 Years of Film History*. London: Sundial, 1974.
Leish, Kenneth W. *A History of Cinema*. New York: Newsweek Books, 1974.
Liebman, Roy. *Silent Film Performers: An Annotated Bibliography of Published, Unpublished and Archival Sources for Over 350 Actors and Actresses*. Jefferson NC: McFarland, 1996.
Lloyd, Ann, ed. *Movies of the Silent Years*. London: Orbis, 1984.
Low, Rachel. *Film Making in 1930 Britain*. London: George Allen & Unwin, 1985.
MacCann, Richard Dyer. *The First Tycoons*. Metuchen NJ: Scarecrow, 1987.
Macgowan, Kenneth. *Behind the Scenes*. New York: Dell, 1967.

Madsen, Axel. *William Wyler*. New York: Thomas Y. Crowell, 1973.
Magill, Frank N., ed. *Magill's Survey of Cinema—Silent Films*. Englewood Cliffs NJ: Salem, 1982.
Magliozzi, Ronald S., ed. *Treasures from the Film Archives*. Metuchen NJ: Scarecrow, 1988.
Martin, Pete. *Hollywood Without Makeup*. Philadelphia and New York: Lippincott, 1948.
_____. *Pete Martin Calls On*. New York: Simon and Schuster, 1962.
Marx, Samuel. *Mayer and Thalberg: The Make-Believe Saints*. New York: Random House, 1975.
Monacop, James. *The Encyclopedia of Film*. New York: Perigee, 1991.
Morley, Sheridan. *Tales from the Hollywood Raj: The British, the Movies, and Tinseltown*. New York: Viking, 1983.
Motion Picture Almanac. New York: Quigley, 1934–35.
Munn, Mike. *The Stories Behind the Scenes of the Great Film Epics*. London: Illustrated Publications, 1982.
Nash, Jay Robert, and Stanley Ralph Ross. *The Motion Picture Guide*. Chicago: Cinebooks, 1987.
The New York Times Directory of the Film. New York: Arno, 1971.
The New York Times Film Review: 1913–1968. New York: The New York Times, 1970.
The New York Times Index. New York: The New York Times.
The New York Times Names Index. New York: The New York Times.
Nollen, Scott Allen. *Boris Karloff*. Jefferson NC: McFarland, 1991.
Nowlan, Gwendolyn Wright, and Robert A. Nowlan. *Cinema Sequels and Remakes*. Jefferson NC: McFarland, 1989.
Parish, James Robert. *Hollywood's Great Love Teams*. New Rochelle NY: Arlington House, 1974.
_____, and Vincent Terrace. *Actors' Television Credits 1950–1972*. Metuchen NJ: Scarecrow, 1973.
_____, and _____. *The Complete Actors' Television Credits 1948–1988*. Metuchen NJ: Scarecrow, 1991.
Reinehr, Robert C., and Jon D. Swartz. *Handbook of Old-Time Radio: A Comprehensive Guide to Golden Age Radio Listening and Collecting*. Metuchen NJ: Scarecrow, 1993.
Rigdon, W., ed. *Notable Names in the American Theatre*. Clifton NJ: White, 1976.
Russo, Dorothy Ritter. *A Bibliography of George Ade*. Indianapolis: Indiana Historical Society, 1947.
Sadoul, Georges. *Dictionary of Films*. Berkeley: University of California Press, 1972.
Schuchman, John S. *Hollywood Speaks*. Urbana: University of Illinois Press, 1988.
Schutz, Wayne. *The Motion Picture Serial: An Annotated Bibliography*. Metuchen NJ: Scarecrow, 1992.
Sennett, Ted. *Great Movie Directors*. New York: Abrams, 1986.
Server, Les. *Screenwriter*. Pittstown NJ: Main Street, 1987.
Shipman, David. *The Great Movie Stars: The Golden Years*. New York: Crown, 1970.
Siegel, Barbara, and Scott Siegel. *The Encyclopedia of Hollywood*. New York: Avon, 1991.
Slide, Anthony. *Aspects of American Film Prior to 1920*. Metuchen NJ: Scarecrow, 1978.
_____. *Early American Cinema*. Metuchen NJ: Scarecrow, 1994.
_____. *The Idols of Silence*. South Brunswick NJ: Barnes, 1976.
_____. *Selected Film Criticism, 1912–1920*. Metuchen NJ: Scarecrow, 1982.
_____. *Selected Film Criticism, 1921–1930*. Metuchen NJ: Scarecrow, 1982.
_____. *Silent Portraits: Stars of the Silent Screen in Historic Photographs*. Vestal NY: Vestal, 1989.
Solomon, Jon. *The Ancient World in the Cinema*. South Brunswick NJ: Barnes, 1978.

Sommer, Robin Langley. *Hollywood: The Glamour Years (1919–1941)*. New York: Gallery, 1987.
Spehr, Paul C. *The Movies Begin: Making Movies in New Jersey, 1887–1920*. Newark: Newark Museum, 1977.
Stedman, Raymond William. *The Serials: Suspense and Drama by Installment*. Norman: University of Oklahoma Press, 1977.
Stewart, John, comp. *Filmarama Volume I: The Formidable Years 1893–1919*. Metuchen NJ: Scarecrow, 1975.
Stine, Whitney. *Stars and Star Handlers: The Business of Show*. Santa Monica CA: Roundtable, 1985.
Stuart, Ray. *Immortals of the Screen*. Los Angeles: Sherbourne, 1965.
Swanson, Gloria. *Swanson on Swanson*. New York: Random House, 1980.
Taylor, Deems. *A Pictorial History of the Movies*. New York: Simon and Schuster, 1950.
Terrace, Vincent. *Radio's Golden Years: The Encyclopedia of Radio Programs 1930–1960*. San Diego CA: Barnes, 1981.
Tobin, Terrance, ed. *Letters of George Ade*. West Lafayette IN: Purdue University Press, 1973.
Tornabene, Lyn. *Long Live the King: A Biography of Clark Gable*. New York: Putnam, 1976.
Torrence, Bruce T. *Hollywood: The First 100 Years*. Hollywood: Hollywood Chamber of Commerce, 1979.
Trent, Paul. *Image Makers*. New York: McGraw-Hill, 1972.
Truitt, Evelyn Mack. *Who Was Who on Screen*. New York: Bowker, 1977.
Variety Obituaries: 1905–1986. New York: Garland, 1988.
Variety Television Reviews: 1923–1988. New York: Garland, 1991.
Variety's Film Reviews. New York: Bowker.
Vazzana, Eugene Michael. *Silent Film Necrology: Births and Deaths of Over 9000 Performers, Directors, Producers and Other Filmmakers of the Silent Era, Through 1993*. Jefferson NC: McFarland, 1995.
Vermilye, Jerry. *The Films of the Twenties*. Secaucus NJ: Citadel, 1985.
Vinson, James. *The International Dictionary of Films and Filmmakers*. Chicago: St. James, 1986.
Wagenknecht, Edward. *The Movies in the Age of Innocence*. New York: Ballantine, 1971.
_____. *Stars of the Silents*. Metuchen NJ: Scarecrow, 1987.
Walker, Alexander. *The Shattered Silents*. New York: Morrow, 1979.
Weaver, John T., ed. *Forty Years of Screen Credits 1929–1969*. Metuchen NJ: Scarecrow, 1970.
_____. *Twenty Years of Silents 1908–1928*. Metuchen NJ: Scarecrow, 1971.
Webb, Michael, ed. *Hollywood: Legend & Reality*. Boston: Little, Brown, 1986.
Who's Who in Filmland. London: Chapman & London.
Wilk, Max. *The Wit & Wisdom of Hollywood*. New York: Atheneum, 1971.
World Film Directors. New York: Wilson, 1987.
Zierold, Norman. *The Moguls: Hollywood's Merchants of Myth*. Los Angeles: Silman James, 1991.

Magazines and Journals

Classic Film Collector/Classic Images
Essanay News

Film Daily Yearbook of Motion Pictures
Film Index International

Film Year Book
Films in Review
The Ladies' World
Life
Motion Picture Classics
Motion Picture Magazine
Motion Picture News
Motion Picture Story Magazine
Motion Pictures
The Moving Picture World
Motography
Newsweek
Photo-Play Journal
Photoplay Magazine
Picture Play Weekly
Saturday Evening Post
Time
Variety

Newspapers

Arizona Republic
Arizonian
Baltimore News American
Baltimore News Post
Baltimore Sun
Buffalo Times
Chicago Daily News
Chicago Daily Tribune
Cleveland Plain Dealer
Cleveland Press
Detroit News
Fargo Daily Courier
Hollywood Citizen News
Hollywood Independent
Hollywood Reporter
Houston Chronicle
Los Angeles Citizen News
Los Angeles Examiner
Los Angeles Times
New York Daily News
New York Herald Tribune
New York Telegraph
New York Times

Recordings

_____. *Francis X. Bushman: Hollywood's First Star Talks About His Life and Times.* Mark 56 Records, 1975.

Index

The Accounting 32, 154
An Adamless Eden 119, 120
Adams, Eadie 225
Adams, Herbert 15
Adams, Mildred 167
Ade, George 21, 32, 38–41, 151, 157
Adler William 43, 47, 52, 158
The Adopted Son 65, 167, 168
The Adventures of Nero Wolfe 196
Aggert, Roy, Jr. 194
Aiken, Robert 162
Albertson, Frank 229
Alias Sargent Billy 111
Allen, George 169
Allen, Irwin 192
Allen, Joseph 116
Allen, Rika 170
Allison, May 166
Allyson, June 98
Alton, John 193
Alton, Maxine 181
The Ambition of the Baron 153
Ambushed 145
Anderson, "Broncho Billy" 21, 22, 26, 39, 98, 111, 151, 183
Anderson, Leona 152
Anderson, Mary 68
Anthony, Marjorie 95
Anthony, Mary Beth 95
Anthony, William 95
Any Woman's Choice 152
Apache Country 92, 190
Aranson, William 44
Arbuckle, Roscoe "Fatty" 53
Archainbaud, George 190
Arnold, Edward 231
Arnold, Sylvia 170

Arthur, John 163
Ashes of Hope 139
At the End of the Trail 113
Autry, Gene 92, 190
Away in the Lead 208
Ayres, Agnes 37

Babille, Edward 143
Baby Garity 135
Baby Harriet Parsons 35, 120
Baby Ivy Ward 171
Baby Lynch 117
Bacon, Frank 48, 158
Bacon, Irving 183
Bacon, Lloyd 187
Backus, Jim 189
The Bad and the Beautiful 92, 190, 191
Bad Guy 224, 225
Baggot, King 29, 182
Bailey, William, 28, 121, 124, 131, 134, 162
Bainbridge, Rolinda 171
Bainter, Fay 229
Baker, Graham 173
Baker, R.E. 23, 105–108
Baker, Richard Foster 21
Baker, Snowy 225
Balfour, Sue 165, 170
Balshofer, Fred 43–52, 158
Bara, Theda 53
Bari, Lynn 197
Barker, Adele 164, 168, 170
Barrymore, Ethel 43
Barrymore, Lionel 43, 218, 231
Bartham, Dorothy 183
Barton, Luke 190

Batman 202
The Battle of Love 151, 152
Baxter, Dr. Frank 101
Bayne, Beverly 6, 21, 22, 24, 26–28, 31–34, 37–39, 42, 44, 47–49, 53–57, 60–72, 82, 83, 90, 97, 115, 117–120, 123, 124, 126, 128–136, 141–143, 145, 147–157, 159–175, 202
Beach, Richard 185
Beery, Chester 155
Beery, Wallace 21, 22, 24, 32, 37, 38, 97, 147, 151, 157, 220
Belcher, Charles 176
Bell, Rex 90
Bellew, Cosmo Kyrle 180
Belmore, Charles 162
Ben-Hur 5, 40, 48, 58, 71–79, 81, 82, 89, 97, 101, 175–177, 201, 202, 214
Bennett, Charles 192
Bennett, Edith Barker 183
Benoit, George 180
Bergman, Henri 163
Berquist, R.J. 164, 167–171
Betty and Bob 195
Bey, Tema 193
Bey, Terza 157
Big City 225, 226
The Big Surprise 199
Bill Bumper's Bargain 109–110
Billy and the Butler 116
The Bishop's Carriage 21
Bitter, Karl 15, 30
Blackton, J. Stuart 183
Blackwell, Carlyle 24, 29, 166
Blackwood, Peggy 174
Blair, Thomas A. 193, 194
Blaisdell, George 57
Blake, Thomas 165, 171
Blakemore, Harry D. 163
Blanchard, Eleanor 131
Blood Will Tell 140, 141
Blow, Lila 171
Blythe, Betty 91
The Bob Hope Show 200
Bodeen, De Witt 193
Bogart, Humphrey 191
Bolder, Robert 140, 143
Bond, Ward 223
Boots and Saddles 54, 164
Borden, Eugene 171
Borge, Victor 198

Boring, Edwin 164
Borzage, Frank 225, 228, 229
Borzage, Lew 225, 228, 229
Bottomley, Roland 175
Bowker, Virginia 37
Bowman, William 43, 47, 158–159
Boyd, Stephen 75
Brabin, Charles 71–74, 167, 168, 171–173
Bracey, Sidney 178
Bracken, Eddie 197
Bradley, David 193, 194
Bradley, Estelle 182
Bradshaw, George 190
Brady, Alice 166
Brady, Fred 189
Brand, Max 167
Branscombe, Lily 21, 112, 118, 119
The Brass Check 169, 170
Brennan, Edward 161, 165
Brennan, Walter 218, 223
Brent, George 187
Breslyn, Otto 28, 131
Breyer, Maggie 168
The Bribe 165
Brickert, Carl 162
Bromley, Milton 152
Bronson, Betty 176
Brooks, Thomas 161
A Brother's Loyalty 128
Broussard, Walter 168
Brown, Betty 133
Brown of Harvard 87, 209
Bruce, Bella 163, 165, 173
Bruce, Virginia 231
Brundage, Marilda 165
Buffington, Adele 180
The Burglarized Burglar 108
Burnett, Dana 177
Burnette, Smiley 185
Burr, Raymond 98, 201
Burton, William H. 164
Bushman, Bernadette Soubirous 5
Bushman, Bruce 6
Bushman, Edith Philimena 5
Bushman, Frank 95
Bushman, Iva 90, 99, 198, 199
Bushman, John Henry 5
Bushman, Josephine Fladuene 6, 17, 61, 66, 67, 83
Bushman, Lenore Konti 5, 15, 61, 87, 203–205

Index

Bushman, Mary Josephine 5, 7
Bushman, Mary Magdalen 5
Bushman, Merlin Valentine 5
Bushman, Myrtle 95, 96
Bushman, Norma 88, 90, 96
Bushman, Ralph Everly (Francis X. Bushman, Jr.) 6, 87, 124, 162, 206–234
Bushman, Robert A. 16, 37
Bushman, Robert Aloysius 5
Bushman, Robert L. 11, 13
Bushman, Sam 70
Bushman, Stella 70
Bushmanor 20, 58–61, 66, 67, 94, 96
Butler, David 174
Butler, Fred J. 174
Butler W.J. 165
Butt, W. Lawson 164
The Butterfly Net 117
Buttram, Pat 190
Buzzell, Eddie 180
Byrd, Anthony 168
Byrd, Ralph 91, 185
Byrnes, Edd 200
Byron, Paul 158

Cabanne, W. Christy 21, 63, 121, 165, 170, 173, 175
Cabot, Bruce 187, 225
Calhoun, Alice 179
Calhoun, William 165
The Call of the Circus 86, 181
Calvert, E. H. 21, 33, 38, 48, 129, 136, 137, 139, 140, 142, 143, 145–149, 157
Cameron, Donald 166
Capra, Frank 179
Carewe, Edwin 167, 168
Carleton, H.O. 161
Carlyle, Aileen 181
Carr, Harry 131
Carridine, John 192, 200
Carroll, Richard 114
Carson, Robert 165, 171
Carter, Monte 180
Carver, Margo 196
Caryl of the Mountains 223
Cashman, Harry 21, 106, 109, 114–116, 121, 122, 124, 126
Cassinelli, Dolores 109, 110, 113, 114, 116, 125

Castle, William 189
Caward, Neil G. 156, 157
Chadwick, Cyril 182
Chadwick, Helen 86, 179, 180
Chains 35, 123
Champion, Cyril 183
Chandler, Robert 167
Chaney, Lon, Jr. 216
Chaplin, Charlie 21, 39, 41, 42, 53, 63, 97, 166, 183
The Charge of the Gauchos 86, 180
Charles, John 170
Charters, Spencer 187
Cheron, Andre 177
Chichester, Emily 173
Churchill, Winston 47
Clark, Marguerite 53, 62, 63, 68
Clayton, Ethyl 166, 181
Clayton, Marguerite 111
Clemens, George 183
Clifford, Ruth 183
Clifford, W.C. 180
Clifford, William 46, 48, 158
Clive, Vincent 183
Coburn, Charles 192
Coleman, Charles 182
Collier, William, Jr. 87
Collyer, June 211
Colman, Ronald 192
Commerford, Thomas 33, 38, 133, 137, 143, 144, 146–149, 151–154, 156
Comont, Mathilde 180
Compson, Betty 183
Conklin, Chester 175
Conley, Ligo 180
Connelley, Edward 165
Conte, Richard 91, 189
Conway, Jack 6, 87, 123, 124, 204, 206, 211, 213, 218, 219, 230–233
Conway, Michael 61
Conway, Pat 96
Coogan, Jackie 101
Cook, Clyde 181
Cook, Elisha, Jr. 186
Cooper, Edna Mae 179
Cooper, Gary 183
Cooper, Ollie 170
Cooper, Robert 194
Corby, Ellen 191
Corrado, Gino 180
Cortez, Stanley 194

Cosgrove, Jack 174
Cossa, Thomas 38
Cossar, Hohn 138, 141–144, 147, 148, 150, 154
Costello, Dolores 87
Costello, Helen 87
Costello, Maurice 21, 24, 26, 29, 30, 183
Cotton, Carolina 190
The Count and the Cowboys 111
The Countess 141
Court of Last Resort 200
Cousins, John 182
Craig, Blanche 175
Craig, Nellie 152, 155, 230
Crane, Ward 178
Cravat, Nick 192
Craven, James 189
Crawford, Joan 211, 229
Crolius, Louise 158
Crossroads 233, 234
Crute, Sally 172
Cruze, James 45, 182
Cummings, Robert 161, 162, 164, 183, 184
Cuneo, Lester 21, 33, 38, 45, 48, 52, 146–154, 157, 158, 159, 162, 163
Currier, Frank 170, 176
Curtis, Mel 193
Cushing, Sidney 161
Cyclone Higgins, D.D. 169–171
The Cyclone Kid 215
Cytron, Morris 159

Dailey, Joseph 164
D'Albrook, Sidney 169, 170
Dalmorez, Juanita 28, 130, 131
The Dan Carson Story 197
Dane, Karl 173
Dangerous Traffic 209, 210
The Danny Thomas Show 200
D'Arcy, Hugh 170
D'Arcy, Roy 175, 183, 184
Daring Hearts 68, 173, 174
The Dark Romance of a Tobacco Tin 108
Darmond, Grace 177
Davenport, Alice 181
David & Bathsheba 12, 91–93, 97, 189, 190, 199
Davidson, John 161, 162, 164, 165
Davidson, William 163

Davis, Clayton 12–15
Davis, Will S. 169, 170
Dawn and Twilight 136
Daydream of a Photoplay Artist 27, 28, 125, 126
Dayton, Frank 21, 28, 114, 116, 117, 122, 128–132, 147, 155
Dear Old Girl 28, 32, 131, 132
Dearing, Ed 184
Death on the Diamond 218
De Bruiler, Nigel 176
de Chett, Marie 165
De Conde, Syn 170
de Cordova, Rudolph 163
De Fore, Don 101
de Gresac, Fred 63, 165
de Lara, Frederic 183
Delmar, Thomas 157
Demarest, Drew 182, 230
Demarest, William 225
de Maupassant, Guy 118
Dempsey, Jack 225
Dempsey, Pauline 168, 175
Des Lyon, George 174
De Vin, Shelby 167, 169, 172
De Vinna, Clyde 176
Dick Tracy 91, 185
The Discovery 127
Dr. Kildare 202
Dodd, Claire 221
Dodge, Henry Irving 178
Donaldson, Arthur 174
Don't Bet on Blondes 221
Douglas, Kirk 92, 191
Douglas, Melvyn 229
Douglas, Royal 143
Dove, Billie 84, 177
Dowst, Harry Payson 174
Dresser, Marie 213
Drew, Ann 158
Drew, Lillian 38, 45, 115, 128, 137, 143, 148, 150, 151, 153
Drew, Lowell 184
Drew, Sydney 45
The Dude Wrangler 86, 181
Dudley, Robert 177
Duff, Howard 200
Duffield, Harry 174
Dumas, Alexandre 217
Dunbar, Helen 21, 24, 28, 35, 38, 48, 58, 60, 114–116, 122, 125, 129–133,

142, 143, 147, 149, 150, 151, 152, 155–159, 161–165, 171, 173
Dunlap, Scott R. 180
Dunkinson, Harry 33, 115, 143, 146, 147, 149, 150, 151, 154, 155–157
Dunn, Eddie 184
Dunn, Jack 171
Dunn, William 171
Dunne, Phillip 189
Duryea, George 181, 182

Eagler, Paul 176
Eddy, Nelson 231
Edney, Annie 138
The Elder Brother 141
Elfstrom, Katherine 194
Ellerhusen, Ulric 11, 17
Elton, Edmond 163, 164
The End of the Feud 122
Esher, Efe 52
Essanay Film Manufacturing Company 21–42, 44, 48, 49, 90, 97, 105–157
Ethier, Alphonz 179
Eubank, Victor 153, 156
Evans, Frankie 175
Every Inch a King 150–151
The Eye That Never Sleeps 115
Eyes Right 210

Fabersham, William 52
Fable of the Bush League Lover Who Failed to Qualify 38, 151
Fairbanks, Douglas 166
Fairbanks, Douglas, Jr. 87
The Fall of Montezuma 90, 183
A False Suspicion 109
Fang, Charles, 163, 165, 171, 173
Farley, James 179
The Farmer's Daughter 126
Farnum, Dorothy 174
Farnum, Franklin 166, 216, 218
Farnum, William 184, 189
Farris, William 159
Fate's Funny Frolic 107
Father's Day 212
Fawcett, George 182
Fetchit, Stepin 215
Fildew, William 165, 170, 173
The Film Parade 90, 183

Finger Prints 141, 142
Fitzgerald, F. Scott 229
The Flag 84, 179
Fletcher, Cecil 168
Fletcher, Johnny 184
Florey, Robert 183
Flowers, Bess 191, 212, 229
Flynn, Errol 221
For Old Time's Sake 131
Forbes, Madeleine 188
Ford, Glenn 97
Ford, James 184
Ford, John 211
Ford, Tennessee Ernie 200
Four Sons 211
Fowler, Norman 129
Francis, Kay 221
Franklin, Edward 144
Freeman, I.K. 160
Freeman, Kathleen 191
Fremyear, Mabel 171
French, Charles K. 180
French, Daniel Chester 11, 15, 19, 30
Fulbright, Tom 63, 33, 68
Fuller, Dale 176
Fury 223, 224

G.E. Theater 202, 202
Gable, Clark 203, 230, 232
The Gallantry of Jimmie Rodgers 153
Galloping Ghost 215, 216
Garland, Judy 186
Garson, Greer 198
Gay, Dorothy 181
Gay and Festive Claverhouse 173
Gebhardt, Fred 193
George, Gladys 227
George Burns and Gracie Allen Show 199
The Ghost in the Invisible Bikini 94, 194, 195
Gibson, Helen 189
The Girl at the Curtain 135, 136
The Girl from Missouri 218, 219
The Girl Said No 213
Gish, Dorothy 53
Gish, Lillian 63
Glazer, Benjamin 178
God's Inn by the Sea 106
God's Outlaw 68, 172, 173
Going Some 6

The Golden Years of Hollywood 201
Goldwyn, Samuel 175
A Good Catch 26, 115
The Good Old Days 91, 188, 189
The Goodfellow's Christmas Eve 110
Goodman, Jules Eckert 158
The Gordian Knot 107
Gordon, Alice 161
Gordon, C. Henry 184
Gordon, Eva 169
Gordon, Julia Swayne 181
Gorey, Lou 172
Gould, Chester 185
Grauman's Chinese Theater 99
Graustark 39–41, 48, 62, 156
Graves, George W. 166
The Great Secret 54, 63–65, 165, 166
The Great Silence 155
The Great Train Robbery 22
Greeley, Evelyn 158
Green, Alfred E. 186
Greene, Joseph J. 188
Greenstreet, Sidney 196
Griffin, Eleanore 186
Griffin, Gerald 172
Griffin, Merv 202
Griffith, Corinne 84–86, 99, 178
Griffith, D.W. 124
The Grip of the Yukon 84, 179
Grover, Leonard 164
Guissart, Rene' 176
Guthrie, Carl 189

Hagney, Frank 180
Haines, Rhea 174
Hall, Ella 166
Hall, Norman Shannon 190
Hall, Thurston 188
Hall, Winter 176
Halliday, John 184
Halligan, William 186
Halsey, Forrest 187
Hamilton, G.P. 111
Hamilton, Neil 179
Hamlet 6
Handworth, Octavia 24
Hanna, Franklyn 169
Hannan, Joseph 97
Hannan, June Bushman 10, 16, 97, 102
Hannan, Kathleen 95, 97

Hannan, Marie 96
Hansen, Einar 84, 178
Hardwicke, Sir Cedric 188, 192
Harlan, Otis 179
Harlow, Jean 218, 219
Harper, Thomas 138
Harris, Major Sam 188, 192
Hart, Bill 71
Hasbrouck, Olive 180
Haunted Island 212
Hawks, Howard 219
Haydel, Dorothy 165
Haynes, Dick 193
Hayward, Susan 91, 92, 189, 190
Hayworth, Rita 197
Hazard, Lawrence 186
He Fought for the U.S.A. 110
Healy, Ted 227
Hearst, William Randolph 88
Hearts and Flowers 134
Hecht, Ben 231
Hedda Hopper's Hollywood 200
Hennessey, Ruth 128, 140
Henry, Miss C. 158
Henry, Robert "Buzzy" 186
Hepburn, Audrey 191
Her Dad the Constable 106
Her Hour of Triumph 118
Herbert, Alexandre 164
Hering, Henry 16, 18, 19
The Hermit (of Lonely Gulch) 28, 120
Herrin, John 193
Heston, Charlton 75, 94, 98, 100, 194, 201
Heyward, Louis M. 194
Hill, Ramsey, 198
Hill, Walter K. 172
Hillburn, Percy 176
Hilliard, Ernest 175
Hines, Johnny 230
His Friend's Wife 23, 105, 109
His Stolen Fortune 142, 143
Hitchcock, Charles 33, 115, 137, 142, 143, 146, 147
Hitchcock, Walter 116
Holden, William 191
Holles, Antony 183
Hollis, Jack B. 171
Hollywood Boulevard 90, 183, 184
Hollywood Story 84, 91, 97, 189
Holm, Celeste 197

Index

Holmes, Gerda 137–142
Holmes, Rapley 115, 137–139, 141–145, 151
Holmes, Stuart 172
Holmes, Taylor 21
Holmes, William F. 182
Holt, Tim 87
Honky Tonk 231, 232
Hope, Bob 98, 200
Hopkins, John 180
Hopper, Dennis 192
Hopper, Heda 82
Horton, Edward Everett 182, 192
Hostile Guns 94
Hough, Horace 186
The Hour and the Man 134, 135
Houry, Henry 173
House of Pride 123, 124
Houseman, Arthur 168–170, 228
Howell, Dorothy 179
Hudson, Eric 164
Hull, Henry 189
Human Targets 216
Hunt, Marsha 184
Huntsville 94
Hyer, Martha 191

I Found Stella Parrish 221, 222
Ibsen, Henrik 194
In the Diplomatic Service 163
In the Glare of the Lights 148, 151
In the Moon's Ray 137, 138, 141
Ince, John 188
The Iron Heel 124, 125
It's a Great Life 206, 207

Jabs, Henrietta 95
James, Alan 185
Jeffrey, Hugh 169, 170
Jeffries, Jim 48, 159, 225
Johnny Madero, Pier 23 197
Johnson, Arthur 29
Johnson, Orrin 43
Johnston, J.W. 167
Johnston, William Allen 187
Jory, Victor 101
Joy, Leatrice 174
Joyner, Frank 170
Judge, Elwell 172

Judge, John 172
Julian, Rupert 166
June, Ray 180, 218
Just a Gigolo 204
Justice, Maibelle Heikes 148

Kahn, Eleanor 116, 134
Karloff, Boris 94, 194
Kavanaugh, Katharine 171
Keaton, Buster 207, 208
Keckley, Jane 178
Kelly Alberty 180
Kelsey, Fred 178
Kendall, Henry 183
Kennard, Pop 171
Kent, Charles 174
Kent, Lois 184
Kent, S. Miller 43
Kerrigan, J.M. 188
Kerrigan, Warren 29, 30, 49, 53, 62, 63
Key, Kathleen 72, 176
Kibbee, Guy 221, 229
Kimball, Alonzo 11
King, Carleton 180
King, Henry 187, 189
Kirby, William Cotton 181
Knox, Alexander 188
Kohner, Frederick 189
Kolker, Henry 180
Konti, Isadore 11, 15–17, 19
Kramer, Cecil 187
Kramer, Samuel 173

Lady in Ermine 84–86, 99, 178
Lady of Lyons 5
Laemmle, Carl 44
Laemmle, Edwards 178
Laemmle, Ernst 179
La Garde, Henri 177
Lamarr, Hedy 192, 234
Lane, Priscilla 187
Lang, Charles, Jr. 191
The Last Frontier 216
The Laurel Wreath of Fame 113
Lawrence, Ed 165
Leach, John 165
Lehman, Ernest 191
Leiber, Fritz 164
Let Freedom Ring 231

Let No Man Put Asunder 128
Let's Talk About Hollywood 197
Levine, Albert Shelby 167
Lewis, Mitchell 176
Linder, Max 21
The Little Black Box 112
The Little Substitute 133
The Little Theater Off Times Square 196
Live, Love and Believe 108
Livingston, Margaret 179
Loan Shark 26
Lockhart, Caroline 181
Lockwood, Harold 166
Logan, Jacqueline 180, 181
Logue, Charles A. 167, 178, 179
Lombard, Carole 232
Lonesome Robert 114
Lorre, Peter 192
The Lost Years 23, 109
Love Crazy 232, 233
Love Is a Headache 227, 228
The Love Lute of Romany 28
Love Wager 203
Lowe, Edward T., Jr. 154–157, 206, 211
Loy, Myrna 228, 230, 233
Lucy, Arnold 175
Ludlow, Patrick 183
Lupino, Ida 200
Lux Radio 198
Lyles, A.C. 94, 99
Lytton, L. Rogers 174

MacBeth 6
MacDermott, Marc 24
Macfadden, Bernarr 7, 8, 21
MacLaine, Shirley 97
MacLane, Barton 222
MacLeod, Elsie 171
MacRae, Gordon 198
Madeiro, Addison, Jr. 153, 154
The Madman 110
The Magic Wand 35, 120
The Mail Order Wife 111
Mailes, Charles Hill 180
Main, Marjorie 229, 230
Mainhall, Harry 121, 122, 143
Man and His Soul 54, 160, 161
A Man for A'That 138
The Man Life Passed By 207
Man-Proof 228

The Man Without a Conscience 53, 160
Mann, Hank 189
Mansfield, Etta 161, 165
Mantell, Ethel 164
Many Loves of Dobie Gillis 201
Marano, John 95
Marburg, Charles L. 14
Margo of Castlewood 196
Marlie the Killer 212
Marlowe, June 179
The Marriage Clause 84, 177
Marry the Poor Girl 69
Marsden, Aileen Pitt 183
Marsh, Mae 53, 184
Marsh, Oliver 175
Marsh, Vera 214
Marshall, Robert 158
Marshall, William 193
Martin, Peter 102
Marx, Chico 192
Marx, Groucho 11, 192, 202
Marx, Harpo 192
The Masked Bride 79–82, 175
The Masked Wrestler 145
Mason, William "Billy" 35, 115, 116, 120
Masquerade 197
Massey, Raymond 189, 190
The Master Thief 69
Mathis, George 72
Mathis, June 72, 74, 168, 170, 171, 173
Matton, Martha 178
Maturi, Richard 16, 23
Matzen, Herman 15
Maude, Arthur 182
Maupain, Ernest 155, 156
Maxwell, Barry 164
Maxwell, Edwin 188
Maybeck, Bernard R. 17
Mayer, Louis B. 43, 63, 73, 74, 81–84, 87, 93, 165, 175, 198
Mayo, Edna 154, 156
Mayo, Frank 184
Mayo, Virginia 192
McAvoy, May 74, 76, 98, 176
McConnell, J. Parker 174
McCoy, Tim 181
McCoy, William 173
McCrea, Joel 98, 189
McCutcheon, George Barr 156
McDaniel, Hattie 229
McDonald, Norman 124

Index

McDowell, Armorel 171
McDowell, Claire 176
McElravy, Robert C. 171, 173
McGovern, Evelyn 96
McHugh, Charles 174
McHugh, Kitty 184
McIntosh, Burr 179
McKinney, C.R. 168
McLarin, Jimmy 226
McMackin, Arthur 130
McManamon, Pauline 95
McQuade, James S. 146, 152
McRae, Duncan 168
Mead, Dwight 114, 116
Mead, T.S. 154, 155
Meadows, Jayne 189, 190
Meakin, Charles 177
Meechan, George 176
The Melody of Love 112
Menchen, H.L. 5
Mercie, Jean Marious Antonin 14
Meredyth, Bess 74, 175
Messimer, Howard 106, 107, 115, 117, 124, 125, 127
Metro Pictures Corporation 42–68, 157–173
Meyers, Harry 24
Midnight Faces 210
Midnight Life 96, 180
Milland, Ray 203, 204
Miller, Liza 163
Miller, Walter 170
Miller, Winston 185
A Million a Minute 54, 162
Milne, Peter 47, 157, 161
Minnelli, Vincent 190
Minter, Mary Miles 43, 52, 63, 166
The Mis-Sent Letter 115
A Mistaken Accusation 127, 128
Mr. Adams and Eve 200
Mr. Celebrity 91, 186
Modern Marriage 69–71, 174, 175
Mohr, Hal 177
Mongrel and Master 139, 140
Montana, Bull 226
Montgomery, Frank 169
Montgomery, Robert 213
Mooney, Martin 186
Moore, Marcia 158
Moore, Mary 162
Moore, Victor 53

Moorehead, Agnes 192
Morgan, Frank 232
Morgan, Ralph 227
Morris, Francis 184
Morris, William 164
Mortimer, Charles 183
Mortimer, Henry 167
The Motor Buccaneers 144, 145
Mott, Valentine 173
Moulton, Zita 175
Movie Town Radio Theater 198
Murder Man 222
Murray, Mae 79, 80, 175
Musuraca, Nick 180, 192
My Dear Miss Aldrich 226, 227
Myers, Carmel 72, 74, 176, 211
The Mystery of Room 643 138, 139

Napatia, the Greek Singer 114
National Association's All-Star Picture 166, 167
Neff, Pauline 175
Neptune's Daughter 121
Neumann, Harry 187
Never Too Late 208
The New Church Organ 119
The New Manager 106, 107
New Theater 198
Newman, Paul 226
Newton, Joel 169, 170
Niblo, Fred 74, 76, 175, 214
Nicholson, Elwood J. 193
Night Hawks 143
A Night with a Million 142
Nilsson, Anna Q. 83, 98, 178, 234
Noble, John W. 161–165
Norman, Gertrude 167
Norris, Edward 225
North, Wilfred 181
Northrup, Harry S. 167, 168
Norton, Edgar 172
Novarro, Ramon 74–77, 81, 98, 101, 176, 177, 201

O'Brien, Pat 197
O'Brien, William 182
O'Connor, Frank 181
O'Dell H. 159
Oland, Warner 177

The Old Wedding Dress 119
Olmsted, Gertrude 72, 180
O'Malley, Charles 186
O'Malley, Pat 167, 184
Once a Gentleman 86, 182
One Man's Family 195
One Wonderful Night 29–32, 34, 143, 144, 182
Ortega, Arthur 165
O'Sullivan, Maureen 227
The Other Girl 136
The Other Man 38, 148
Our Hospitality 207, 208
Out of the Depths 112, 113
Out of the Night 114
Overton, Evart Emerson 166
Owen, Garry 225, 227

Paddock, Jane 33, 146
Paige, Jean 174
Paine, Ralph D. 161
A Pair of Cupids 171, 172
Palace of Fine Arts 17–19
Panama-Pacific Exposition 12, 17–19, 51–53, 96
Paris Interlude 219
Parker, Franklyn 184
Parker, Fred 181
Parsons, Louella 34, 35, 94, 98, 120, 123
The Passing Shadow 116
The Pathway of Years 128
Paul, Edward F. 175
Payne, Louis 181
Peck, Gregory 91, 92, 190
Pederson, John 27
Peer Gynt 94, 193, 194
Pemberton, Baring 182
The Penitent 124
Pennington's Choice 48, 159, 160
Pepsi Cola Playhouse 199
Perrin, Jack 210
Perry Mason 201
Pessin, Leo 190
Peter Gunn 201
Petrova, Olga 43, 52, 63, 66, 166
The Phantom Planet 94, 193
Phillips, Augustus 170
Phillips, Dorothy 21, 98, 105–109, 129
Physioc, Louis 181
Piccori, John 185

Pickford, Mary 24, 37, 49, 53, 62, 63, 68, 74, 98, 166
Pidgeon, Walter 178, 191, 198, 227, 228, 230
Pierce, Evelyn 182
Pigeon Island 160
Playter, Wellington 159
The Plum Tree 32, 147, 151
Pole, Colin 183
Ponder, Jack 180
Ponsella, Carmela 88
The Poor Rich Man 172, 173
Powell, Dick 191
Powell, William 233, 234
The Power of Conscience 129, 130
Pratt, Bela Lyon 14, 19
Prescott, John 171
Price, Vincent 188, 192
The Pride of the Force 208
Prince, Charles H. 161, 162
Prince, Hal 184
The Prince Party 38, 149, 150
The Private Officer 38, 149
Prout, Eva 119
Providence and Mrs. Urmy 157

Quackenbush, Jo Anne 201
Quality Pictures Corporation 42–68, 158–173
Queen of the Moulin Rouge 6
Quinn, Arthur 173
Quirk, Billy 24

Raas, Paul 145
The Railroad Hour 198
Raine, William MacLeod 179
Rainer, Luise 226
Ralph, Jessie 227
Rankin, Arthur 179, 180
Rathbone, Basil 175, 194, 234
Raymond, Frances 174
Raymond, Jack 168, 218, 229
Reagan, Ronald 201
The Red Mill 5
The Red Mouse 54, 165
Red River Range 204–205
Red, White and Blue Blood 65, 168, 169
Redden, Arthur 174
Reed, Luther 170, 171

Reichenbach, Harry 44, 47, 52
Reid, Elizabeth 60
The Return of Richard Neal 155
The Return of William Marr 116
Reynolds, Ben 178
Reynolds, Genevieve 164
Richard Carvel 47, 48, 53, 160
Richardson, Jack 181
The Right of Way 28, 130, 131
Rin-Tin-Tin 195
Ripley, Charles 165
The Rivals 114
Rivers, Joe 226
Roberts, Fred 165
Roberts, Kenneth L. 170
Roberts, Marquerite 183
Robertson, Sir Forbes 6
Robinson, William 144
Roff, Arthur 173
The Romance of the Dells 27, 28, 126
Romanoff, Constantine 221, 231
Romeo and Juliet 6, 40, 48, 56–58, 63, 65, 67, 97, 163, 164
Romero, Cesar 98, 192
Rooney, Mickey 186, 218, 227
The Rosary 105, 106
Roscoe, Albert 156
Rose, Jackson 179, 182
Rosemary 48, 53
Rosenbloom, Maxie 226
Roth, Richard 194
Rowland, Richard A. 43
Ruben, J. Walter 186
Rubin, Dr. Theodore Isaac 189
Ruckstull, Frederic Wellington 13
Russell, Martha 116–118, 121, 122
Russell, Rosalind 228

Sabrina 93, 191, 192
Saint Gaudens, Augustus 11, 13
Sale, Virginia 181
Saved from the Torrents 108, 109
Say It with Sables 86, 179, 180
The Scarlet Arrow 212
Scars of Possession 38, 150
Schlitz Playhouse of Stars 199
Schnee, Charles 190
Schofield, Paul 174
Schubert, Bernard 187
Scott, Betty 33, 146

Scott, Helen 174
Seay, James 186
The Second in Command 46, 47, 51, 158
Seddon, Margaret 181
Selznick, David O. 191
77 Sunset Strip 200
Sewell, C.S. 168–171
Shadows 137
Shamroy, Leon 187, 189
The Shanty at Trembling Hill 152
Sharkey, Sailor 178
The Shining Hour 228, 229
Shipman, Barry 185
Shirley, Thomas 114
Short, Gertrude 182
Siegmann, George 178
Signal Lights 117, 118
The Silent Voice 47, 54, 62, 158, 159
Silliphant, Leigh 101
Silver Queen 91, 187
Sinatra, Nancy 94, 195
Sinclair, Ronald 186
Sins of the Children 212, 213
Sittenham, Fred 161, 165
Skavlan, Olaf 164
The Slim Princess 22, 38–41, 157
Smiley, Charles 174
Smiley, John 167, 170
Smiling All the Way 69, 174
Smith, C. Aubrey 186
Smith, Clara 133, 134
Smith, James 96
Smith, Leonard 186
Smith, Oscar 177
Smith, Thelma 95
Snow, Marguerite 21, 43, 45–48, 51, 52, 63, 98, 159
Snowden, Caroline 177
Social Quicksands 171
Sojin, Kamiyama 182
Sokoloff, Vladimir 234
Sonnenberg, Gus 226
Sothern, Ann 197
Sparks of Fate 38, 146
Spell of the Circus 214
The Spirit of the Madonna 138
A Splendid Dishonor 38, 147
Spy's Defeat 128
Stanhope, Cecil 21, 183
Stanton, Fred 165

Stars and Their Courses Change 154
Stars of the Silents Saluted 202
Steadman, Lincoln 87
Steck, H. Tipton 149, 154, 156
Steene, E. Burton 176
Steinguard, Arthur 144
Stephens, Harvey 222
Stepmother 195, 196
Steppling, John 21, 116, 117, 128
Steppling, Margaret 125, 129
Sterne, Elaine 172
Stevens, Craig 201
Stevens, Jessie 172
Stewart, Anita 166
Stewart, James 222
Stidwell, Ernest 183
The Stigma 133, 134
Stone, william 171
Stonehouse, Ruth 21, 24, 35, 38, 40, 41, 115, 121–123, 125, 127, 128, 134, 136, 138–140, 142–144, 146, 147, 149, 151, 157
The Story of Mankind 94, 192, 199
The Story of Mary Marlin 195
Stowe, Leslie 167, 171
Stretton, George Dudgeon 183
Struss, Karl 176, 183
Stuart, Virginia Bushman Conway 6, 8, 10, 15, 16, 19, 20, 43, 44, 61, 82, 87, 124
Sullavan, Margaret 229
Sullivan, Barry 191
Sullivan, Ed 200
Sullivan, Frederic 182
Sullivan, Lillian 165
Sunlight 130
Surteen, Robert 190
Suspense 198
Sutton, Charles 172
Swanson, Gloria 21, 37, 38, 97, 153, 183
Sweet, Blanche 53

Tabler, P. Dempsey 174
Tangled Fortunes 216, 217
Taylor, Charles A. 162
Taylor, Elizabeth 97
Taylor, Ray 185
Taylor, Robert 229
Taylor, Samuel 191

Thalberg, Irving G. 74, 81, 175
Theater 201
Their Compact 65, 167
Thew, Harvey F. 159
They Learned About Women 213, 214
Thin Ice 88
Thirteen Down 153
The Thirteenth Juror 83, 84, 178
The Thirteenth Man 127
Thirty 156
This Is My Best, Miss Dilly Says No 197
Thomas, Danny 200
Thoroughbreds Don't Cry 91, 186
Thorpe, Jim 226
Thorpe, Richard 181
Thorton, Norma 199
Those We Love 196
Three Comrades 229, 230
The Three Musketeers 217
The Three Scratch Clue 137
Through the Storm 135
Thurston, Adelaide 43
Titus, Lydia Yeamans 174
To the End of the World 160
Toast of the Town 198, 199
Todd, Mike 97
The Toll of the Marshes 132, 133
Tone, Franchot 219, 227–229
Tony (Antoine) the Fiddler 28, 131
Too Hot to Handle 230, 231
Tooker, William H. 168
Toones, Fred "Snowflake" 187
The Top o' the World 56
Totten, Lester 21, 153
Townley, Robert H. 131
Tracked Down 112
Tracy, Louis 143
Tracy, Spencer 222, 224, 226
The Trade Gun Bullet 126
Travers, Richard C.
Treacher, Arthur 220
Treacy, Enerson 182
Treadwell, Laura 186
Trento, Guido 180
Trevor, Claire 232, 234
Trinkets of Tragedy 142
Trotti, Lamar 187
Tucker, Sophie 186
Turner, Lana 92, 191, 232
Turpin, Ben 21, 183

Twelve to the Moon 94, 193
Twilight 121

Ullman, Elwood 194
Under Royal Patronage 33, 145, 146
Under Suspicion 169
The Understanding Heart 211
The Understudy 118
An Unplanned Elopement 149
Unsell, Eve 158, 160

Valentine, Grace 161
Valiant Lady 196
Van Loon, Hendrik Willem 192
Vane, Derek 175
Varconi, Victor 226
Verhalen, C.J. 137, 138
Vinton, Horace 164
A Virginia Romance 54, 162, 163
The Virtue of Rags 125
Viva Villa 219, 220
The Voice in the Wilderness 140
The Voice of Conscience (Essanay) 122
The Voice of Conscience (Metro) 65, 168
Voice of One 169, 171
Von Betz, M.C. 142–144
von Winther, Carl 165
Voyage to the Bottom of the Sea 202

Wales, Ethel 181
Walker, Joe 179
Walker, Johnny 179
Walker, Lillian 166
Walker, Robert 131, 223
The Wall Between 54, 161, 162
Wallace, Lew 176
Walling, Richard 87
Walters, William 112, 121, 122, 124, 127, 128
Walthall, Henry 62, 166, 220
Ward, Ivy 165
Warfield, Irene 137, 138, 140
The Warning Hand 122, 123
Warren, Fred 175
Washburn, Bryant 21, 24, 33, 35, 38, 106, 110, 112–115, 117, 122, 123, 125, 127–129, 137–141, 143, 145–147, 150, 152–157, 184

Watch Beverly 90, 182, 183
Watrous, Howard 143
Watson, Bobby 192
Watson, Minor S. 129
Way Out West 214
The Way Perilous 132
Wayne, John 203–205, 209, 217
Webb, Jack 197
Weber, Lois 177
Webster, Henry McRae 121, 128, 129, 140
Weinart, Albert 11, 12, 19
Weinman, A.A. 13
Weir, Hugh S. 169
Weis, Don 194
Weitzel, Edward 167
Welles, Orson 197
Wenstrom, Harold 178
Weston, Mildred 123, 124, 127
Wharton, Theodore 22, 28, 35, 120, 122, 125, 128, 131, 140
When Lightning Strikes 220
When Soul Meets Soul 125
When Wealth Torments 123
The Whip Hand 130
White, Leo 115, 143, 151, 175, 176
White Roses 117
Whitlock, Lloyd 178
Whitney, Eleanore 184
Whitney, Raymond 127
Who's Your Friend 209
Wilbur, Crane 24, 29, 63
Wilder, Billy 191
Williams, C. Jay 172
Williams, Earle 49, 62, 63, 166
Williams, Frank D. 172, 173
Williams, Guinn "Big Boy" 187, 209, 227
Williamson, Robert 170
Wilson 82, 91, 187, 188
Wilson, Carey 74
Wilson, Cary 175
Wilson, Jerome 162
Wilson, Jim "Sunburst" 181
Wilson, Lois 182
Wilson, Marie 192
Windom, Lawrence C. 174
With Neatness and Dispatch 170
Wolheim, Louis 172
The Woman Scorned 133
Woods, Walter 182

Worts, George D. 182
Wray, Fay 220
Wulf, Fred 122, 125
Wyler, William 75
Wyndham, Joan 181
Wynn, Keenan 97

The Yellow Dove 53, 161
Yorty, Sam 98

You Bet Your Life 202
Young, Carleton 185
Young, Clara Kimball 24, 166
Young, Howard Irving 162
Young, Robert 219, 229
Young, Tammany 165, 221

Zanuck, Darryl F. 188, 190
Zimbalist, Efram, Jr. 200